1981

252, 276

"YOUR FATHER'S NOT COMING HOME ANYMORE"

"YOUR FATHER'S NOT COMING HOME ANYMORE"

BY

MICHAEL JACKSON AND JESSICA JACKSON

Edited by Bruce Jackson

RICHARD MAREK PUBLISHERS
NEW YORK

Grateful acknowledgment is made to Farrar, Straus and Giroux, Inc.,
for permission to reprint "The Ball Poem" from *Short Poems* by John
Berryman. Copyright 1948 by John Berryman. Copyright renewed ©
1976 by Kate Berryman.

Library of Congress Cataloging in Publication Data

Jackson, Michael, date.
  "Your father's not coming home anymore."

  SUMMARY: Records interviews with teenagers in
which they discuss how they coped with their
parents' divorces.
    1. Divorce—United States. 2. Children
of divorced parents—United States—Interviews.
[1. Divorce] I. Jackson, Jessica, joint author.
II. Jackson, Bruce. III. Title.
HQ834.J3   306.8'9   80-25263
ISBN 0-399-90109-4

To all the children of divorce,
and especially to those we interviewed,
who made this book possible

CONTENTS

Michael Jackson: INTRODUCTION   13

Bruce Jackson: Editor's Foreword   26

MAUREEN (16) *"It's the bad things I remember,
just all bad things."*   36

RICHARD (16, John's brother) *"Nobody likes to
beat up their mother."*   41

JOHN (19, Richard's brother) *"I had finger
marks on my neck."*   50

LOUISE (17) *"Her arm was broken in twelve places."*   68

JOANIE (15) *"It's a very sad situation—incest is."*   76

PATRICIA (17) *"We can't prove he's dead."*   78

JIM (15, Alice's brother) *"I don't know if the
crime would have happened."*   89

ALICE (16, Jim's sister) *"I didn't know who
my father was."*   92

TONY (16) *"I put my hand through a window."*   98

MARGARET (18) *"Everything is mostly
stemming from financial things."*   109

CHRISTINE (15) *"It wasn't a good kind of different."*   118

ALEC (18) *"He took my brother and threw him
through a glass door."*   124

JENNY (16, Linda's sister) *"I never did meet
anybody's standards."*   139

LINDA (16, Jenny's sister) *"There's his side,
her side, and the truth."*   151

ALAN (15) *"She kicked Teddy square in the balls."*   163

JOE (16) *"I think divorce is dumb."*   169

MARYANNE (21) *"My mother never told
us she was divorced."*   172

DIANE (17, Ellen's sister) *"Michael, I don't
want to remember."*   181

ELLEN (16, Diane's sister) *"She took the lead pipe
and hit me with it."*   194

CHARLIE (16) *"Something happened along the way."*   208

MARY (17) *"I'm happiest when I'm out
of the house."*   215

ANN (16) *"I've learned to swallow my pride."*   219

PETER (15) *"Then he attacked my dog."*   235

CAROL (17) *"My father would take me to
the zoo every Sunday."*   237

FRED (16) *"She wants an abortion sixteen
years too late."*   247

ED (18) *"I was in the way."*   251

SALLY (14) *"I used to think it was all my fault."*   254

ANGELO (17) *"It was better for all of
us all around."*   258

GINA (16) *"The judge—you wouldn't believe . . ."*   264

JANE (16) *"Four times a year I'm part of his
life for a week."*   275

ALICE (13) *"I was scared to be living without
a dad."*   280

JOSEPH (17) *"It's all your fault, it's all
your fault."*   284

JUDY (15) *"She tried to kill herself with pills."*   288

BARBARA (17) *"Your father's not
coming home anymore."*   292

SHAUN (18) *"Don't be manipulated like I was."*   300

MARY (16) *"I'm a survivor."*   306

SUSAN (17) *"You just can't know it all."*   309

Jessica Jackson: CONCLUSION   316

The Ball Poem

What is the boy now, who has lost his ball,
What, what is he to do? I saw it go
Merrily bouncing, down the street, and then
Merrily over—there it is in the water!
No use to say 'O there are other balls':
An ultimate shaking grief fixes the boy
As he stands rigid, trembling, staring down
All his young days into the harbour where
His ball went. I would not intrude on him,
A dime, another ball, is worthless. Now
He senses first responsibility
In a world of possessions. People will take balls,
Balls will be lost always, little boy.
And no one buys a ball back. Money is external.
He is learning, well behind his desperate eyes,
The epistemology of loss, how to stand up
Knowing what every man must one day know
And most know many days, how to stand up
And gradually light returns to the street,
A whistle blows, the ball is out of sight,
Soon part of me will explore the deep and dark
Floor of the harbour . . . I am everywhere,
suffer and move, my mind and my heart move
With all that moves me, under the water
Or whistling. I am not a little boy.

John Berryman
Short Poems

Michael Jackson: INTRODUCTION

A parents' divorce is the kids' divorce. The purpose of this book is to show the effects divorces have on kids' lives and let the kids say something about how they cope with those effects. The book is intended for both parents and kids.

I think it's important to understand that all the interviews in this book were done by younger people—by my sister and me. I'm seventeen now, and Jessica is fifteen; we started the book almost two years ago. I believe the people we interviewed were more open with us than they would have been with adults. I think they were more open with us than they would have been with a therapist, because they knew we were serious about this and not doing it just for money. And they knew that we had also gone through a divorce and that we could relate to and understand the problems they were talking about.

One night at the dinner table we were talking about the craziness caused in my family by my parents' divorce. Jessica told a story about one of her friends whose parents had just separated. That reminded me of something that had happened to one of my friends. Jessica told about another one, and so did I. I don't think I had ever realized before how many of our friends were involved in divorce and separation. My stepmother, Diane Christian, and my father listened to us talk. My father said that when adults get divorced they hardly ever know what is really happening with their kids.

"Including you," I said.

"I suppose so," he said.

"Why don't you do something about it?" Diane said.

"Like what?"

"Write a book about it. If there's that much that people ought to know about, you should tell them what you know."

That was two years ago. Since then, Jessica and I have been interviewing kids, mostly middle-class, all between the ages of thirteen and twenty-one. Most of the kids we interviewed were friends of ours or friends of friends. I think we are normal kids, and I think our friends are normal, so I believe these kids are a fair representation of middle-class "divorced kids."

Most were quite open with me and weren't afraid to show their true feelings. Several got very emotional during the interviews. I learned that for a long time they had been repressing many bad memories and feelings, and our conversations opened old wounds. Some didn't know exactly how they felt and what they thought before they started talking. I had a list of questions ready, but many kids needed hardly any questions. It seemed that they had been waiting for someone to ask these things, waiting for someone to talk to about their parents' divorce. Several thanked me after the interview—just for listening. They said they had never talked to anyone about the problems before. I could identify with that: I have never really talked about mine yet.

There is no standard divorced child and no standard situation. Parents never seem to ask kids how they feel, and many children are forced to deal with problems and responsibilities that some adults can't even handle. Many parents believe if they impose no physical abuse, they are doing well. The truth is that mental abuse, which is hidden, can do real and permanent damage, damage more serious than any done by a simple beating.

It fascinates me to find that some of the kids who tell their stories here do not hold grudges against their parents. After all the abuse—conscious and subconscious, physical and mental—most kids still love their parents. They accept the abuse, see it as a problem the parents have, and say it is not really them. It is almost as if the problem is detached from the person doing the abuse.

Money is the cause of a great deal of pain and instability in divorces. A father's refusal to pay alimony or child support only makes the situation more bitter. The father of one girl I interviewed refused to pay his alimony despite a court order. The mother was forced to work two jobs, and the kids were left unsupervised. The girl, at the age of thirteen, was put in charge of her twelve-year-old brother and her nine-year-old sister. She and her brother have both been in trouble with the police, sometimes about drugs. She once took her own father to court to try to get some money, but she got nowhere. Her father is a lawyer.

Many kids I interviewed used dope as an escape from depressing scenes at home. When stoned or drunk, one can forget about problems for a while. Dope and alcohol are means of releasing frustration and escaping reality. Kids use those things the same way adults do. Some kids were messed up more than others by this form of escape. There are kids who admit it and others who think the idea of using dope for an escape is nonsense. The ones who can't admit it to themselves usually got into more trouble. When people realize they are using dope as an escape, they can usually stop or not let it become a problem. I'm talking about using dope in a bad way, in a way that just creates more problems in the long run, as opposed to getting stoned once in awhile to relax or occasionally having a couple of beers.

Family situations sometimes are the cause of kids doing poorly in school. Anger and guilt can build up in a child's head, and with no healthy form of release, temper tantrums, poor social relations, and negative attitudes can result. That happened to me.

I have learned that many problems that are stereotypical of the lower class exist and are often just as prevalent in the middle class. The difference is that in the middle class these problems are hidden—mostly by money. There is alcoholism in the parents of the middle

15

class, a surprising amount. It has been the cause of many divorces, and it has made a lot of them more miserable. There is child abuse in the middle class, which can sometimes be attributed to irrational acts of drunkenness and sometimes to one or both parents projecting their unhappiness on the kids because of their own misfortune or misery. This abuse can be mental and physical. Physically, kids are beaten; mentally, kids are guilt-tripped. Sometimes the kids are puppets for the parents: they are pulled back and forth with no say about anything.

My youngest sister, Rachel, who is now ten, has been torn between which parent to live with for years. She has no real choice; her life is run by a piece of paper—the contract. Mother guilt-trips her and tells her she is all she has left. Rachel is in a tough position. She wants to live with my father, but the guilt feelings overpower her desire. My mother has defined such a move as betrayal and abandonment.

I remember one particularly nasty incident. Diane had made a special dinner and Rachel was looking forward to it. Rachel was over here, where I live with my father, Diane, and Jessica. Rachel and my mother were on the phone. Rachel told my mother that Diane had made this special dinner. Then my mother told Rachel that she too had made a special dinner and she thought Rachel should come home. If Rachel didn't come home, the dinner would be wasted and my mother would be lonely. Rachel was trying to deal with this as well as she could, but it wasn't easy for her.

I picked up the phone and asked my mother what was going on. She told me that Rachel's affairs were none of my business. Then she told me that I was "no son of hers" because I wasn't supporting her. (What a guilt trip!) She began to yell so loudly I held the phone a foot from my ear. Then she told me to "fuck myself" and said that I "should have been born to 'that nun,'" referring to Diane, who was a nun at one time. Then she hung up. The outcome of this was that Rachel went home in tears to be a baby-sitter for her mother.

Sometimes I would think about incidents like this and think my mother was especially thoughtless or dependent. Then, after I did a lot of these interviews, I learned that there are a lot of parents like that. They use children to answer needs that should be answered by themselves or by other adults. The relationships get turned upside down.

I was nine years old when my parents separated, but they had marital problems before that. We lived in California at the time. One morning, I remember, I walked into the kitchen and my mother was sitting at the table, crying. I asked her what was wrong and she told me, "Your father is leaving; we're getting separated."

I was crushed. I ran into my room and cried all day. I was really mad at my father. Not only was he leaving my mother, but he was leaving *me*. He tried to talk to my sisters and me to explain why they were splitting up. I would not listen or talk to him, so he wrote me a letter, which to this day I am glad he gave me. It says things I think all parents should say to their kids during a divorce. This is the letter:

November 10, 1971

Dear Michael and Jessica,

I thought I would write you a letter because some things are so hard to talk about and I know sometimes it's easier if you can think about them while you're by yourself. That's what I'm doing right now, thinking about things by myself, and that's maybe what you'll do when you read this.

I didn't know Mom was going to tell you this morning that we were going to separate and that I was going to move out of the house soon. I knew we would have to tell you before long, but I didn't know when we would do it. I had a notion that we would maybe take a walk down in the canyon—you two and me—and somewhere down there we would sit down and I'd explain everything.

The problem is, there isn't any way to explain everything.

In fact, for you, there probably isn't any way to explain *any*thing. So the way she told you was probably best. There aren't any secrets now. Secrets are usually bad things, I think. If she hadn't told you, you would have been wondering what was wrong with her, why she was crying and red-nosed, and you would have been mad that we were just treating you as children.

I said there isn't any way to explain anything. What I mean by that is there is no way to explain things that would make sense to you now, that would make it seem all right now. Later, when we're all older, things may make more sense. You won't like them any more than you do now, you won't approve any more than you do now, but they'll at least make a little more sense to you.

(I think this letter maybe should be full of false starts and cross-outs. But it isn't. I knew exactly what I was going to say to you when I started to type. So much of my life is here on this typewriter and it is where I go when I am pained. Everyone must have some place to go when he is pained, I think, but when he goes there for that reason he hates it a little just because he is there for that reason.)

So far, all you know is Mom and I aren't getting on too well and I'm moving out. And you maybe wonder about that because we don't fight the way a lot of people do, we don't shout or yell at each other. But you've both suspected things weren't right with us.

Michael, remember you told someone last summer that if your parents ever separated you'd run away so they would have to come back together again? You must have had feelings that things were wrong if you were saying such things. (It wouldn't work, you know. It would only make everyone more miserable. I hope you won't do anything that will make any of us more miserable than we are.)

And Jessie, remember how extra-affectionate you've been lately? You always were cuddly, but the past few months you've been even more huggy and squirmy. Were you maybe a little worried I was going to go away and hoping you'd get me to stay? I bet maybe you were.

We're not separating because we're mad at each other or even because we don't like each other. We do like each other a lot. You know that Mom and I have known each other for over half the time we've been alive. That is a long time. We've had a lot of fun in that time and done a lot of things, and the nicest part of all was you kids.

But something happens. People grow, they change. Kids grow, you know that; grown-ups grow too, the only difference is you can't see that kind of growing so easily. You grow in your body and you grow in your mind. You learn things you hadn't learned before, you think things you never thought before, you understand things you never understood before. Sometimes grown-ups grow very differently from one another, even though they live in the same place and see each other every single day. That happens very slowly and you don't notice it happening.

Until one day, when you look up and say, "Gee, we really are very far apart. We have very little in common now. We are interested in different things. We have different needs. We look at the world differently. When we were young, we looked at the world alike, but we don't do that anymore. We're different people now. So maybe we should try living separate lives to see how the older people we are can develop into what we really ought to be."

What happens is, we look around and the only thing holding us together is the children. But that isn't a fair reason to stay together, because what happens after a while is the parents start resenting each other, and they think, "I'm not here because of *you,* I'm here because of Jess and Mike and Rachel." And so they get mad at each other a lot and start not liking each other at all. And everybody gets mean to everybody.

So we're trying to separate before things get like that. We know we can't live together anymore because the things that should exist between grown-ups who live together just aren't there for us anymore, and we know that we love you all very much and we're very sad because it means I won't see as much of you as I do now and I won't be around to answer a lot of the questions you think up, and we're very sad because it all means you're going to be unhappy and we don't want you to be unhappy.

Maybe it's like having your appendix or tonsils out: it

hurts a lot when you have it done, but if you don't do it when the time comes things are worse later on.

Or maybe it's like brushing your teeth every day: it's a real bother and annoyance, but if you don't do it your mouth gets all rotten and you're not much fun and you can't eat apples.

I think it's a drag.

I know you're unhappy, but I think this is a good time for you to try especially not to make your mother unhappy. She's unhappy enough. And so am I. We should all try to be especially nice to one another now because we're all so sad anyway.

I didn't make a copy of this letter for Rachel. She's too little for a letter. You're going to have to be my letter to Rachel. You're going to have to help her with the things I'd help her with if I were there. I hope you'll do that for me.

Parts of this letter are confusing for you and parts of it probably just don't make any sense at all to you. After you read it, put it someplace safe for when you're older in case you want to read it again. Or rip it up and burn it if you never want to look at it again. It's your letter and you should do what you want with it. Letters are like your life: once you get them, they're your responsibility. They're nice to get, but you should take them seriously because you only get each one once.

I guess the only other thing to say is I'm sorry we have to make you sad like this, and you must remember that we both love you very much and we wouldn't be separating like this if there were any other way for us. But there isn't.

Love,
Dad

The letter helped, but events were a lot less mellow. My parents fought quite a bit before and after the separation. They were violent fights—verbal, not physical. Often I would hide under a table and listen. It hurt me. I would sit there and cry while I listened to them

20

fight. I don't remember what they fought about. Like many kids, I never talked about it with my friends.

We spent the rest of the year in that house in the Berkeley hills. My father lived on Russian Hill in San Francisco. He used to see us weekends and sometimes in between. When the year ended, my mother and the two girls flew back to Buffalo, and I drove back with my father. We took two or three weeks for the drive. We went to a drag race on a mesa near Albuquerque, we visited friends in Austin, we went to a rodeo in Arkansas.

We got back to Buffalo. My dad moved in with Diane and my mother and we kids moved into our old house. I hated Diane for a long time even though she was extremely nice to me. I thought the separation was her fault, that she was a home wrecker, and that she had stolen my father. I was very confused for a long time. I didn't know what to believe. My mother and father always told me bad things about each other. (All the talk of mutual goodwill my parents had when they separated disappeared somewhere as the divorce became more and more real.) For a couple of years I was on my mother's side.

My parents' playing me against each other caused me a great deal of frustration and anger. I had a terrible temper until about eighth grade, and I did poorly in school until tenth grade. I just didn't care. I used dope as an escape from my home situation starting in about sixth grade and continuing through the ninth. I can remember times when I stormed out of the house in a rage, and all I wanted to do was get so wasted I wouldn't have to think about it.

About the time I started smoking marijuana and cigarettes, my relationship with my mother began to decline. I was in a phase of rebellion, and she didn't know how to deal with me. At the same time my relationship with my father began to improve, and I accepted Diane. Many times I would get in trouble with my mother and get grounded. I would just call up my dad and go to his house. I switched back and forth quite a few times. I got away with just about everything. If my mother said I couldn't do something—like go to a concert—I would go to my father's, and he would often let me go. But if my father said I couldn't do something, I wouldn't do it. It ended there.

I can remember only one scene of physical violence between my parents. I was about twelve. My father was picking us up, and he went inside the house and took a lamp. It was an antique lamp which both parents claimed as theirs. As he was walking out of the house, my mother came home and they had a loud verbal confrontation in front of us and the neighbors. Then my mother grabbed his hair, pulled it quite hard, and kicked him a couple of times. He never hit her back.

One of my mother's ways of manipulating my sisters and me was by guilt-tripping us. The guilt trips worked on Jessica and Rachel more than on me, maybe because they were younger. My mother would say to me, "How can you do this to me, your mother? Where have I gone wrong?" My sisters would hug her and tell me I was mean. I would say, "Mom, it's not going to work." I would get so mad, I just wanted to go out and get stoned. (So what she was doing *did* work, but not the way she planned.) Her method of manipulation still gets me furious. She denigrates almost everything I do, and it is rare when we have a peaceful conversation about anything.

The divorce proceedings seemed to take forever. Mom and Dad argued over money and visitation rights for us kids. Neither parent asked us what kind of visitation rights *we'd* like. We had nothing to do with the negotiations. That didn't bother me, as I recall; I don't think I was aware of the implications of the legal arguments. I was confident that things would get better for us after the proceedings, and in some ways they did. That was because my parents had fewer occasions to communicate and some of the bitterness was toned down.

When my father and Diane got married, I was his best man. I thought it was great; being best man made me feel important. My mother disapproved of my participation in the wedding, and I think she disapproved of the wedding itself. The bitterness was toned down, but that doesn't mean it wasn't still there. I don't think she wanted to see him happy or see him married to someone who might win over the kids.

My mother married her divorce lawyer. She didn't invite my sisters and me to her wedding. She didn't even tell us when it was happening. We found out afterwards. She got married while we kids were away on a trip with my father and Diane. I came home, she was married—and I was insulted.

At first Harold, her husband, was nice to me. I could not respect him at that time because I was still in shock from the divorce. My father's getting married was different because I did not live with him then and I was not in the position of having to accept a surrogate mother. My father was important to me, as with any young boy, and I was not ready to accept the authority of a new father. I think Harold's niceness at the beginning was an act, because it wore off about a year after their marriage.

Harold has three children—two girls and one boy. One of the girls once said to me, "Let's think of a plan to split up your mother and my father." I was mad at her for this. Even though I didn't like Harold, I didn't want to split them up because my mother was happier than she had been for some time. I said I'd have no part in such a sneaky plan. Now I understand why she said that: she just wanted her father back, which is reasonable.

A series of incidents led to my moving in with my father and Diane. My mother and I were not getting along at all. We fought all the time. During one fight she said to me, "Leave! Go to your father's! Pack your bags and go!" She had said that to me several times before, but I never left. This time I did leave, but I didn't pack my bags and I didn't go to my father's.

I grabbed my bankbook and went out and had a good time for about three days. She was frantically looking for me, calling mothers and talking to my friends. Finally one of my friends talked me into going home. I was told that my punishment would be "grounding for life." She denied kicking me out of the house. "I'm your mother; I wouldn't do that." I told her that she had done that; I quoted the conversation. "No," she said. "I'm your mother, I wouldn't do that." After about three days the tension between us became unbearable, so I moved in with my dad.

The main problem between my mother and me was and still is a complete lack of communication. My relationship with my mother has not changed in the three years since I left, except I don't get as mad at her anymore because I'm not there. I do get mad sometimes.

Sometimes I feel like banging my head against the wall, but I don't verbally abuse her with the intensity I used to. We don't talk very often, and when we do, we usually get into arguments. Most of our conversations are on the telephone. I rarely talk to Harold because we have nothing to say to each other. I don't respect his values and he doesn't respect mine. Rachel told me he says bad things about me and deliberately goes into his room and watches TV whenever I come over to avoid seeing and talking to me. Recently, though, he called to congratulate me on my report card, which surprised me.

One time about two years ago, my mother and Harold were having a terrible fight. I was no longer living there, but I happened to be over for dinner. My mother was distraught; her second marriage seemed to be falling apart. There could be no peace in the house at that time, so my mother, Jessica, and I went out to dinner. My mother said to me, "I don't know what to do." She was crying.

I said, "Divorce him, Mom. You'll be a lot happier."

She said, "What would I do then, go back to my mother's? Then your father would get Rachel."

She is pretty dependent on Harold if her only alternative in life is going back to her mother's. And what kind of position does that put Rachel in—having to live in all that combat because her mother won't let her live with her father?

It isn't easy for me to say harsh things about my mother and Harold. I don't want to regret anything I write or write anything damaging. It is hard to weigh the good and the bad and form a final opinion that is to be published in a book.

I get along well with my father and Diane. We have strong mutual respect for one another and they treat me like an adult. This environment is more intellectually stimulating than the environment at my mother's house, and that played a major part in sending me in the right direction. I'm doing well in school, I've been working on a book, and I'm going to college next year.

My parents are still very bitter toward each other. I would say they loathe each other now. They still have occasional violent confrontations on the phone—always over Rachel's visitation. Jessica has been living here for about two years now.

I'm telling you all this so you'll understand that I'm one of the kids this book is about, that the conversations I had with them were about something I was part of, too.

One of the hardest parts for me, while it was all going on, was not having any way of knowing I wasn't alone. It is important to know that terrible things can happen in your life, but that doesn't mean you're a freak. Even if an adult tells you that, the way my father did with his letter, it's not enough. They have different problems from us.

I hope by reading this book kids can identify with other kids' situations and feel better about their own. I also hope that parents can read this book and realize that kids do care and do have strong feelings, and that parents' actions have serious effects on their children. I hope parents will learn what they look like from where we are, and I hope kids will learn they're not alone in seeing what they see.

The above "Introduction" describes my relationship with my mother at the time I worked on this book. During the past two years, our relationship has improved considerably.

Bruce Jackson: EDITOR'S FOREWORD

We've attempted here to present directly and objectively some extremely subjective narratives. Like everyone else, these kids perceive themselves as central in the scenarios of their lives. Like everyone else, they try to get their scenarios to make sense. Unlike fiction, the facts of life do not have to make sense, so that job is often not an easy one. These children may empathize with their parents, they may have moments of remarkable insight into the motivations of their parents and themselves, but finally their statements are about their own pain. If we did another book based on interviews with the parents of these same children, those interviews would doubtless show many of these children as troublesome, selfish, uncooperative, and unsympathetic. Part of that would be true: some of these kids are those things—from the point of view of the parents. But that doesn't matter, because the kids' pain is real, their defenses are either necessary or the best they can manage at the time. They are in the position of someone in a dentist's chair who screams and who is told by the dentist that what just happened didn't hurt that much, or that what just happened is

26

merely a normal aspect of this kind of work: "Fine. *You* can say that. But from in here, it *hurts*." They cannot indulge in the luxuries of comparison and relativism and contextuality that observers enjoy. Those do not exist from the inside.

These interviews and conversations deliver a kind of information you don't get from a psychologist or sociologist or a social worker. Michael and Jessica are now seventeen and fifteen years old; they are in the middle of the age group telling their stories here. Children talk differently to one another than they do to an adult clinician. There are some things they will perhaps feel they have to explain in greater detail to an adult, but there are other things they will discuss more directly with someone who inhabits their own world.

When someone goes to a clinician, it is with a specific problem in mind. The conversation focuses on the problem, on the need, on a solution or resolution.

The conversations are about how things are, not how they might or should be. The participants are teenage children comparing notes with other teenage children.

This is a book of conversations by children about how they perceived what was going on in their families. It is probably fraught with misinformation: parents don't tell them much so they have to infer a lot; their data are always partial, their concern is always subjective. Like the rest of us, they read cataclysmic events in terms of one question first: What is this doing to *me*? These kids talk about their hurt and how they try to cope. They talk about the unintentional injuries done by adults who are so caught up in their own bent lives they don't see the wreckage they make of other lives around them.

With only a few exceptions, these are not kids who were ever brought to a psychologist for treatment. These interviews are with "normal" kids, kids whose voices never get heard by anyone. Some of them got into a lot of trouble or appear very troubled, and they were "seen by someone." But most come from families that, except for the divorce, appeared normal, and the kids appeared to handle it.

They tell you how they handled it. Some of what they have to say is not very nice. They are more critical of us than we probably know, they patronize us more than we could probably stand, they manipulate us more than we would tolerate—if we knew.

They do these things to survive.

The numbers are staggering. Last year in America, there were more than 61 million children under the age of eighteen. Nearly 7 million of these children lived with one parent because of divorce or separation. There were 2.1 million marriages in America that year and 1.1 million divorces; the marriage rate was 10.3 per 1,000, the divorce rate was 5.1—one divorce for every two marriages. In that one year, well over 1 million children suddenly found themselves living with just one of their parents as the result of divorce.

The kids who find voice here are almost all middle-class and white. Mike and Jess simply talked to their friends and to friends of their friends. Like most Americans, they live in a world of de facto economic and racial segregation. A sociologist might challenge the sampling technique for representativeness, but I suspect there is a neatness about it. I think the microcosm Mike and Jess explored is not unique to a single county up here in the north country. We're too mobile a society for that. We take our white middle-class problems into white middle-class communities that accept us and incorporate us as easily as a General Motors car accepts a replacement part.

I know many of the families. From the outside, they look like perfectly normal white American middle-class families. What frightens me is the suspicion that they *are* normal—that the massive amount of psychic and physical injury these kids detail represents all-too-common patterns, not some special stream of idiosyncratic pathology.

There is a lot of alcoholism and a lot of violence in these stories. That may tell us nothing about alcoholism and violence in families in general, but it does say something about alcoholism and violence in families that break up. If the factors aren't causal, they are at least concomitant. There is a lot of drinking when things go bad, people hurt one another in a lot of ways, and often the target of the violence has little to do with the cause of the anguish producing the violence. Children become victims of the broken relationship and they are punished within the break.

Most parents I know worry about the supposed epidemic of teenage drug use. They worry about pills, about grass, about cocaine; a few remember to worry about alcohol (though a depressing number have told me how relieved they were to find out their kids were "just going out and drinking a case of beer with some friends after school; they're not into drugs at all"). What few of those parents know is how acutely aware their children are of their parents' drug use. They keep score. They watch the liquor bottles, the beer cases, the pill prescriptions. Some can tell by their parents' behavior what chemicals they've been ingesting that day or evening. If you can take what these kids say seriously, you'll learn that the source of the youth drug problems won't be found in the schoolyard—it's in the family medicine chest and liquor cabinet. The drug takers the kids observe most are their own parents.

What is perhaps surprising is how well so many of these children seem to cope. They become like refugee children in war areas: they develop and demonstrate an astounding resilience, creativity, self-possession. The ones who don't, don't survive very well.

It doesn't mean the others are healthy; it doesn't mean they won't spend years burrowing out of the holes. All it means is that many of them fight very hard to keep from being destroyed by a psychological and often physical violence not of their making and over which they have no control.

Sexual problems—either as manifestation or cause of other problems—figure significantly in many divorces, but there is little of that here. That is because few teenage kids are capable of dealing with their parents as sexually active beings; the kids are having trouble enough coming to terms with their own sexuality. They deal with their parents in terms of things they see, things they think they understand: money, alcohol, pills, physical and psychological violence, property. Some of their reasoning about new spouses is simplistic and naive. Several say their parents or stepparents married for money. It is hard for them to assume love. I don't think any of them specify love as a significant factor in their parents' remarriages.

Kids in divorces have secrets. They know things the parents aren't telling them, things they cannot say to anyone. Saying makes it real, and most kids are still hoping it won't happen or it won't continue. It's a little death. That means the kids go through those years with enormous unarticulated anxiety and anger. Sometimes the anger erupts in apparently meaningless violence; sometimes it boils inside, eating away.

Kids manage their parents a lot. They have to, once the rules of the game are proven to be only provisional. A divorce says to a kid, "The roles and rules and boundaries you thought fixed your place in the world are insubstantial things we just pretended were there as long as it was convenient for us to do so." Confronted with that relativism, kids work hard to establish their own place, their own boundaries, their own roles and rules. Few are willing to remain passive victims. Sometimes they participate in violence; sometimes they try to defuse or deflect it; always, they try to manage it.

Few parents, it seems, know how much children know about what is going on, and few seem to credit them with the ability to infer very much. That leads to another problem: since little is said directly, the children are dependent on what they can deduce, and their deductions are not always accurate. In protecting the children from some unpleasant truth, parents let them wander into more complex and debilitating untruth.

Instead of being small communities in which lives occur symbiotically, the homes in most of these families become battlegrounds in which the kids develop complex strategies for survival. Parents rarely tell the kids the truth about the divorce, rarely do they seem to know it themselves, and even when they do they are burdened with anger or hurt. The absent partner is not there as a focus for the anger or hurt, and the child may become a vehicle for expression of it. If a child is not to be a mere victim, he or she must develop defense strategies. If a child maintains contact with both parents' households, there are often two completely different battlegrounds to be negotiated, each with different rules, each requiring different strategies. The dissonance between the two makes matters even more complex, forcing the children more and more to rely on external bases of support, external notions of community. All teenagers have to work at normal problems of moving toward adult definitions of identity and boundaries; the task is brutally accelerated for these kids. Few of them seem comfortable in both of their homes, and most are fully at home in neither.

At the time of separation and divorce, the parents are going through profound changes; their definitions of their social networks and roles are changing. It takes a long time for most divorces to occur, and it takes far longer for the separate lives to achieve any kind of stability after that. Sometimes the divorce turns out to be merely the symptom of a problem rather than the solution to one. Each parent worries about his or her balance and locus. The kids worry about the same things, but they are at far greater risk. The divorce has told them that the ground rules they assumed about protected space do not apply; they are not constants. It shouldn't be surprising that they are both terribly rebellious and terribly dependent in this time (part of that is a normal aspect of adolescence anyway), and that a long season of reestablishing trust should follow. The process is made more difficult by the fact that usually none of the participants can describe the state or stages they are going through. Talk between parent and child about things that count is rare.

A father who has just moved out may flee his children because they seem to keep him from creating for himself the new role he envisioned; he may also for the first time be able to deal with them directly because he can see them outside the context of the unhappy marriage. A recently abandoned wife may work very hard to establish a new identity for herself; she may also hold tightly onto the aspects of her old identity that still remain. The kids may respond to this ambiguity with fear, mistrust, claustrophobia, and panic.

There is, in many situations, an inversion of the usual roles. The children in divorce are often called upon to parent the parents, to ratify the legitimacy of the parents' existence. This seems particularly the case for women who have no career. The breakup of the marriage fractures and reduces their basis of self-identification; whatever the effect of this on the parent, it often means a doubling of the burden on the children.

Michael and Jessica did about seventy-five interviews. Most were by

Michael. He is old enough to drive, he has greater mobility, his circle of acquaintances is larger. After Ann Christian transcribed the tapes, Michael, Jessica, Diane, and I read all the transcripts and marked the ones we thought interesting enough for inclusion. There were far too many for a book like this.

Next, Michael and Jessica read through the transcripts again and marked the sections they thought should go into the book. A few sections they thought unimportant struck me as having some significance; we discussed those and some of them were included. The final selection was impressionistic: we tried to give a sense of the range and the repetitions. After we selected the texts, the segments of each interview were assembled in what seemed the most coherent order; some interviews here present the material in the exact order of statement. I took the liberties anyone transcribing conversation to a printed page takes in that translation: I eliminated false starts and unintended repetitions, I deleted phrases common in adolescent speech but rare in writing ("you know," "like," "man," and so on). I didn't put in anything that wasn't there, and I tried to make sure the reorganizations didn't create any meanings not intended by the speakers. Our few rephrasings, all done for clarity, are indicated by brackets. We changed all the names and most of the places. Diane Christian gave critical assistance at all stages of this process.

As a sociologist used to working with personal documents, with interviews, with reconstructions of events past, I know that some of the statements purporting to present facts here aren't factual at all. They are reconstructions, imaginings, wishes, fantasies. I also know that many more are extremely accurate descriptions of what happened. The difficulty, for a reader, is that there is no way to tell on the basis of these data only which is which.

I don't think that problem is very important, because the facts of each of these broken families are not the substance or subject of this book. This book is about how those events seemed to the participants in the divorce who are virtually never given any notice at all: the children.

How the events appear to them, how they perceive what the situations are doing to them, is more important than the objective reality—if in fact any such thing exists in these cases. People act on the basis of what they believe happened.

I don't think that a participant in a situation is necessarily capable of telling the truth of the situation, that a person in a context can explain the meaning or the significance of the context. But it is with their words that we must start. They form the vocabulary for understanding, for analysis, for comparison. Their words accurately document the way they perceive their experience and the way they choose to present that experience.

What is special about this collection of interviews is that it was done by peers. Michael and Jessica are divorced kids. They went through it and, as well-educated and sophisticated as their mother and I are, they did not have an easy time of it. We played games with their minds, games I didn't fully appreciate until I read the comments of some of the children in these pages—and until I read some of the comments in those conversations offered by my own children.

My divorce began in calm, but it quickly degenerated into acrimony, and far too many times the children became the battleground for that. They were the only conversation point we had; we struck out at each other through them. Were it not for the children, we could have avoided each other forever; the children bind us more tightly than the defunct marriage contract did. They know that and they pay for it.

Divorce is a rotten mess and hardly anyone handles it well. Most adults think they've done a fine job if they get out without physical fights and a knockdown court battle. If these kids are a fair sample of anything—and I think they are—very few adults do anything but a lousy job of managing what happens to the children in divorce. Children are argued over, their support terms are fought over, their custody is hassled over. But their hearts and minds are a dark continent. Parents in divorce have a hard enough time talking to each other; they seem to have little left to say to their children, and much of what they do say is an expression of frustration or bitterness or loss—which is to say, they talk about themselves and their own hurt and seem to be blind to the other hurts they are causing as they go about attempting to make their own lives more comfortable or felicitous.

Lawyers become the meeting ground; they are the passionless agents who fix the terms. They have no personal interest and no moral center in these affairs. Their concern is getting their client the best deal possible, and kids in divorce never have their own lawyers. If the lawyer represents the wife, he tries to get as much alimony and child support as possible (it is still rare for the father to get custody); if he represents the husband, he tries to keep alimony and child support as low as possible. Lawyers urge the guilt-ridden spouse, the one leaving for a new life of choice, to pay less; they say, "You feel guilty now, but you'll know I'm right later." They urge the understanding wife to demand more: "So what if that doesn't give him enough to live on? He's the one who wants out." Lawyers set patterns for visitation.

Only in the most vicious divorces do any of the agents ask the kids anything. Judges don't ask, lawyers don't ask, parents don't ask.

Some kids get lost in the interstices. The breakups occur, the kids fit neither of the new life patterns, and instead of altering the new patterns, the parents pretend the children aren't there. It's like a driver who unscrews the plates from his malfunctioning car and abandons it on a city street: let someone else, some public agency, take care of it; I don't have a car anymore. Throwaway cars, throwaway kids.

Because I am a sociologist, these interviews strike me as important human documents. They give voice to an enormous population traditionally kept mute by the rules of our adult game.

I have spent a lot of my professional career studying social pathology—crime, criminals, prisons, criminal justice agencies, government malfunction, and the like. When Michael and Jessica began this book, I looked upon it as an interesting exploration of another pathological area, an area of disease. What happened, though, was that the work Michael and Jessica did made me rethink my easy definition of social pathology, made me wonder about "normal."

They didn't have to look very hard for these conversations. They went through their friends, they talked to kids they met at parties. They could have quintupled their interviews and not exhausted the local supply. I said earlier that the families don't look abnormal or freaky from out here and that I know some of them and I know of

34

more of them. They're mostly comfortable middle-class folks: lawyers, teachers, store owners.

The marriages broke up, the children of the marriages knew my children, the stories wound up in this book. I don't think the children or the parents are all that anomalous. Many of these stories could have been told about people whose families still look nice and neat to me, about people who live on either side of you, maybe about you.

These conversations tell you some of the things your own children may think and experience if your marriage does what over a million other marriages do every year, if it falls or breaks apart. A close reading of these conversations may help you avoid doing more damage than you intend; it will make you privy to conversations that will not otherwise occur in your presence.

You will learn that these kids have an enormous tolerance. A few hate their parents, but most, beyond reason, love them still; they assume that things will somehow work out, that the parents mean well. The real level of malevolence or incompetence is still denied. They are kinder to us than we probably deserve.

It's the bad things I remember, just all bad things.

MAUREEN (16)

We knew they were going to separate. It was obvious because they fought a lot. One day he was out. I'm not sure where he was. He might have been away for the weekend. We just packed up and left. She told us then, me and my brother. He's nineteen now. My other brothers are twenty-seven and thirty and my sister is twenty-nine.

There were physical fights. He used to beat her up.

The first one I remember was after they had been to a wedding. They came home and I was sleeping, but I woke up because I heard them yelling. My father was an alcoholic, so when he used to get drunk he would get violent. I heard them fighting about something and I remember hearing him slap her. I called my mother in the room because I didn't want her out there. I said, "What's going on?" My father came in the room and I said, "Why are you hitting her?"

He said, "I'm not hitting her." I just looked at him. He thought I was stupid because I was a little kid—but I heard him hit her.

How old were you then?

Oh, God, I don't even know. I think I was in kindergarten.

Do you remember how you felt about it?

I didn't like him. I was really scared of him. I can't remember it very well. It's like I've blocked a lot of it out. I can remember little things, little bits of things that happened. I don't remember detail.

I remember one time that was really bad because they were screaming a lot. I was in bed. I couldn't sleep. Me and my sister shared a room. I don't know what they were fighting about, but I know he had gotten drunk.

I remember that he used to come home, he'd go in her room, and all of a sudden you would hear him say, "Don't start." 'Cause she could tell by the look on his face which way he was going to be. That night they got in this really huge fight. We lived in a flat and the people downstairs called the police. My sister called the police, too. They came, but they couldn't take him away because he didn't bruise her or something stupid like that.

I think the next day is when we left.

There were a lot of times when he just beat her up. He'd fight with my sister, too, and my brothers. He never touched me because I was too little, but he hit everybody else.

After the divorce he had visiting rights at first. We saw him twice, but I was always so scared of him that I didn't want to see him. He'd walk by our house about ten times to see if he could see us, but whenever he came, I ran away.

I read about him in the paper because he was in the Olympics. I read in the paper how he said he was divorced and how he hopes his family will come and see him and all this bullshit. Like he never did anything wrong.

It made me feel like he's such a fool to say that. He was such an asshole to my mom. He has never once sent alimony or child support or anything. He wrote once and he said, "If I can see the kids, I'll send child support, otherwise I'm not going to send anything." She asked us and I didn't want to see him and neither did my brother. My brother hates him more than anybody; he had, probably, the biggest effect on my brother. I just think he's an asshole. I don't feel anything toward him. I don't even know him, really.

When was the last time you saw him?

I've seen him from a distance. I've never actually talked to him. The last time I talked to him was about the second grade.

And then one time we were having a block party. He knew where we lived and he came to the block party. He was figuring we'd be there. I guess it had been three or four years, so he wasn't sure what I'd look like. He came up to me once and he asked me, "Maureen?" and I said, "No," and I took off and I ran away. I was too scared. I ran all the way home. It was really funny.

Did the court ever tell your father to give your mother alimony?

Oh, yeah. They subpoenaed him and then he took off. He lived in New Mexico and they followed him there, and they subpoenaed him and he left. He went to California and to Hawaii. He stays down there, mostly. Whenever they get him, he just takes off.

Erie County wrote us a letter about a month ago, and they told my mother that they looked him up and found out he's been dead for two years. So my mother called his sister and his sister said that was bullshit. I guess he's been married twice since my mother.

Does your mother see other men? Has she remarried?

She hasn't really seen anyone. Once when I was younger. She won't get married again. She's too old.

What was the most painful or hardest thing to cope with during or after the divorce?

When they got divorced I was pretty young and I didn't like him, so there was nothing I would miss. But until recently he had a big effect on my brother. My brother was right at the age where it would be affecting. Like if you said something and my father didn't like it, he'd beat you up. My brother, when he started getting older, was really shy and he couldn't let out his feelings. And he couldn't associate with other people very well. He was really shy. He had a bad time in junior high. And watching him, the things he went through—that probably hurt me the most. And remembering the fights that they had. My brother would actually come home and cry, it was so bad.

How old was he?

Oh, God, it didn't even end until last year. He graduated high school in seventy-eight. He was really bad. He couldn't talk to people. He saw a social worker and that helped him a lot, but he's going to college this year and he's really scared. He wants to go, but it's a whole new thing. He's not the type that can make friends that easily, that can just go up and start talking to someone.

How do you think the divorce affected you?

I grew up without a father. If I had had a father when I was growing up, I would have been a lot different. I wouldn't have been so wild. Right now I have a lot of freedom. I can mainly do what I want.

Usually you can remember things from kindergarten and even when you were four, but I can't really remember anything. I remember just little parts of things that I did. I remember him once taking us to the drive-in. And a couple of times going to the beach. I remember once seeing my mother and father actually hugging each other.

It's the bad things I remember, just all bad things.

I was scared to death of him. And she was scared of him, too. He was so violent when he got drunk. He just went crazy. She couldn't have stayed with him. There's no way.

Did he want you kids?

He did. He'd probably take us; yeah, he'd take us. He's the type of guy, if I saw him now, he'd just bullshit to me.

I can remember the one time he took us, when he was visiting, and he kept saying, "Your mother is crazy. She's crazy."

There's nothing wrong with her. It's him. They say alcoholism is an illness, but he wouldn't go get help for himself either. My mother tried. He'd go to the hospital maybe for a weekend. But you can't do it in just a weekend.

But yeah, I'm sure he'd want us.

Did it bother you when he bad-talked your mother?

Yes, it did, because it was like I was Mommy's girl 'cause I was the youngest one. I don't know why I just always liked her more. And when he would do it, I'd get so scared. I didn't like him at all.

Did you show him? How did you react? Do you remember?

I just cried, 'cause it would always be late at night. It would always make me start crying. And my sister would tell me, "Be quiet, 'cause if he comes in here, he's gonna hit you." And I'd just kind of go under the covers and cry. I'm sure he could tell I was scared of him because I would never go near him. I'd just stare at him.

After they broke up, my mother had to go to work and it was the first time. She didn't go to college, so she can't get that good a job. She had to work and she had a babysitter for us when we came home from school. Then it became my brother—he's two years older—and when we were older, he would be the one to watch me. That was a lot of responsibility right there, because I had to be more or less on my own. My brother would say, "Yeah, I'll watch her," and then he'd take off. That made me look at things in an older way.

Do you think you'll ever get married?

It's hard to say. Usually, when I think about it, I think no. But I don't know. Who knows by the time I'm that old? I might not be around. The world might not even be around. I don't think about it much.

What about divorce? Do you think of that?

It's not that great for the kid.

When you're younger, I suppose it's probably better to happen then. You can't understand it, and when you're older, you have to choose between your parents, especially if you love them both. I don't think divorce is that good an idea, but it's better to be divorced than to be fighting.

"Nobody likes to beat up their mother."

RICHARD (16), John's brother

They got divorced six years ago.

I woke up one morning and my father was gone. I didn't see him for three years after that.

As far as I knew, my father had been arrested and he was in jail in Europe. My mother told me this. It turned out to be total bullshit.

When I saw my father three years later, he told me that it was not true. I presume my mother did this just to make us like her more and put my father on the bad side, that she thought it would make her look better if my father was disobeying the law.

Who was it that finally told you they were divorced?

My mother. She just said they were divorced.

I knew this beforehand. I don't know how. It was just a sense, a feeling. I told my brother that they were going to get a divorce about a week before they were. I just knew it. I don't know why. Even at a young age I just knew it. At that age I couldn't handle it because when you're that young, you need a father. And when you find out that he's a fuck-up, or he supposedly is, you don't want to believe it. It crushes you inside. You don't know what to do.

Our family then wasn't together anyway. None of us were close to each other. But my mother is mentally sick, which doesn't help any. And at that time I didn't realize that. My biggest problem was, I was living in her sick world doing things that weren't normal, but that I thought were. That's what really fucked me up.

It was a game. Once I started seeing my father, I didn't know who to believe. They were both telling me different things about each other, about the past. And at that age I didn't know. I couldn't sort out things because at that point I'd been living with my mother for three years. And after three years, not hearing the other side of the story, you're going to believe what your mother tells you.

It shocked me when I finally found out. As a matter of fact, I never really understood and sorted the truth from the bullshit until the last two years or year and a half.

What was the truth?

That my mother was definitely sick.

How do you mean "sick"?

She's disturbed. She lies constantly and doesn't know that she's lying. She'll say something and it won't make any sense. I never realized my mother was sick until she started doing really strange things. She'd sit in her room, two or three days at a time. And I finally found out that she was on something, some kind of drug.

She smokes weed constantly, probably a half ounce a day, which is, to me, insecure. She can't live with reality. And she's been doing this ever since I can remember.

The first time I knew she smoked was when I was about eight years old. But I didn't know what it was, so it didn't bother me then. Not that it bothers me now, but anybody that smokes a half ounce a day has problems to begin with. They can't live and cope with their own problems.

That's her problem: she has no sense of values. You can't even have a conversation with her. She'll flip out on you. One minute she'll smile at you, the other minute she'll tell you that you're sick in the head.

There's no sense in having any kind of relationship with a woman like that because her values are so dented, they're different every time you talk to her.

She's now living about eight hundred miles away from here and I don't see her anymore, and she's fucking up my brother and sister just like she tried to do to me. And I feel helpless. I can't do anything about it.

I hope they get through it like I did.

She's remarried to a sixty-five-year-old doctor who is using her for bed purposes, let's say. He doesn't pay for anything in the house. He doesn't pay for the food. He doesn't pay to do anything. He just sits around and generally gets laid.

I've gotten into physical fights with him. Well, with him and my mother. He told me he was going to strangle me when I saw him a year and a half ago.

I don't think he's sick. I think he knows what the hell he's doing. He's got a free ride in life. My mother has money. So he's got it made. As far as us fighting, I couldn't handle that at a young age. I fought with him many times physically, and he's too old. I never really lost, but I felt bad about it. You don't want to fight an old man. It just doesn't make you feel good.

As far as my mother goes, we got into sick fights. I would drop an ice cream cone and she'd get so pissed off at me, she'd throw something at me. And that would start a fight. This happened for a year, probably once a week. We got into fistfights. At one point I had to put her into a headlock.

I couldn't handle fighting with my mother every week. It was somewhat against my morals. Nobody likes to beat up their mother. It hurts, but when your mother attacks you with kitchen cutlery, belts, lamp shades, glasses, anything, it's human instinct to fight back.

Most kids don't fight back.

I was at a point where I couldn't handle it.

The first time I physically fought with her, I had gotten caught sneaking out of the house. I came back in and she told me to take off all my clothes and she was going to beat me with a belt ten times. I told her she wasn't. I let her know right there that I didn't want to get beaten and I didn't think it was that bad a crime. Right there and then I knew there was something wrong with her if she had to beat her own son for something ridiculous like that. I knew there had to be a problem.

From then on, it started. Anything I did wrong, she'd go physical. And I got beaten up sometimes, and let's say I beat her up sometimes, too, but I regret it now. You can't live with the guilt of beating up your own mother. It's just not normal. But it's something in the past and we have to forget about it.

I got a knife pulled on me once and at the point I was, I couldn't handle it. I went down to my room and I swallowed probably fifteen various pills trying to commit suicide. I was eleven. I couldn't handle it, I couldn't handle life. I didn't even want to live anymore because it was too much hell.

I didn't die, obviously, but I'll never forget it.

I was in bed for four days, literally crying because my stomach hurt so much. And the bad thing about it is, finally my mother asked me what I had done and I told her and she didn't even want to take me to the hospital. She told me that it was my fault I had done it and I'd have to suffer. That's sick.

Did you ever feel that you were responsible for the divorce?

Yes. Many times. Because I was told that I was. My mother told me many times that I was the problem in the divorce, that me and my brothers were the problems of the family.

At that age we couldn't handle the guilt feeling that it was our fault. We weren't old enough to know that it wasn't our fault. I probably lived with that one for three years.

I finally realized that she was sick. I didn't realize it until I had actually moved out and looked at the situation that I used to live in, and then I realized that I had nothing to do with it, that I was too young. Obviously the problems were between my mother and father.

Small kids can't be the cause of a divorce. What she was doing was giving me guilt to let her off the hook.

She didn't want to take the responsibility of the divorce because she couldn't handle it, so she had to put it on somebody else. It made her feel better. She had done this many times.

Anytime any one of us did something wrong, she would take the rest of the family out and do something for them, like buy them clothes, but that one would stay home. That was sick. It was, in her viewpoint, to make us feel guilty for what we did, so we wouldn't do it again.

It didn't work. It ate inside us. We didn't know what else to do.

How else did she guilt-trip you?

Many different ways. Blaming things that my brother and sister did on me, for instance. My brother was sent to a mental institution for a year, and she said the reason my brother went crazy was because he and I always fought. I don't think that was why. It was her.

My brother and I are great friends now. The problem was the family and neither one of us came together on our problems. So we just fought.

It turns out my brother isn't mentally ill. He's out now, and it put a dent in his life, too. I feel guilty, not so much that he was there; I just feel sorry for him because that was a trip that he didn't have to take.

Do you ever feel that you got the worst of it?

No. I regret the divorce and I regret all the problems, but I feel that I'm a stronger person because it makes me aware of the sick people that are in the world. If I come across it again, I'll know how to handle it, exactly how to handle it. And I think it made me tolerant of a lot of my problems. It has taken me a long time to come out of this, but I finally have.

It makes you a stronger person because you have to be strong to come out of the bullshit, the divorce, the fights, all this shit. And if you can come out of that, then you can start working on your own problems and work things out.

I won't say it helped me, because I'm sure it didn't, but I'm a lot happier now than if my parents had never gotten a divorce. I don't even want to think about how I'd be right now if they hadn't.

Did you ever think or dream about your parents getting back together so things would be normal again?

Yes, but that didn't last very long because my mother was giving my father the image of being a menace to society. Therefore, I didn't want him back either. The first time I saw him after he left, I was really scared of him. I didn't know what to expect.

I don't remember how old I was, seventh grade I think, and I was seeing my father regularly and he asked me if I would like to live with him. It was a quick decision, because I didn't want to live with my mother. I didn't really know my father, but it was the better of two evils. Obviously I was not happy with my mother, so why not try something else?

And there I learned how really sick my mother was and the things that she did. My father is still messed up from this, too. The divorce and the marriage with her screwed him up and he's still having problems with it.

I don't know whether he'll totally come out of it, but there's no comparison between the two of them. My mother is literally sick. She can't even talk correctly. She wrote me a letter about a year and a half ago and literally talked about nothing. The sentences weren't complete. No major reason for the letter that I could see. All I saw was bullshit. It looked like some retarded child's letter done with good handwriting. I couldn't believe I received it.

When was the last time you talked to your mother?

I said hello to her last Easter, but that was all. I said hello to her and she didn't answer me and that was the end of it.

My father married this lady that also has extreme problems. She's been sick for the last three years. She lies in bed and cries and eats all day. She weighs over two hundred pounds.

Right now I'm having a lot of problems with them, too. I don't know what to do.

How did you feel when your father got remarried? How did {your stepmother} feel about you?

The deal my father made was that if he was going to marry this lady, she had to get along with the two of us kids. She was very nice to us for about a year and a half after my father met her. When they got married, I don't know what happened. It all fell apart.

I didn't want my father to remarry. She certainly turned on us. Now I look back on it, and it's a free ride. She had two kids and she, to use an expression, has my father by the balls. He'll do anything for her and she doesn't do much of anything.

What are her kids like?

Very sick. For instance, a couple of months ago, one of her kids took a bag of beer bottles and started smashing them over his head. That's an instance of sick. She doesn't realize that her kids have problems.

I don't think their problems are as bad as when I was their age, but it certainly defects the family when nobody's in reality, when they don't realize that they have problems. That's the worst. If you realize the problem, then you can at least work it out. But when you don't know there's a problem, then you can't do anything for it.

She told me many times that I should act like her two kids, which is sick to me. Her daughter is a bitch. She's just like her mother. She's fat, too, and she doesn't do a hell of a lot of anything. I look at [my father's wife] and I can't believe she's saying that. She kicked my brother out of the house five months ago and the reason she gave was, she couldn't trust him. Personally, I can't trust her. I don't know what the hell she's going to do. She told me just the other day that she wouldn't bother if the house burned down. I don't know whether she's sick, but there are some problems with her.

When they were divorced and you had a problem at one house, did you run to the other; then if you got in trouble there, would you go back? Did you ever use the situation for that?

Yeah, but I ran into problems with that. In the storybook it's "The grass looks greener on the other side of the hill." In this case it was fucked in both directions. More so in my mother's.

You don't realize the problems with a person until you live with them. And you can't go back to your mother. I ran into problems with my father that are nowhere as severe as my mother's, so I can cope with that.

But, yes, I did run into problems with not getting what I wanted from one so I ran back to the other. But it doesn't work out. You can't play both ends against the middle.

As I said before, I moved in with my father after the trouble with my mother, but things haven't gone too well lately at all.

I went away to school in September and things were not going all right for me. The communication between my parents was not going well. I talked to them over vacation. I went home for Thanksgiving vacation, but it was very trivial: hello and good-bye.

I got kicked out of school over Christmas for something that was just a dent in my life. My father kicked me out of the house right after I got kicked out of school and I had nowhere to go. To be honest, it scared the hell out of me. I had had pretty good grades, so I got into another school. It's a public school in a really small town in New England. I'm still getting good grades. I plan to finish up this year, then go on to another school.

I'm on my vacation right now and I just came back to Buffalo. I had gotten a letter from my father and I didn't know what to make of it. He just said that he didn't want to talk to me anymore. He said that things between me and what he called "his family" were finished. In the letter he told me that he didn't want to see me again and that he'd blow my head off if I ever came back to Buffalo.

I guess I didn't take the letter seriously enough. I thought he was just blowing off steam, that he really wasn't serious about it. When I went home this evening to get some of my stuff at my house and talk to them, my stepmother came to the door and she invited me in and called my father. My father went up to his room and he got a gun and he came downstairs and talked with me.

I didn't know what to make of it. I'll probably not have communications with my parents at all or for a long time because of that, because of what they've done.

Did you bring anybody with you when you went to your father's? Were you apprehensive?

I was. I brought four friends with me. If he wasn't going to shoot me, I didn't want him to get physical with me. I thought he would think twice if there were four people with me.

I don't know what his problems are . . . whether he wants to help himself. I think there's something wrong with him and I don't know what it is. I've been thinking about myself more. Maybe that's pigheaded, but I don't want to deal with any of his problems right now.

I'll always respect my father because he's my father. But I really don't have any feelings for him at all right now.

Has anything happened in the relationship between you and your mother?

I just got a letter from her. I haven't read it, but it surprised me that I got a letter from her at all. I don't know what she's doing right now. I don't think she's gotten much better, though, as far as her illness goes.

So what are your overall feelings about divorce?

In my case, or I'll say in our family's case, it was probably for the better. But for a kid to grow up with a family that's never been divorced, I think that's good. I'm very much against divorce.

I'll make goddamned sure the lady I marry is something to keep.

"I had finger marks on my neck."

JOHN (19), Richard's brother

It was a long, drawn-out thing. Richard and I both knew they were going to split up just because of the way they were acting.

My mother had some money problems, I guess you could say. You know how some people get corrupt? Too much money in their hands and they screw up and try to buy people's love and things like that? She got in the habit of spending a lot of my dad's money. And my dad didn't really treat her too well and they just kind of split up.

There was some throwing stuff. I saw a huge ashtray fly through a plate-glass window once.

Who threw it?

My mother.

I was bummed out first, especially because of the age Richard and I were at the time. It's hard not to have a father or a mother. My mother was really losing it. When they got divorced, she had a pretty bad breakdown right afterwards. And Richard and I did just what we

50

pleased. We ran the streets. We had no direction in what we were doing.

We stayed with my mother then, but she was never there. She was always out having a good time with other guys, getting smashed and smoking weed.

I guess the courts right away granted my mother custody because they figure that the mother could take care of the kids better since the mothers are the ones who stay home all the time. But then Richard and I made our own choice and lived with my dad.

Did you have to go to court for that?

We did go to court, but it wasn't a big, drawn-out thing. The judge could clearly see that Richard and I knew what we were doing, that it wasn't working out.

It was good with my father for a year. Richard and I were both going away to private schools so we didn't spend that much time with him. When we came home for vacations, we got treated really well. He was still single and he thought he was a stud. He was pulling in some money. And he treated us really well. He played golf with us all the time, and tennis, too. Bought whatever clothes we needed.

As soon as he got married to my stepmother, it changed. She was an attention seeker in a sense, and she started carrying an aura of power in our family when they first got married. It soon came down to, "Edward, I'm not getting enough time from you. The kids are fucked up. Get them out of the house right now."

She tried to get me put into the navy, but when I went to the recruiter, I gave him a really long drug background, really played it up well, and he said to my dad that they couldn't accept me with such a bad attitude.

They tried to send you to the navy?

Yeah. My old man did. He wanted to give me some direction, make a man out of me. That's what he said.

Your mother sent you away once, didn't she?

That was really strange. As I told you, my mom had a nervous breakdown after they got divorced. I came home from private school in my sixth-grade year. I was going to a private school in Connecticut then. One day she came home and started bitching at me and bitching at me. It was the day after I came home from the airport as a matter of fact.

My hair was pulled back in a ponytail. I was wearing a top hat, a pair of overalls, and sneakers. I came home and she got really uptight. "What kind of kid goes out dressed like that?" Because of the clothes it means I had no respect for authority, smoked cigarettes, and would go out and get drunk. She thought it was abnormal, but she knew it wasn't.

She couldn't handle Richard and me because we were growing up faster than she could ever handle. We were just normal kids like anyone else. We played hockey, got into sports, had a lot of friends, were pretty popular around people.

But one day she attacked me with a pair of scissors. She wanted to cut my hair. I got away from her. I ran away from home after that and I came home two days later. I talked to Richard, and he didn't know what was going on. My mom kind of had me swayed on her side for a little while. I wouldn't stay long, just a little while.

The minute I walked in the doorway, my stepfather grabbed me from behind, pulled me down on the floor, pulled my arm behind my back, and she cut my hair off so short. Really, really short. Cut it right off with the rubber band still on, just chopped it right off. She purposely fucked up one side so I'd have to get it shaved even shorter. I was eleven then.

After that I got into a real big hassle with my mom and she locked me in my room.

Richard had a real fucked-up life. He was in casts for a long time and he had a bone disease and he had to stop playing hockey for a while. I don't know if you know about that shit. He's really hurt with his legs. My mom used to treat him like shit; she'd get him at the top of the stairs and she'd kick him down the stairs. I'm serious. But Richard handled it all the time.

One time he really went bullshit. [My father and stepmother] tried to get him to pull down his pants so she could whale him with a belt. We were supposed to be baby-sitting my little sister. No kid ten or eleven years old should be baby-sitting a three-year-old sister anyway. So we used to take off all the time.

At the time it was Christmas; Richard and I were in the market of stealing light bulbs, the big spotlights that go in front yards. And we got about fifteen of them in one night. We came home. My little sister had gotten scared, and she called up the neighbors or wherever it was my mom had gone. She got home right before we did. And here we walk in the house with two coatfuls and armfuls of these bulbs. They were in our pants and in the pockets of our down coats. We went in and stashed them in the closets as quickly as possible and my mother goes, "Go out and pick yourself a belt from the belt rack and I'll be up in just a second." Supposed to be funny. She just looked at me and she goes, "Okay, boys, pull down your drawers." We were both really scared for sure and then Richard goes, "Blow it off, Mom," and he just stood there. You know how he is; he's straightforward and if something's bothering him, he'll just blow it off really fast.

He said, "I'm not going to pull my pants down for you. You're gonna get my pants off of me if you wanna beat me."

So he had a really big struggle with my stepfather and my mother. They got him down, but every time my mother tried to swing the belt, she hit my stepfather's hand instead of Richard. Richard had this cast on one of his legs and he was really hurting, but he got around okay. He had just gotten sick of it. He was a really good athlete when he was young and he tried to stay in good shape.

She came to my room one day. She said, " Come on, let's go for a drive." I said, "Sure." This was during the time when she had me locked in my room quite a bit, not giving me dinner sometimes, or I'd get a bowl of cereal for two meals. I'd just be sitting in my room. A friend brought some cigarettes to my window so I could have a few smokes, and I had gotten a bottle of wine that he took out of his cellar, so I made myself happy for a few days. I had little collections of things. I had started photography that year, so I had quite a few pictures that I was checking out. And I kept notes on things and tried to keep my life together because I knew how not together my mother was.

When she said, "Come on, let's go for a ride," I figured, maybe she's going to be nice to me. She hasn't been nice to me in three weeks. Maybe she's turning over a new leaf.

We were just driving around and all of a sudden we pull up to West Seneca. It's a psychiatric clinic of some type. I got out and I couldn't believe it: I got dragged in there by my mother.

Everything there is really secure. The guy's got to come out and unlock the door. We go into the head shrink's office. Now I'm sitting and I'm getting talked to by this big, fat shrink that's a lady and she's about fifty years old and she's just a total pig and I can't believe my mother is doing this to me. I was handling it okay at first. I just said to myself, I don't know what kind of shenanigan my mother is pulling, but I'll check it out.

They asked me about my problems with my mother. I talked to my mother and she wouldn't talk to me at all. She played like I was crazy as hell. And she keyed it up really bad. She's a really good talker.

This was her easy way out. The state would pay for my living if I was committed. She was hurting on money so bad after my dad left and screwed things up.

They said to me, "Would you like to get away from your mother and stay here at this place?"

I weighed both sides and said, "What are my options?"

"We can give you special privileges and you'll come in for a two-week"—I'm trying to think what they called it—"examination period." They check out your mental health and how your head is and all these shrinks just toy with your head.

I was a pretty good talker when I was a little kid. I was pretty sharp about what people said. I listened to them. She said to me, "You can stay here and it's not too bad and for two weeks you can get away from your mother."

I said, "I've been treated like shit for a long time. I might as well do it."

In the end my mother got a court order to keep me in that place. That was after the two weeks were up.

It was total hell there. There were a lot of strange people. A lot of them were palsied. Some were retarded and some had family problems, severe child beatings and shit like that. It was a huge ward.

Did you ever see *One Flew over the Cuckoo's Nest?* There you go: same scene.

Were there fags there?

A lot. I saw quite a few. As a matter of fact, my second day there, there were two of them in the shower getting it on. It just blew my head.

If you saw *One Flew over the Cuckoo's Nest*, the whole place was laid out the same way. A big nurses' station in front with two RNs. They have double shifts. They're behind this window and they give out medication. They drug you up so they can handle you. You were some kind of little nothing to them and with the drugs they can tell you exactly what to do and you will be passive about it.

I used to always spit them all out. They give them to you in little cups and you can tip your head back and shoot them under your tongue. Take your hit of water and still talk and they don't know. I didn't take my medication for a long time.

I just got into myself, reading and shit like that. I was bumming out, though. I tried to talk to the people at first because if it's people I'm going to be around, it's nice to talk with them. But there was no one in this place that I could talk to 'cause they were all so fucked up. They were really fucked up. I got in a few fights while I was there. None that I started. I was just defending myself.

I think I had a problem when I was there, an identity problem, about what kind of kid I was: I must be pretty screwed up to be going through all this, and what the hell is going on?

I started getting to be good friends with two counselors. One was about twenty-five and he took me to a concert after I got out of the place. When I first got out, we went horseback riding. And there was this chick who was a hot-looking lady, but she was really comforting, too. She'd talk to me. She'd say, "Look, we know you're not screwed up. Don't let anyone else try to fool you." They kind of pacified me so I could get through it.

I had brought with me all my stuff pertaining to sports. I would sit there and look at my things and remember the good old days when I could still play hockey and not be locked up in my fucking room.

The hockey season started and this lady—I don't even remember her name—looked at my stuff and she said, "Well, you must be a pretty good hockey player to have all these things."

I said, "I enjoy hockey and I played it for a few years."

She knew of my enthusiasm and I had said to her that I'd really love to play and keep my mind on something and keep my head open and not stuff it up and get fucked up. She had a lot of pull in the league because her son was playing and she was head of a lot of different women's clubs. She had to go through the state and through some different counselors and shit, but she got permission for me to play hockey. She was okay.

So I got into hockey. I couldn't play in the games, but I went to practices on the weekends. This was only on three different weekends, but it was good because I could get my mind off things and just skate my ass off. I'd line that puck up twenty yards from the boards. I'd practice my snap shot and each time I'd crack it harder. That was the only way I could get out, flush my system of all the bullshit I had been going through.

It's really hard. You have to keep your guard up and try to be strong in a group like that. Because you'll fall right in with them and follow what they do and you'll even begin to believe that you're crazy. Not the kids. I mean the people who are accusing us.

The eighth month came and I was still living there. My mother wouldn't come to pick me up. She wouldn't speak to me. She wouldn't speak to any of the administration. So they started looking for foster homes for me and that made me go bullshit even worse.

I didn't know what to say. We looked at one foster home with one of the social workers and they were definitely just out for the money. The state pays the people who take in kids. You're not adopted, so the state pays. The lady looked at me and I asked her some questions. She was an old Italian lady and it was in the downtown section of Buffalo. I didn't get into her at all, I didn't like the idea whatsoever.

We left and I was supposedly to go there in three days. I was supposed to make a decision. Meanwhile, I talked to Richard on the phone and I told him he's got to get hold of my dad and tell him what's going on. I hadn't talked to Richard in a long time.

56

I saw Richard on two different weekends toward the end of my stay and he kept straight with me. He didn't give me shit about it and he gave me a healthy attitude. He said, "Look, you know it's not you." But he used to kind of joke about it, too. He'd say, "Hey, John, how the hell's it going in the bin?" He used to call it "the bin" all the time.

They finally got ahold of my dad and my dad just went bullshit because he never knew this was happening.

Hadn't he ever gone to visit you?

I guess he was out of Buffalo for a while. Maybe out west or something. I don't know the story.

So he was gotten hold of by the administration and my dad said, "I'll be right over." He hung up the phone and left that minute. He was furious that they were doing this to his son that he hadn't seen in a long time.

I think he was feeling guilty about getting divorced because he was seeing how fucked up our lives were getting.

Then he took me in and he was good to me and Richard for three years.

A month after I started to live with my dad, Richard came and lived with us, which was really cool because he was going bullshit with my mother, too. So Richard and I got to be reunited again and became even closer. That's why he and I mean a lot to each other: because we've been through so much together and the only way to make it is to stick together, keep helping the other person. He and I have our little scraps, but we never had any physical fights. He's been really good to me and I try to be good to him. I love him more than any other kid in this world, any other anything. That's how much he means to me. He has gotten his head together, too. We had a good time this year in private school as roommates because we hadn't seen each other in quite a while.

Why do you go to private schools?

Better education. I started going to private schools to get away from my family. I don't know much about the family background, I know that my great-grandparents were wealthy to some extent because they owned a factory and all this other shit, and they started a trust fund for Richard and me for school. They thought it would be a good idea for me to start going to private schools, so I did.

I hated it my first year, but after that I got into it because I could play hockey. And you meet nice people. It was a bunch of fine people from all over the country. They were hand-picked by the administration. I don't know how, but they look at you and they take a certain class of person. They were all really wealthy. They weren't very stuck up about their wealth. They handled themselves really well with people. They didn't give them the "I'm better because I have more bucks" attitude. They were down-to-earth people and they didn't flash anything. But they had a good time and they lived comfortably. People like that, that come out of good, caring families, give the kids a lot.

Sometimes it hurts them if it's done too much, if it's an oversheltered life.

And I met a lot of caring teachers there, too. As I got to be liked in eighth grade and started my adventurous climb toward females, there were a lot of nice chicks around there. A lot of really nice ladies.

How often did you come back from school and who did you stay with?

For the last two years I haven't stayed with my parents at all. Either I stay with friends or I sleep in vehicles. It kind of sucks, but I like to come back and see my friends.

Why don't you stay with your parents?

I can't. I'm not allowed to. I'd get my head blown off.

What do you mean?

My old man is really screwed up and I think he's losing his head right now.

Did he tell you not to come back?

Yeah, quite a few times. He just said, "John, don't come back here." Last year he said, "Don't come into this town unless I have two weeks' advance notice or I'll run you out of town." This time, since I've come home, I haven't talked to him. But he's been following me all over town. I did see him just two days ago when I was driving Richard's car. I blew him off. I didn't want to talk to him.

I have to go to my house and get some of my stuff that's been there for quite a few years, and I wouldn't be surprised if it's destroyed. I'll go get whatever's left before I leave. But I'm not going to talk to my dad. That's a lost cause as far as I'm concerned and as far as my brother is concerned, too.

Have you ever had any physical scraps with him?

For sure. We had one this past Christmas. I was so stoned and so coked out I didn't know what I was doing. You know my friend Annie, don't you?

Yes.

Well, I wanted to give her a Christmas present. I hadn't seen her in a long time and I'm really fond of her. As a matter of fact, when I was in the bin, Annie's church group came to play there. I had known her for two years before that. She and I—I don't know how it was figured out, but somehow we are distantly related. Nothing by blood. And when I was in junior high, I used to give her hell. I used to tease her and kid her because she was just starting to fill out. I used to tell her what a little peach she was and me and Carl Ogleby used to give her a lot of shit. All of us did. We had a good, wild time. I was really fond of her.

So about the seventh or eighth month, their church group came and played. I was sitting almost in the front row of the auditorium and I saw her up there. I couldn't believe it. She was so gorgeous to me and I hadn't seen a person from the outside in such a long time. After I saw her, I just ran up to her. I couldn't believe it. It made my whole day. It really did.

When I got out, I got back to being really close with her, and she and I have seen each other off and on for the past five years.

Back to the Christmas present.

Carl and I decided that we wanted to get some coke and I wanted to give Annie a really nice Christmas present. I was going to split a gram of coke with her. I think we ended up getting two grams altogether. Carl brought a gram and I got a gram. And we got four Thai sticks. We were going to celebrate Christmas heavily, so I stopped at a liquor store and got two bottles of Mateus. Then we went over to Ann's house and started cutting up lines. We were buzzed as hell.

It's such a good feeling to be coked out. You talk to someone you haven't seen in a long time and you relate to them so much. You're both on a set level, and with a nice buzz you can communicate very well. We had a great time. We got smashed as hell drinking wine.

We had gone from [Ann's] house at three in the morning and we slept in the basement of my house. I got up the next day and we went to Canada and screwed around. Then I met Richard at the Tavern. We were supposed to leave for Boston that day and go see a friend of mine down there before we went back to school.

My dad, for some reason, was being super-nice and said he'd give us a ride down to the bus station. Our bus was supposed to leave at twelve-thirty. I said, "Okay, Dad. I'll pack my stuff and we'll leave. I'm going to go to the Tavern and see my friends and we'll leave at eleven-thirty or quarter to twelve."

So I was in the Tavern. I did a few more toots with Carl because we had some left over from the night before. Not too much, but we finished it off and got a little buzz, and I saw so many people that I hadn't seen in a long time. People were saying good-bye to me, buying me shots and drinks. I saw Bob Green and I hadn't seen him in four years, so we did three shots of gin. People were buying me beers. I was having such a fine time, seeing all these nice ladies around that I hadn't seen in a while and saying hello to them and them kissing me good-bye. I was really psyched up.

So Tom's brother gave me and Richard a ride home. And I was with Jerry, too. You know Jerry? He's a sick guy. We were smoking bowls [of marijuana] too, just to top it off.

When I came home crocked as hell, my father really took advantage of me. He had discovered that I had taken my twenty-two-caliber rifle out of the house. He kicked the shit out of me. Richard was standing behind me, and Richard was getting ready to hit him or choke him. He had a sick look in his eye because he was so drunk and he was seeing that my dad was taking advantage of me. My dad laid into me four times. I just tightened up my chest and let him blow me against the wall four times.

I didn't feel it too much because I was so numbed out. It was like shakes. Then the last time he cracked me in the chops, and that hurt. And he grabbed me by the neck and I had finger marks on my neck the next day. Ripped a button off my shirt and then ripped my shirt.

I looked at him. I said, "How can you do this to me? How can you do this to your own son for doing something like that?"

I got kicked out of the house before, two years ago, for taking a goddamned shower. For taking a goddamned shower.

I was out doing yard work for my father. I was doing this work for him and he never paid me for work. Richard and I painted the whole fucking house two years ago and we didn't get a red cent. We worked a month and a half straight, six hours a day. This time I was doing some yard work for him and my stepmother goes, "John, make sure you take a shower before three because Susie wants to clean it at three-thirty because we're having company tonight."

I said, "Fine." That was no problem.

I'm out doing the work for my dad, I'm working all day, and I happened to work past three-thirty. It was eighty-five, ninety degrees in the sun, and I had dirt all over me and was sweating like a fucking pig, with shit in my hair. And there was no way I was going to go out without taking a shower. So I went up and told Susie—she's my stepsister—I said, "I know you just cleaned the tub, but I'm very dirty. I'll clean it just as clean as you did, because I know you just cleaned it." I didn't see my parents—my father and my stepmother—around the house then.

So I was really considerate about it. I got downstairs, we eat dinner, not a word said at dinner. My friend comes to the door. "Okay, Dad, see you later."

"Where are you going?"

"I'm going out."

"No, you're not."

"What are you talking about?"

"You took a shower tonight after your stepmother told you you weren't supposed to. Now what the hell is wrong with you, you asshole? You always blow us off all the time. You never listen to us."

I said, "Dad, is taking a shower a goddamned offense, a crime?" He kept on bitching at me, bitching at me, and I said, "Fuck you. I'm leaving. I'm going out of this house. You're not going to tell me. I'm seventeen years old right now and I'm old enough to take care of myself. I'm more fucking responsible than you half the time." I said, "Later."

I walked out of the house. I got all my stuff, packed it in my friend's car, and said, "Much later."

I've gotten kicked out of the house on three different occasions. That whole scene is really fucked up.

Tell me about your stepmother.

I hate her. She's a bitch. A real bitch. She plays mind games.

Richard and I call her the "Mindfucker" because she plays mean games in your head. She's good at it. She's a bright lady, but she comes from a shitty family. She happened to see an easy snag with my old man, snagged him for a good vehicle—a lot of clothes, bucks, traveling all the time.

Because of her, Richard and I don't get money from my old man. Everything is channeled her way, basically. Whatever she says, goes. She takes care of all the books, the checkbook, the credit cards, everything like that.

I just hate her. She's a total bitch.

She plays little mind games, and I've caught onto her mind games because I've gone to different schools, been around so many different people, and you get accustomed to picking out certain things about people and using different sentence structures to set them up, to counteract what they have to say. So I burned her ass a few times. In the last year and a half she hasn't talked to me.

62

What do you mean, "burned her ass"?

Just certain things that have been said. She tries to be real smartassed and tries to blow me down. I go into a fucking rage. Not that I would ever hit her or kill her. I'd like to, but I wouldn't lose my head that much. I'd get up and I'd start going bullshit and she'd go, "John, John, settle down, you're sick, you're a sick kid."

Then I'd stop and I'd look at her and she'd try to twist my head up a little more and I'd just tell her to fuck off.

One time she said that Richard and I couldn't use any of the kitchen appliances—the stove, the oven, the toaster, electric can opener. Anything. Not even the dishwasher. We weren't allowed to use them because we weren't responsible enough. That was because Richard had supposedly started a fire in the toaster oven. I think cheese spilled on the fucking fryer and started a fire. No major problem. It's very forgivable. Well, just because of that incident, we couldn't use anything.

Then one day I got pissed. I said, "Fuck you. Excuse me." I walked out of the way and I just blew her off. I put a piece of toast in there and popped it down.

She went apeshit. She said, "I can't believe you're doing this in front of me." She went nuts. It was a good thing.

How many kids does she have?

Two. Marsha's really cool. Marsha's a very bright chick like her mother, but she is not that bad a mindfucker. She's very smart for her age and she can be very testy. She and Richard don't mix because they're both very strong people. They never got along. But I get along with Marsha well. And David, my little stepbrother, Richard and I could have beaten the shit out of him on several occasions. The kid would be going on, "John, you're an asshole, nah, nah, nah." Shit like that. I'd walk up, I'd grab him by the neck, and I'd cuff him across the top of the head. It doesn't hurt that bad. It really doesn't. I just wanted to knock some sense into this little kid. Richard would get out of hand; I used to have to tell him to settle down. When Richard's string breaks and he loses his temper, he'd just grab the kid

63

and *bam, bam, bam*. David would start screaming. "Mom, Richard is beating the shit out of me!"

"Richard, Richard," she'd go.

"Shut up," he'd say to her.

After a while Richard and I didn't respect her at all. I think we hated her so much because we already had one mother that was fucked up and we weren't about to accept another one. When I first met her, I thought she was really nice, but as a mother, she sucks.

There were too many bad memories with my old mother for me to take on another one. I said, "Fuck that, Dad. I get along with you, but I'm not going to listen to your wife."

I felt I had every right not to accept her because when he got married, it was his decision. It wasn't all of us. He didn't even come and talk to us. Here our life-styles were going to be changed again and he didn't talk to us at all. So he said, "Screw you. I can dump you kids out in the street. You know, if it wasn't for me, John, you'd still be in the fucking loony bin, and Richard, you'd be off with your crazy mother."

Did your father use drugs?

On Christmas my dad would have a few drinks just because of the season, but he doesn't drink other than that. My old man has smoked weed, but when we found it, he played real stupid with us. I guess we were about ten or eleven years old. It was when we were getting fairly heavily into weed and we knew what we were doing.

At ten and eleven?

Yeah. Richard and me. We would buy a bag. It was little kids' stuff, though. We'd buy a dime and split it four ways and save it for two weeks. But we knew what the fuck was going on. My old man had a nice-size ounce in his dresser drawer.

This was when he was still single. He asked us to do the laundry, so we did the laundry. I was putting my dad's socks away in his dresser. We had never been allowed in there before, but we had just moved in with him. Big fucking ounce sitting there. And it was really funny.

64

The next day he had a party. Richard and I came home earlier than expected. He had some friends over and one guy just tossed a joint behind the couch and it was still smoldering when we walked in. Everyone mellowed out and tried to get a grip on themselves. My dad's sitting there. "What are you doing here? You told me you were going to be home at twelve o'clock. I told you you could stay out until two."

After that we talked to him. We said, "Dad, we love you a lot. It's cool that you smoke dope because we smoke dope, too."

He didn't handle that well. He totally blew it off. He said, "I didn't smoke weed. This guy Dave was going to be busted for smoking; I was holding it for him."

I looked at him and said, "Dad, you're crazy. A dealer doesn't give you an ounce to hold onto. He'll give you a pound if he's going to get his house checked out by the pigs. He won't give you an ounce. I don't know who the hell you're trying to kid." He kept saying he was holding it for this guy.

My mother smokes a lot of good weed. She lives out in New Mexico. We got really buzzed with my uncle for three days and he was telling us that while he was out there seeing my mother they had done some good 'shrooms. I thought that was funny.

What about your stepfather?

I don't know. I don't even know him. What I know of him, he's an asshole. I don't even care. In my mind he doesn't even exist because I was in West Seneca most of the time.

What kind of feelings did you have about your mother after you got out of that place?

I hated her, and thought I'd never forgive her. It hasn't been until just recently that I've been open-minded about it and said, well, hey, maybe she made a mistake. She wasn't well then and maybe I can forgive her. She wrote me a nice letter recently. I'm getting a transfer at the end of the year and I'll go to the University of New Mexico, hopefully. She doesn't live far from there. Even if she's still fucked up, I'll get to see my brother and sister. I don't know them because they were so little. My little sister is about fifteen and is getting to be blooming and beautiful and I'm going to check it out. And my little brother, I'm going to help him get into sports. If you ever saw him or looked at a picture of him, he'd be a cross between me and Richard.

Do you think you'll ever get married?

Not for a long time. When you go through so much shit like that, after a while you wonder what's wrong with these people. Why do they get married?

My mother, I think she had me when she was seventeen or eighteen years old. That's asinine. Just think: that's *our* age. I couldn't handle a family right now. I couldn't handle bringing up a kid. I can't even fucking handle taking care of myself. Some days I can't even eat. It's just so fucking hard on me. I'm getting there, though.

So I won't get married for a long time. I want to know exactly what the hell I'm going to be doing. I want to see my share of women and what kind there are available all around the country. I'd like to check that out. Maybe in my late twenties. I want to do my traveling and be financially secure before I bring up any kind of family.

Divorce—I think it's pretty stupid. That's why you can't get married when you're young: your mind is still young. My father was a wild guy when he was my age. He used to do a lot of races like the Daytona and he had some hot cars and poured all his money into it. I think he hates Richard for owning that Trans-Am because he's jealous. There's Richard, only seventeen and owning a car like that. I think it pisses him off. He said, "No kid your age should drive a car like that."

Richard blew him off. He said, "Later, Dad." Laid some rubber out in front of the house.

And my mother was wild, too. She used to pose for all these fucking photographers. She was a beautiful lady. I've seen pictures of her when she was young. I don't know how her life got so fucked up.

Do you think it was good or bad that your parents got divorced?

It was great. I'm not saying that sarcastically. It was good because things would have been even more fucked up if they hadn't. Two fucked-up people in one house. They would have killed each other.

Did you go to your parents' weddings?

No. Neither of them. It bothered me to have them get married and me not be a part of it. But I wasn't invited and I wasn't going to ask them to go to their wedding.

Have you any relationship with either of your parents now?

No, none at all. I'm on my own and having a good time, busting my ass and trying to get an education.

Going through it has made me a hell of a lot stronger. Everything that I've gone through lately has made me more aware of all the problems in school and all the problems in the world and how to deal with them, how to take them in a good frame of mind.

I was really foolish when I was younger. My sophomore year of high school was a total blow-off. I just got buzzed all the time. Had a fine time. Went to more concerts than I have in any other year and just blew off life. Then I went back to private school again for my junior and senior years and did pretty well. Did well scholastically, did well in journalism and photography.

Things will work out well for me. I'll get a break sometime.

"Her arm was broken in twelve places."

LOUISE (17)

I have one brother, a half brother. I had a twin sister, but she's dead now. She drowned. My mother's been divorced five times.

Which husband were you born to?

Her third.

They are mostly younger, a lot younger than she is. Ten years apart. I'm trying to remember all their names.

Her fourth husband, Jim, was twenty-six and she was thirty-five at the time. He was weird. He wasn't wrapped too tightly. He was a Marine. He spent a lot of time with my mother. I was living with my father then and I don't know too much about him.

I know a lot about the one she's married to now. He's a really great guy.

Jim and I used to fight a lot. He's a lot like my real father. Really strict. Everything had to be his way. And I guess I'm the same kind of person. I like things my way and we used to fight a lot. I didn't like his age; I kind of resented that. I'd say, "Listen, you're not too much older than me, so don't tell me what to do."

I didn't like him. I always thought, You're not my father. So I couldn't respect him. I respect Steve, her husband now. I think he's a really great guy.

My mother and father were married twice. The first time they got divorced, my mother got custody of my brother and me. My sister had died before then, when I was eight; my brother was ten. Then they got remarried and divorced again, and she got custody of us again. Then she turned me over to my father.

Why?

I got into trouble. She wasn't very strict and she gave me too much freedom and I got into too much trouble. She couldn't handle it, so she gave me to my father.

Did you want to go to your father?

No, no. God, no.

What sort of trouble had you gotten into?

A lot of trouble with the police. I stole a car. Shoplifting. Drugs.

Do you get in trouble now?

No.

Why then?

I don't know. I got into the trouble after they were divorced. My mother gave me a lot of freedom and I just took advantage of it. My father, when they were together, did not give us any freedom at all. It was, "Do this, do that. Don't talk back."

The first time they got divorced, I was thirteen, maybe just turned fourteen.

Did your life change when {your father} left?

Just a little bit. I'd always heard about divorce and I wasn't sure how to handle it at first. Then I got used to it and it didn't bother me at all. When he first left I was glad, because I never got along with him. My mother and I got to spend more time together, but we fought a lot. Just little stuff.

I kind of resented the responsibility. A lot of things that my father used to do, little things like taking out the trash. That was the only time I missed my father: when he did his stuff. I had to do them and I didn't like it.

Have you ever gotten close to any of your stepfathers?

No. I should have, though, because they were pretty close to my age. I guess they understood what teenagers go through. I never got a chance to get used to them. I think I resented them more than anything. I didn't want them there. I wanted it to be us three, like it was in the very beginning.

Did your mother ever tell you about her previous husbands?

She told me about my brother's father. That was her second marriage. My brother always called my father Dad; that was the only father he knew. He said one day that he'd like to find his real father, and he put a lot of thought into it and a lot of time into it. He talked to people trying to find his father. My mother told me that his father was dead and she didn't have the heart to tell him. I used to ask her about him and she said that he was a cruel man. She didn't like him. They weren't married that long—eight months, nine months, something like that. Right after my brother was born, he left. He was an alcoholic.

Were any of the others alcoholic?

I think my father is, but there's no way to be sure. I really think he is. He drinks so much. And his personality changes completely when he drinks. It's scary.

How do you deal with him then?

I hide, because he can get violent. He broke my mother's arm one time. And he used to smack her around. The fights were unbelievable.

Can you tell me about some?

There's one that I will never forget in my whole life. When I think about it, I almost cry.

I heard my mother screaming and my brother and I were upstairs. I heard my father yelling. And like a jerk, I looked down the stairs and my mother saw me and she looked straight at me and she said, "Run!" My father was very drunk at the time.

I couldn't run. I was paralyzed 'cause I was so scared. He had her arm behind her back all the way up till it touched the back of her neck. And she was screaming and crying, and she kept saying, "Run! Run!"

My father told me not to come downstairs. When he says something, you should stick by it. So I ran upstairs and my brother ran with me and we ran in my room and locked the door. We had wood steps and I heard my father coming up the stairs. My mother was screaming behind him and she kept saying, "Hide!"

He broke down the door. My brother attacked him, he jumped on him, and my father threw him till he hit the closet; he just threw him. Then he grabbed me and picked me up and was yelling at me, "I told you not to come downstairs!"

My mother's arm was bleeding and it was all scratched up. It looked so bad. It was so gross. And she hit him on the back with an iron. And it knocked him out or it did something to him, and he was lying there all spaced out. My mother grabbed us and ran downstairs. She couldn't drive, so we ran next door. They took her to the hospital.

Her arm was broken in twelve places. Her arm was destroyed, and a year later she had to get money for an operation on her arm or they were going to amputate. And it was all because of my father.

I'll never forget that. It was so scary. God.

He gets so violent when he drinks.

They stayed together after that, surprisingly. Her arm was in a cast and they got into a little picking fight. They were picking on each other until they got really mad and she threw a plate at him. He came after her and she picked up a knife. And he just left. That was the last

71

time I saw him for about three months. She had to sell the house because she didn't work.

There were millions of fights. They were all physical. My father is the kind of person that if you do the littlest thing wrong, it gets him upset. She didn't prepare dinner right one night and he got mad. She was in a bad mood and we were all at the dinner table and she threw something at him for self-defense. She couldn't yell back at him, so it was like self-defense. He really got violent and he picked up the table. It was a big table. He just threw it over to the side and me and my brother hid. My father was slapping her around and her arm was still broken at the time. Her face was all cut up and all bruised on one side from him hitting her. It was terrible.

How old was your brother at the time he jumped on your dad?

Twelve. Didn't do any good.

My father hit my brother one time. I can't remember for what. He broke his collarbone. It was basically an accident.

My brother had a little animal, a gerbil or a hamster, and it got out of its cage and we couldn't find it and my father was mad. He was picking my brother up and shaking him. My brother likes to fight back. He doesn't like to be put down. So he hit my father. And my father hit him in the side of the face and slammed him up against the wall and broke his collarbone. I don't think he ever hit him again.

He used to hit me, but bruises was all it was. Nothing really serious. Well, I guess it was serious, but he didn't break any bones like he did to my mother and brother.

How did you feel toward him at the time?

I hated him. I still hate him. I've always hated him and I always will, no matter what. He treated us like we were robots. We had to do things. Everything had to be his way and it still is. If you don't do it, watch out. He is the kind of guy that will come after you. And it's scary. He's not that big; it's just the tone of his voice and you know what he can do. And it scares you.

Is your mother violent naturally?

No. God, no. She's a beautiful person. How my father ever treated her like that, I don't know.

She lives in Hawaii now. The last time I saw her was her wedding day, last June. I don't hear from her very much. It's too expensive to call. We tape to each other, but that's only every two weeks or so. I miss her.

She wanted me to come out after graduation and see her, but it's too much money. Plus I'll only be seventeen and my father won't let me. He hates my mother. They hate each other, I should say.

My father has custody. He won't let me go. I tried to fight it in court two years ago. Well, they fought it in court and I didn't have much say. But what I did say didn't help, so they fought it out and he still got me.

He's got custody because she turned me over to him. I think it was a spur-of-the-moment thing, but I don't know.

I think she'd want me, but her husband is only four years older than I am, so I think that would kind of endanger her marriage. So I don't think she'd want me back now.

That fight when your brother jumped on your dad—why was your father so mad?

I couldn't tell you. I think my father is very suspicious. And I know my mother would never cheat on any of her husbands. She never would. And she supposedly said that he had an affair with some girl, and I think he did. And he thinks that she was having an affair and I think that's what brought it on. Jealousy even though they hated each other at the time.

Tell me about your stepmother.

I don't like her. I don't like anything about her. She's twenty-eight, she's a diabetic, and she's almost blind. She lost an eye a couple of years ago and she has a glass eye. She's so weird. I hate her. She's the kind of person who's ten years behind the times. And won't change. We never get along. We never have and we probably never will.

She lies to me constantly about everything she did. She used to tell me weird stories. I was only twelve or thirteen at the time and I believed them. It was just so she could win me over. She used to take me places and do things. She would always keep me away from my father. It was like she wanted me to be close to her and not close to my father.

My stepmother lived with my father at the time I had to come and live with him. I think that's why they got married: because my father thought I needed a mother. I don't need her.

What sort of stories did she tell you?

I'm a roller-skating freak. My brother was state champion and we love to roller-skate. The first time I met her, we were at the roller-skating rink and she and my father came over and she said, "I used to be in the roller derby." She carried it on and carried it on, so I said, "Well, come on and teach me how to skate. Teach me how to do some of these things you used to do, like spin around."

She'd never skated before. You could tell. She got out there and fell.

She'd work up these stories, then say later, "I'm only kidding" or something like that. She was trying to make herself better than what she is, which isn't very good.

Were you invited to your parents' weddings?

To all my mother's, but not to my father's. He didn't invite anybody. It was a little wedding.

Were you insulted?

Yes. Very. I didn't feel it was right.

Did you say anything to him about it?

No. I didn't want him to get mad.

Do you think you got the short end of the stick in your parents' divorce?

Not when they were first divorced, but I did after she remarried. Because after her fourth marriage I had to go live with my father. I felt like, she's got a new husband, she doesn't need me, so she's giving me up. And I said, if she doesn't need me, fine, but it wasn't fine at all.

You know, something happens to my father in February every year. It's because of my sister. She died in February and we were twins. He changes completely. He gets in his own shell and he freaks out sometimes. He cries and then he starts laughing. Then he starts throwing things around. It's weird. I hate February.

How do you deal with it?

Usually I hide from him. He was pretty close to my sister. He spent a lot of time with her. She was really talented. She could do a lot of things, like gymnastics. I guess he always wanted me to be like her and I could never be like her. He was so close to her and I just have to hide because of it.

I've joined the army. Graduation is the twenty-second and I'll be going in on the twenty-fourth. It's just to get away from my father. My father wouldn't pay for college. He wouldn't let me go live with my mother. So I had no choice if I wanted to get away.

Don't you get custody of yourself at eighteen?

Yeah, but I would have no way of getting out to where she lives. She lives so far away. The army gets me free.

"It's a very sad situation—incest is."

JOANIE (15)

I moved more because of my stepfather than anything else. I could handle my mother pretty much. She used to bitch at me about everything, but that didn't have much of an effect on me. I didn't pay any attention to it after a while. The guilt-tripping was harder. I never did learn to deal with that well. That worked more to keep me living at her house. She used to make me feel terrible when I even talked about the possibility of living at my father's for a while. She made it so moving there would be a terrible betrayal of her. It was always put in those terms—what it would do to *her*. I didn't have much to do with it, at least not from her point of view. I didn't understand that until later, though.

So what got you to make the move?

My stepfather—as far as I'm concerned and surely for anyone who knows him well—is crazy. He did the weirdest things. You probably wouldn't believe me if I told you all of them. I truly believe that he's troubled mentally.

The thing that triggered my leaving just scared hell out of me. He used to wake me up for school. One morning, the last day of exams, he got into my bed. I woke up and he was trying to get on top of me. I've never been so scared in my life. I didn't know what to do. He was totally nude—and trying to have sex with his wife's thirteen-year-old daughter!

I got away from him and I screamed for him to get out of the room. He left without saying a word.

That was the day I moved out. For good. I moved in with my father.

I still can't look at my mother's husband without contempt and without wanting to smash his face into a thousand pieces. I still have massive hostility in me against him and against my mother.

Why against your mother? Was she there when it happened?

No. I told my mother what happened. She had a conversation with my stepfather and the two of them concluded that I made up the whole story to break them up. I told her I would never do such a thing. She said, "Then why did you make up that awful story?"

I think it came down to this: she had to believe one of us. If she believed me, then he had to go. How could she live with a man who tried to rape her daughter? So it was easier for her to believe his version.

It took me two years before I was able to tell my father about it. Now I can talk about it and laugh it off and say, "Harvey is crazy. He's sick-minded. And my mother's just scared about losing another husband."

It's so horrible, especially because it happens to so many kids who never report it. Who's going to believe us? A friend of mine is adopted and her father tried to get into bed with her when she was fourteen. She thought it was great because there he was, hugging her and telling her he loved her, something she wasn't used to. Then he started getting under the covers with her. And when she was crying and shrieking for him to leave, he said, "I love you! Why won't you let me love you?"

It's a very sad situation—incest is.

"We can't prove he's dead."

PATRICIA (17)

My parents knew each other since they were little kids, since they were about seven. They set up housekeeping in a treehouse. They knew each other all their lives. When they first got married, I guess they were very happy. They lived in South America for a while and they had my sister there.

We lived in Maryland and we were your typical happy family. Then my dad got a job up here in Buffalo and we moved up here.

But alcoholism runs in my father's family a lot and he started drinking. He started drinking heavier and heavier. We had a nice house then. He started drinking more and more and he lost that job because of his drinking.

He got another job, an even better job, so we moved to a nicer street. Then he lost that job and he started drinking a lot more. He was unemployed for about six months. That's when my parents really started fighting. Things got bad.

He got a job in Cleveland, Ohio. It was a good job. They told my sister and me that we were staying here because of school, that we were going to sell the house. It was actually a separation, but I didn't know that. That kept up for maybe four or five months, then they decided that for the kids they'd get back together again. We moved outside of Cleveland. It was a nice house, out in the country.

But my father's drinking kept getting worse. He lost his job there and he was unemployed for another six months. It wasn't that he couldn't get a job, but he'd just sit home and keep drinking. He started coming home late at night. And he couldn't hold down a job.

Then he got another job. It was a good job. It was with a government agency and he was a systems analyst. He designed computer systems. His superior there was a doctor and he realized that my dad had a drinking problem and he tried to help him. Things were looking up for a while. He was drinking less.

And then—oh, I always hated the government for this—they phased out the program that he was in, that he was working for. They decided to cancel it in a budget cut. So then he was just working while they were winding down the program. The drinking got worse and worse. And for that last year he was working there, he would start coming home early in the morning and I couldn't stand sleeping in the house anymore because he'd come home and my parents would fight and I couldn't sleep. We had a screened-in porch out in the back and I slept there until late in January, when my parents made me come inside because it was getting so cold out.

My schoolwork started suffering because I couldn't sleep at night. I was so scared that he'd be drunk, he'd be out on the road somewhere and he'd be in an accident, or that something had gone wrong. I couldn't sleep until he came home. Every night I was awake until he came home.

When that job finally ended, it was in the summer. He'd be so drunk when he came home sometimes he couldn't get out of the car. He'd just stay in the car and sleep in the car all night. Sometimes I'd take a blanket out to him.

My sister took it differently. She became really withdrawn and she tried to run away to California. She was maybe in the ninth grade and she got a bus ticket. My parents caught her.

Things just kept getting worse and my mom took my sister and me to a family psychiatrist to talk about all the problems. My mom got into Al-Anon and we went to Alateen for a while.

I finally decided that the only thing that will make [an alcoholic] stop drinking is himself. I asked my father, "Daddy, would you stop drinking?" So he went into AA for about three weeks. He did okay for a while. The guy that sponsored him in AA was a lawyer and he handled my parents' divorce later.

Things were looking good for my dad. He was talking a lot better. Before, sometimes I'd hear him at night say, "I just don't want to go on living" and stuff like that. And then one night he said he had a job interview for the next day. We had all gone out for a while in the car and we came home and he said something was wrong with the car. He said, "I'm going up to the gas station."

He never came home. He went up to his old hangout and I guess he got really drunk that night. He just took off and about a month later the police found his car in a state park in Ohio. The car had been there for about a week and it had been stripped. And nobody has heard from him since. I was fourteen then.

We talked to people at Social Security and for almost four years nothing has been deposited in his Social Security account. The FBI had a tracer on him and he hasn't worked for anybody under his name, under his license.

I think he's dead.

He was in really bad shape when he left. I think if he started drinking again, he couldn't have held down a job.

My mother immediately asked for a divorce. He wasn't around and you have to have two people for a divorce. But they printed a notice in the paper and they ran it for five weeks. It said that my mother requested a divorce because of abandonment and cruel and inhuman treatment of the children and stuff like that. And she got it. She got a divorce in about five months. It was bad, though, because we can't prove my father is alive, so we don't get alimony or child support, and we can't prove he's dead because there's no body, so there's no life insurance or Social Security.

So my mother had to go back to work. She hadn't worked in twenty, twenty-five years. She took some courses at business school. She used to be a secretary before she got married. Now she works as a secretary. But it's kind of tough, supporting two kids, trying to get them through college on a secretary's salary, when you're used to living in a nice house.

I started getting kind of fucked up about the seventh grade. I started doing badly in school 'cause I was always staying up late. I always wanted to be out of the house, especially on weekends, because I hated to hear my parents fight. That's when I first started to smoke a lot of pot. And I drank a lot.

Then we moved here because we had to sell our house [in Cleveland]. We came back to Buffalo because we had our friends here. My mom thought it would be good if my sister and I were near old friends.

The first couple of summers I was here, the kids I hung around with—I can't believe I hung around with them. Some of the most disgusting people. Jerks. Some of them were nice; some of them were okay. But it was just that I was really into drugs for a while and I used to hang around with the cool kids and I got into trouble a couple of times.

I got caught in a bar one time—being extremely underage. They threatened to call my parents and give me a Person in Need of Supervision or something card, but I managed to get out of it because I was with a bunch of kids who were also underage, but they were older than I was, so they figured—there were maybe ten of us—that's too many, and they said, "Okay, just get out of here."

Another time I was really drunk and I was walking down the street and I got picked up by the cops. Just for being drunk. It was around two in the morning. And the other time was for trespassing. We were at Park Pond and all the cops came and chased us out. They yelled at us. My mother had to go to court.

I think recently I've pulled myself together pretty well. I'm doing pretty well in school and I'm looking forward to going to college. And I have some good friends.

What sort of drugs did you take?

Nothing really hard. I smoked a lot of pot. And I did pills—speed and tranquilizers. It was an escape from what was going on, especially if my parents had a big fight. All I wanted to do then was get out of the house, go have a couple of beers and get drunk and get in a good mood and forget about things.

Did you recognize at the time that it was an escape?

No. My mom took us to Child and Family Services out in Williamsville and I went to a lot of Alateen meetings and some AA meetings and stuff like that. And I realized why I was doing a lot of stuff—to get back at my parents.

I still love my father a lot. I understand—this is all AA philosophy, that detachment—I realize that his drinking problem was what messed up his family. I don't love that about him, but I still love him. And I forgive him for a lot.

I know that one reason he left was he knew he was falling apart. The tension and stuff at home were just so terrible. When my sister tried to run away, that almost killed him because he knew that we couldn't stand it anymore. He knew it was him being lost.

But I think that was just the easy way out for him—just leaving. I think he should have tried sticking it out, or sticking with AA, trying to get off booze. That just ruined him. That is what happened to his father.

My father supposedly killed his father. My grandfather was really drunk one time and he was beating up my dad, and my dad grabbed him and beat him up and he died from a heart attack. So the family always said he killed his father.

Alcoholism runs in my family. I know that I'm a prime target for it and I worry about it. I worry that when I have kids I'm going to do the same thing to them, that I'm going to drink and mess up the family.

Then don't.

I know, I try not to. I don't drink a lot. It's really hard to tell when somebody is an alcoholic and when they're not. Sometimes it's just heavy drinking. It's weird, but a lot of it is hereditary.

My mother really scared me. She's a very kind woman, but she took me one time to Bry-Lyn Hospital in Buffalo, which is a small hospital for recovering alcoholics and people with drug problems, an expensive hospital, and I talked to a doctor who's head of it. He said that one of the scariest things is that daughters of alcoholics have a seven out of ten chance of marrying an alcoholic. It's because of the behavior pattern of their fathers, the way they were. The kind of people you're attracted to treat you like your father did. And also granddaughters of alcoholics. It's just the way you are. You tend to choose friends who are going to drink a lot or who need drugs a lot.

Did the shrink do you guys any good?

The first one I went to did. She helped me because she's the one who explained what alcoholism was and the reason my dad did a lot of stuff he did was because he drank. That helped me. But a lot of the stuff she did—I don't think it hurt me, but I don't think it helped at all. It confused me, a lot of the stuff she said.

'Cause I was doing badly in school at the time and she and my mother were saying, "Get tutors. You've got to do your homework. You've got to do this and that." "Don't go out" and "You know you've been drinking. You've got to stop drinking." And a lot of bullshitting at me.

Who did you go with?

Mostly my mother and my sister. A few times the whole family was there. My dad had to be dragged there, he didn't want to go at all. Then when we came here, I went to Child and Family Services out in Williamsville. The people there were really nice. I went with my mother a couple of times. And my mother and sister. And I went by myself a couple of times. But I think the people there are mostly just social workers.

Have you ever gone to friends and just let out all your frustrations on them?

When I lived in Ohio, before I really knew what was going on, I kept it inside so much. I didn't want anybody to know that my family was different in any way from anybody else. I didn't want people to know when my dad was out of work, I didn't want people to come over to the house because my dad might be drunk. Or he and my

83

mom might be in the middle of a fight. I always went to other people's houses as much as I could because I wanted to get out.

[My friend] Emily knew. I told Emily 'cause we've known each other all our lives. At the same time she was going through a lot because her mother was dying. We kind of cried on each other's shoulders.

My sister and I are very close and got through a lot of it together. She got in a lot of trouble, though. She's a year older than I am. But she's really good now. She went off to Europe for five months and now she's in college and she's got a 4.0 average. She's really pulled herself together. But I don't believe the stuff that happened to her. If we hadn't had each other, I think we would have gone under.

I think she took it harder than I did because she bottled it up inside her. She didn't let it out. She's kind of a quiet person anyway. She doesn't make friends as fast as some people because she's not really outgoing. She had two good friends when things were going really badly. One was a boyfriend she had been going out with for about three years. It was really sad because they both moved away at the same time and she had no close friends through the worst part of it. That's when we got really close, I think. It kind of pushed us together.

What do you recall about the fights?

Mostly, my dad would be almost always drunk. My mother would be saying that something had to be done and my dad was losing another job. They'd just scream at each other.

Right before they got their separation, when my dad was working in Cleveland and we were in Buffalo, it was a lot about my mother wanting him to drink less and come home earlier and try to keep a job. Then he was always screaming and yelling, "Oh, you're just nagging me. And you're neurotic and you're worried about little things."

He never hit us. He wasn't a wife beater or a child beater. There wasn't any abuse like that. The cruelty my mother meant in that thing in the paper referred to the strain of living like we were. And then he abandoned us.

He never hit you?

Well, mostly it was when we had disobeyed and had done something. He never hit me real hard in the head or anything. But when I was little, a couple of times, I remember him spanking me real hard for doing nothing. I was about six and I didn't understand why. But what was worse were the times he started cutting me down or cutting my mother down in front of us, stuff like that. And when they fought.

I have asthma and it's something wrong with you, but a lot of it can be brought on by stress. And I remember one time when I was in about third grade and my parents were having a fight. My dad was drunk and they were screaming at each other. I came down and I sat on the steps and I remember thinking, oh, my God. This can't happen. And I had an asthma attack. All of a sudden. It was a real asthma attack, but it was brought on by that, I'm sure. So they had to rush me to the hospital and I had to have medicine. But it broke up the fight.

How would your dad cut you down?

It was only when he was drunk that he would do it. One time he said, "Oh, you're just a rat. You're a failure. You'll never do anything. You're just like your parents. Just like your mother."

I know he loved me and my sister a lot because sometimes when he'd come home really late and it'd be early in the morning, I'd make him a cup of coffee and we'd sit and talk. He'd say things like, "I just want you to know that whatever you do in your life, we'll always stand by you. I'm your father and I really love you and please, don't forget that I will always love you."

That was shortly before he left. So I think he left because he loved us, because he knew what he was doing [to the family].

He cried once. He was very drunk. He was down on himself and I went and put my arms around him and said, "Daddy, I love you," and he started crying. We were really close then. I'd make him breakfast. I'd fry him an egg or something. I liked doing that for him. We were always close at times like that.

How did you react that time he said he didn't want to go on living?

I felt so bad. I was so scared and insecure for a couple of years. I was just so terrified. I'd stay up until he came home every night. I was so scared that he wouldn't come home. Then, when he didn't come home, it was a relief because I didn't have to worry about it. It's kind of ironic.

Probably the hardest thing is not knowing. I mean, if he's dead, then we can accept it. If the parents are divorced, you can accept that. But when you don't know if you're ever going to see your father again, if he's ever going to turn up . . . What if he suddenly turned up in my life? What the hell would happen?

You told me your dad went to Ohio and it was actually a separation. When did you find this out?

I think I kind of knew at the time, but I wouldn't admit it to myself. It was, "My daddy is working. Everything is fine. Everything is going to be okay."

Then maybe a year later, after we had moved and they had gotten back together again, when my dad was losing another job and my mother was going nuts with him, she said, "I don't see how this is going to work. Maybe I should just get a divorce right now. When we were separated last year . . ." And blah, blah, blah. That's when I found out it was a separation.

I felt really bad. I was just terrified thinking about them getting a divorce. It really scared me. And I felt guilty. I thought, I've got to try harder to keep things together.

Did you ever think it was your fault?

I don't think I thought it was my fault, but I felt that if I tried harder, if I shielded my mom when my dad was drunk, if I tried to keep her from seeing things or seeing him when he was drunk, or if I did things around the house that he was supposed to do, so she wouldn't yell at him—you know: "Go out and cut the grass" or "Fix this or that." 'Cause I was really close to my dad. I was closer than my sister. I used to follow him around all the time. Anything he did, I had to do when I was little.

What grade were you in when you started to do poorly in school?

I think it was the end of sixth grade, 'cause in seventh grade I started to go downhill. And eighth grade was really bad. And ninth grade wasn't too hot, and tenth grade I tried to do better.

Do you think you're stronger mentally now than if none of this had happened and you had led a sheltered life?

Yes. I think about that so much. I think about all the kids at Amherst that live in their nice little worlds, where Mommy cooks dinner and Daddy brings the money home and things are so nice. All those nice clothes. And they live in a nice house. I think, you don't know what it's like. You haven't been through what I've been through. I feel like I can handle so much now.

It's kind of reverse prejudice. I get mad sometimes at people who are rich and have everything they want. I say, "Oh, why does she wear that coat? Aw, fuck you. I can't afford a new one."

But I think it gave me the strength to pull myself together and say it's not going to happen to me. I'm going to do well in life. I'm going to get good grades. It's not going to happen to me. I'm not going to let it.

Some people don't come out of it stronger. They come out weakened by it.

I think the fact that my dad just left and he's not in my life anymore has something to do with that. If he were still around, I'm sure I'd be a mess. I'd be torn up trying to choose between my mother and my dad, who I wanted to live with, or by seeing my dad drunk all the time.

I'd like for my mother to get remarried. She hates working. She's a real homebody type. I think the breakup was mostly my dad's fault, but it drove my mother nuts. I'd say she had a lot of psychological problems—fears and being neurotic. When she knew my dad was losing another job, she'd get really hysterical. If I broke a dish, she'd have this unusual anger. She'd throw things and say, "Goddamn it! Get out of here!" And she'd scream. Whenever that started happening, we knew my dad was losing a job again.

Do you think you're going to get married?

Yeah. In the future sometime. I want to have kids. It's just that I'm worried. After I talked with that doctor, I'm so scared that the person I marry is going to drink and the same thing's going to happen again. 'Cause he's right. I look at some of the guys I've really liked that were boyfriends and some of them have a list of DWIs and stuff like that just so long, and I think, oh, my God. They're doing it.

You've got to pick someone who's strong and who's going to be strong. Someone who's not going to fuck up my life. That's what scares me: I don't want it to happen again.

What's your opinion about divorce?

I think if you don't have to go through it, it's great. I think about a happy family. I remember when I was little when things were happy and how good it was. In a way I'm glad I went through what I have, 'cause I know I'm a stronger person for it. But it would have been nicer not to.

"I don't know if the crime would have happened."

JIM (15), Alice's brother

It was real gradual. Day after day my father wasn't home. And one day I was told. I don't know if it had a drastic effect or not. I can't compare it to anything, since I haven't had a father since I was so young. I was seven then.

I don't know if the crime would have happened if I did have a father. It may be just myself.

The first time I was in junior high. I sold hash to somebody and they called the police. I had to go to court for that. It was dismissed. The second time it was a real mess. It was pretty awful. The police took advantage. They came in my house, they were searching around. The place was all messed up.

I broke into two houses the same day. One [case] was dismissed, but for the other I was put on probation for a year and a half. And just recently I was caught breaking into a liquor store with two other kids. I don't know what's going to happen with that.

My father didn't want to give my mother any money. He thought it was all her fault. She's been to court so many times with him. She's still going. Right now she gets fifteen dollars a week for each kid, which is nothing, nothing at all. He's an assistant district attorney, so it's not like he's in the poorhouse.

My mother works for an advertising company. Right now she's on vacation. She sells pens and combs to companies. My mother has been a super lady about doing everything; trying to take care of us, she has to do two jobs: she goes out to work and then comes home and makes dinner. It puts a big strain on her. She's been in the hospital a couple of times because she has so much to worry about.

There's nothing there for my father. I don't hate him. I don't even know if I love him.

We would go over there sometimes and he would start getting down on my mother. My sisters couldn't handle it, and they would start crying. We had to go to my father's cousin, who lives around the block, and she had to take us home.

He just can't accept responsibility for his drinking or anything. But my mother's always said, "Try to accept it." She's been great. I don't know how she does it, though. Pretty hard.

My mother would never say anything about him because she had enough to handle without trying to go off and put somebody down. When my father would say [bad things about her], it would be kind of hard for me to understand. I would be saying to myself, "You don't have any right to say this, it isn't true. It just happened and if you want to say it's anybody's fault, say it's both your fault." He doesn't want to accept [responsibility for the situation], so he's trying to push it off on my mother.

Sometimes it's a hassle, but a couple of years ago, when I was ten or eleven, it was to my advantage because my mother would take me especially out to places, to hockey games and stuff, because I was the only boy. She was trying—she still is—to be a father and mother.

Sometimes it's hard for me to go to her and tell her the problems I have, but we get along really well and we can joke around with each other. She's understanding about most everything.

Do you see your father?

The last year or two I haven't at all. I don't want to see him because he's not a part of my life anymore. Before that I would go over just about every weekend with my sisters. They still go, but I broke away.

I always wonder what it would be like if I did have a father. How would my life be changed from the beginning?

"I didn't know who my father was."

ALICE (16), Jim's sister

I was six when I found out they were getting divorced. They were separated for a couple of years before. I've been finding out more lately about why because I'm getting older and ask more questions and I hear from other people.

My father still is an alcoholic and he was an alcoholic when they were married. He worked two shifts: he worked as a lawyer and he had another job in a factory. He'd come home pretty drunk. I can't remember too much because I was really small.

It just happened. My mother didn't tell me anything that I can remember. I just remember my father leaving one night. I can still see it in my mind. I can still see him leaving in his car.

And I remember seeing him every once in a while. He'd come back and pick us up and we would go out for dinner or stay for a weekend. Or not even a weekend—for Sunday afternoon.

He lives nearby now, but back then he lived with a friend of his and she was taking care of him because he had been in the hospital. He was a pretty bad alcoholic.

We used to see him every once in a while. Then he disappeared again for a couple of years.

What happened to him?

I think he went back to getting drunk. I don't know the details, but I know we didn't see him and he was back on the bottle really bad.

At the time I was confused. I can't remember it well. A lot is blocked out of my memory. I know my mother was going through a lot of hassles because she had to go out and get a job. It was hard for her. She's been through a lot of jobs. The first job was as a secretary.

[My father] was paying her fifteen dollars a week child support for each child. Sixty dollars a week, no alimony. Now it's taken out as a wage deduction because he stopped paying for a while. He didn't pay the money and the court ordered him to do it. The court has ordered him to do a lot of stuff.

One of the reasons they got a divorce is that he's a lawyer. He's a really smart guy, but he's full of self-pity. His father was an alcoholic and that doesn't help. His mother died when he was real young and I guess his stepmother was really mean to him.

When they broke up, it was strange. My mother had to start working and I didn't know where he was. I never knew. It was really hard for her with four kids. I was the oldest; I was seven. I never saw my father and then I did see him every once in a while and then he disappeared again and he came back when I was in fifth grade.

My mother would go out a lot and we'd have baby-sitters over a lot. I remember we had this old baby-sitter that was about seventy or eighty, and she didn't show up one night. That was the first night I stayed without somebody there and I remember crying a lot, asking my mother to stay home.

I'm trying to learn more about [my mother] as I'm getting older. I'm trying to forget the past, what's happened, and I'm trying to work on the relationship as it is now.

My father—I don't see him anymore. For a while I saw him, but things got to be really bad. When he started drinking I wasn't comfortable. That was years ago. He stopped drinking when I was around him.

The court had ordered him to fix up the house, since he owns it, and he wouldn't do that, so I went to court in the summertime and tried to get him back into court because my mother's lawyer wasn't doing a very fast job.

You went there yourself?

Yeah. I went and talked with the judge. Nothing happened. I couldn't get the petition back into court because my mother's lawyer was already processing it. She doesn't pay him, he does it for free, and it takes a long time. And my father keeps on getting postponements. So nothing's done on our house.

I've gone through a lot of things just thinking about him—being angry at him for being so selfish. His apartment is nice and our house is pretty much falling apart.

I got money from him one time. I talked to him on the phone and I told him I was going to the judge, and he gave me money that he said was from our trust fund. It was two hundred dollars. I was going to fix up the house with it. Our bathroom is real crappy. There's a hole between our attic and our tub so we can't take a shower. My mother wanted to fix it up. It was going to cost eighteen hundred dollars. I asked him for money and he gave me two hundred. He said that was all he had.

I think about it a lot. Now I just accept it. My mother always brought us up never to hate him.

My father called my mother names. A couple of times when he was really drunk he did that.

I remember when he lived on Grand Island, once he got really drunk. He had a girl friend, the only girl friend I knew that he ever had. I used to stay there sometimes and make dinner for him. He got drunk that night and started calling my mother evil. He said he was going to get custody of me and take me away from her. I went outside and I was crying and this lady he was going out with drove me back home because I didn't want to drive in his car with him.

He got in an accident that night. It wasn't a bad accident. Somebody just smashed into his car as he was turning. He was pretty drunk and he didn't have the right of way.

I remember earlier things. I remember him screaming about

something. I don't remember what it was. In my mind I see a frying pan or a coffeepot that he threw at her. I don't remember it well. I remember I ran outside crying. I see pictures now, but I don't remember stuff.

Our house used to be real nice. Real nice.

After the divorce he had a room near where we lived. He didn't even have an apartment, he just rented a room. My mother wrote him a letter about something and I brought it over to give to him, and he ripped it up before he even opened the envelope.

We still get calls in the nighttime and my mother thinks they're from him. Hang-up calls.

He's said stuff about my mother. He still loves her, I think. He's really bitter. He drinks a lot and he feels real sorry for himself. He gets drunk a lot and he'll start talking about her: "Where is she now? Who's her boyfriend?" That sort of crap.

My mother tried to make it easier on us.

No. No, she didn't. She had so much work and she would go out a lot. That was really hard—not having her home and having baby-sitters. My father disappeared for a while and then he never kept in touch. So it was difficult from both ends.

It was a good thing that it happened, though, because they could never live together. They'd kill each other. They'd fight a lot. It was good because our whole family would have gone through even worse stuff. They had to get away from each other. It would never have worked out.

I was really young and I didn't realize how much it affected my development. I'm sure it did. Early childhood development is an important part of your life.

My mother wasn't around that much of the time. I got real fat. I never had any friends except one.

Sometimes, when I get depressed, I think about it. But then so many kids have it worse than I do. It's worse when I think of so many people who have it better than I do. That's when I start feeling bad. I used to feel sorry for myself for a while.

How did you get over that?

I started having a lot of friends and then I started partying a lot.

I'm trying to stop partying so much. I don't want to get burned out. And I see a psychiatrist now. Not that much, but I used to see her when school was starting. She's done a lot. I used to run to her with my problems.

Do you think if your parents had not been divorced you'd be any different now?

Definitely. I've been through so many experiences, a lot of them with older guys. I think that's a father-complex sort of thing. When I was fourteen, I was going out with a guy who was seventeen. And when I was sixteen, the guy I went out with was nineteen.

I just know a lot of people that are older. I don't think I would have grown up as fast and hung around with older people so much. I probably would have gotten more discipline. I get away with lots of stuff, not being home. I used to lie a lot.

If you were to get married and had a kid that was your age, and you were divorced, what would you say?

I'd try to sit down and explain what love is, or how I loved my husband and how different it is from how I love my child. Then I'd try to explain as best I could that people change.

I think about marriage. I know sometimes that I thought I loved somebody, but if you're going to have children, my feelings are that you can't have children until you know yourself. I don't think either of my parents knew themselves when they got married. I know that because they still don't know themselves.

They didn't know what they really wanted. My father married my mother and my mother married my father for reasons I'm not even sure are true, reasons that I've heard from other people who knew them when they were younger.

My mother was pretty rude. She was spoiled, I guess. And it's hard to grow up when you're forty, like she is now, especially with four kids.

96

I think that you have to be grown up before you can even say to somebody, "Look, I want to spend my life with you."

And then having children—you have to have a license to drive a car and to do all kinds of other things. To have a kid, you just have to do the obvious.

"I put my hand through a window."

TONY (16)

About a year and a half ago my father went to England. My mother decided that they weren't compatible, that she didn't want to go to England with him, and that was sort of the beginning. When he came back from England, she decided that she couldn't live with him again. I guess she had already decided before he went to England that she wasn't going to live with him again. But she never told him.

He was always kind of involved in his work more than his family. He'd get up, go to work, come home, and pass out in front of the TV set. He's a professor and he teaches and does research and gets grants.

Who told you they were separating?

My mom, 'cause she knew a lot before my dad did. He was in England when she started breaking the news to us.

It was pretty obvious because before he went to England, she started sleeping outside. She wouldn't sleep in the same bedroom with him. She kind of went schizo for a while, I think. She slept in a tent in the backyard. You'd have to know my mother.

It was hard. It hurt a lot. It did.

It was a big change moving from our big house to a little apartment with four rooms. It broke up the family. Both my sisters were away at college already, so I suppose that made it a little easier. And the fact that my dad was in England for a year before they separated probably made it a little easier, too.

I could see it coming for a long time, so it wasn't any great shock. I kind of suppressed it, though. I never really thought about it. I pushed it out of my mind until I couldn't anymore. You know what I mean? Sort of don't think about it or talk about it till it's on you.

Have you ever talked to anybody about it frankly before?

No.

Do you think it might have helped if you had had somebody to talk to?

It might have, but it wouldn't have changed anything. I probably wouldn't have done a few of the things I did. Like that scar there on my thumb . . .

How did you get that?

I put my hand through a window. I was coming back from a party at Betty Barber's. I had a little too much gin that night. Everybody was going to Brunner's [Bar] and I didn't feel like asking anybody for a ride, so I figured I'd just walk. I was walking along and all of a sudden—I don't know why—I looked over and I saw this house with two fake trees on each side of the door and I thought, now that's damned ugly. So I went up and I grabbed one of the trees. It had a concrete base. I started swinging it around in the middle of the road. The tree came off the base and I was throwing the base at various things. I was really drunk. I don't know why I did this.

I had a piece of concrete maybe about ten pounds, twenty pounds. I wanted to go look at my old house. I cut through a few yards. I was standing at the house next door to our old house and then I was sitting there looking at it. Just sitting there. I was sitting there looking at the pool and the backyard and the house, and I just went nuts. I threw the piece of concrete through the garage window of the next-door neighbor of our old house, and then I ran across our backyard, and then I broke another neighbor's window. Then I ran over to Main Street and punched the front window of somebody else's house. And then I went to Brunner's. I met Joe and we went out and did some B's [bowls] and a little more terrorism. That was a strange night.

I think it was just a release. A lot of built-up tension. That's how I am. I don't show it and I suppress it for a long time, and then I have a huge release. And usually I take it out on some type of inanimate object. It's not the first time that happened.

Did you use dope as an escape? To forget about what was going on at home?

I used it as a sedative, you could put it. Like a tranquilizer. A lot of times I felt like I didn't have to, but I felt the need to go out and just get high with some of my friends and sit around and forget about it all. I did that a lot [while] going through the main stages of separation, when they were both moving to two different homes.

Did you ever talk to any of your friends about it?

No. You don't talk to your friends about things like that. Just like you don't talk to your friends about girls because when you get drunk, they'll start mocking you out about them. It's one of those things.

What about your brothers and sisters; did you talk to them?

I have two sisters, twenty and twenty-one, and one brother who is nine. When it was happening, I suppressed it a lot and I didn't think about it. I think that's why I had this big buildup to the release point of breaking windows. If they did try and talk to me about it, I'd turn them off or I'd just say, "No, I'm fine. Leave me alone." Something like that. They knew after a while that I did not want to talk about it. They told me that they thought I should talk about it. But I still didn't want to talk about it. I didn't want to think about it.

I feel a lot better about it now because I've gotten used to the situation. I can talk about it more easily. But maybe it would have been better if I had talked to somebody about it when it was harder to talk to somebody about it. It might have done me more good. And I wouldn't have gotten these scars on my hand.

I could accept the fact that my parents did not want to live together. My father didn't want the separation, but my mother made it obvious for a long time. My father was so absorbed in his work that he didn't realize it in time. So I could see that the parents were going to split up, I had some anticipation of it, but my questions were: Would I be going to school with my friends? Would I be able to see them? Would I be living near the area that I'm living in now? That sort of thing.

I realized that they were going to break up and that they probably wouldn't get back together. I realized that better than my father did because he was still thinking he could save the marriage when he came back from England. By then it seemed like everybody in the family but him knew that my mom wasn't thinking about getting back together. It was probably harder on him.

It's helped him to be what you would call maybe a better person, but it's also made him very lonely, I think. And I think it's built up a lot of fears in him of being alone when he gets older. I think he is really afraid of that. So it's brought up a lot of insecurity in my father, but it's helped him to realize how important the family is to him.

For my mother, it is what she really wanted, so I suppose it has been better for her than it's been worse for her. I don't think she was ever cut out to be a mother the rest of her life. That's just not my mother.

And all the kids just accepted it because our parents had always said, when we had a big decision, "That's your decision. It's your life. I think you should do this, but it's your decision." And we sort of looked at them in the same way, saying, "We would rather you didn't break up, but it is your decision and it's your life."

If we had taken it really hard, I doubt they would have separated. But if they didn't get separated, it probably would have been harder on the family. It's probably the best thing. There was a big lead-up to it. My mother would never be nice to my father. In our family I feel it was probably the best thing that could have happened out of the choices we had, given how my mother felt toward my father.

Are they going to finalize it?

I have no idea. They seem to be working out the payments now. My father just got a two-year job somewhere else, so he's going to be in the Midwest for two years.

Now, with my mom living in Buffalo and my father living four or five miles away, we still sometimes get together and have family dinners and stuff like that. The whole family. That sort of keeps the family half going. It's like a phase-out.

At first my mom wouldn't sleep with him, and then he went to England, and then she wouldn't live with him, and now there are still some family ties in that we have dinner together now and then. And now he's going to be moving away.

I don't know if they'll ever finalize it. I don't see that either feels an extreme need to finalize it as long as they're not living together. It's just the fact that she doesn't want to live with him. They don't talk to us about it much, so I'm not sure.

Who did you side with at first?

That's a hard question because I could understand what each was going through. I could see my father being absorbed in his work and still wanting a family unit, but not putting forth the time to keep it together as it probably should be.

My mother felt really cheated. She was going to have a master's degree in psychology, then she married my father and she never finished it. I think she felt that she was ripped off a whole career.

I could see myself in both situations, so it was hard to side with either. I never took a side with either.

It kind of depends on what you mean by "sided with." Like who has better reasons to break up?

A lot of times in divorce a kid will—

Cling to one parent?

No, I never did that. I think I was old enough to want the independence that I might gain through the separation. I was just starting to realize that I wouldn't be living with my parents the rest of my life.

My little brother has really clung to my mother a lot ever since my dad went to England. He's always lived with her and maybe he spends one or two nights a month with my father. I guess you would say he's sided with my mother, although he really loves my father still.

I live with my father, but that's because nobody else lives with him. If I didn't live with him, somebody else would. But it's most convenient for me to because it's right near school and my friends. That's one reason I moved there.

He's a hard person to live with, though. He's hypertense, he's nervous about everything, and he's strange.

I don't see my mother much. Maybe once a week I see her.

I get along with my father, but you always disagree with someone that you live with. I guess you haven't got a healthy relationship if you don't argue sometimes. So I would say we do get along. There's a lot of give-and-take.

He's changed a lot since the separation. He's a lot more liberal and a lot more lenient. I guess that's just out of necessity to try and keep his part in the family.

He's increased his role in the family since the separation, which is strange. It's probably been good for him as a person because he's gotten more understanding, more generous with his feelings and his money. And he's realized how important his family really is to him. I guess he maybe took it for granted before.

My mother sees a lot of other people. But she was seeing other people when he was in England, so that's not much new. But my father—I don't know if he has the facility to do it. He has one girl friend in England who he sees when he can, which is once a year, once every two years. He's had maybe one or two girl friends since then, but never really anybody that I would say he was seeing. But my mother does see a lot of people. A lot of other people.

Does it bother you?

Yeah. It did at first, but then I taught myself not to think about it. That was her life. I was always raised sort of liberal in that society's rules weren't always right, that you should always do what you think instead of what people say you should [do]. I don't know if that makes

103

much sense. But the fact that she was seeing other people was more or less her business. I sort of shut off the separation and said, "If you're going to do it, that's your business. I'm just starting my life."

I gained a lot of independence through the separation, so it was probably fairly good for me in that I was so wrapped up in the family life, in being with my mother and father in the same house, that now that it's all broken apart, it'll make leaving home a lot easier. So it has its good points and its bad points throughout.

It's harder to look for the good points.

Can you elaborate some more on the good points?

Like I said, it will be easier to leave the house now that the family is already broken up, now that I only live with my father. And my father has paid a lot more attention to the family. He's realized how important the family is to him. And my mother has realized that she has her own life. Before, she always wrapped herself up in her children's lives, she was always giving. We were her life. Now she realizes that she has her own life. She's starting a new career. She's got two more years of college before she gets her master's degree in psychology. And it might have helped my little brother some. I think it's helped my sister in the same way that it's helped me. She always clung to the family unit like I did, and the separation will probably help her with getting her own independence.

How old is she?

She's twenty, but she is still living with my mother. She was always a little insecure, I guess. She can never make up her mind. I think this is helping her to realize her drawbacks. Not real drawbacks, but that to get by in life, you have to be able to make decisions and you have to be independent. I think it's helped her realize it.

But, then, there are the bad points. The pain and all that. But I suppose everyone gets through it.

Do you think divorce makes a person stronger or weaker as far as being able to cope with problems and make decisions?

It really depends on the person. It's a good question because there're so many different answers that I could give you. It would make some a little more insecure, seeing that their marriage isn't as solid as it once might have seemed maybe twenty years ago, seeing that a whole family unit can be broken up like that. I think it would help them cope with any other problems that might come up later on because they do realize something of their own insecurities, which might help them be a little more independent.

Have you had to take on more responsibility in the household now that you're living with one parent?

No, I don't think so. I'm lazy by nature. That's just how I am. And my father always makes sure that things are done for me so as to keep me living with him. I think he's really afraid that I'm going to move out. He wants me to go to school there in the Midwest with him. And I don't think I can. I've probably gotten more things done for me since the separation than I had before, which probably isn't good for me. I've probably had more things done for me in the way of work.

By parents?

Yeah. Work around the house. Now that we live in an apartment, there's no work to be done. I used to take care of the pool and all the yard work and all the repairs in the house. Now there's none of that to be done. So it's probably cut down on my responsibilities around the house, but it's helped me realize that I do have to assume a lot of responsibility soon.

My mother hasn't got a job. My father's putting my little brother through Calasanctius [a Buffalo private school for very bright children]. He's going to be putting me through college soon. He's putting both my sisters through college. He's putting my mother through college. That's a lot of money. And now they're trying to cut his salary, but now that he's gotten this job offer in the Midwest, he'll have some more money. I'm going to be going to a state school and both my sisters are going to state schools. We have to, or else he wouldn't be able to put my little brother through Calasanctius and my mother through to get her master's in psychology.

When they fight now, it's mainly over money because of the separation. Before, it was over the separation and the well-being. My father always said, "We shouldn't break up because of the kids." My mother said, "That's no reason not to break up. They have their lives and we have ours."

Once I was up in my room and they started having a big argument down at the bottom of the stairs. I had done some acid that day. I rarely do acid and I don't know why I did it that day. But I was sitting up in my room and they wanted me to go out to dinner and obviously I didn't want to go out to dinner. I wanted to get out of my room, but my parents were arguing at the bottom of the stairs. I felt very trapped there. I started getting really upset because they were arguing and I had to get out of the house. It was the second day that my dad was back from England and it was really the wrong time for me to have done that acid. If I ever have had a bad trip, that would have been the day. It was a hard experience. I sat up there and waited till they went out to dinner. I felt much better after everybody had left.

They never argued much in front of the kids. They tried to keep it out of plain view.

One thing that I do remember is when we were moving out and how lonely it seemed in the house. We had just moved and all the furniture was still in boxes and our old house was empty. That was two or three days, the transition in moving, which made me feel really lonely because I wasn't there with my family. It was just me and my father. My mother was with my two sisters and my little brother. It was hard. That was probably the hardest three days of the whole separation, that transition period of getting settled in a new and much smaller living area.

What happens when one parent says you can't do something? Do you go to the other?

It depends how badly I want to do it. If I really want to do it, then I wouldn't listen to either of them. That's just how I am. If it's staying out late and I really want to, I won't consult the other parent. I'll just do it and then go to the other parent so as to avoid the confrontation. But if it's nothing I really want, then I usually just listen because it's better than starting a hassle in the family.

Does your dad ever threaten to send you back to your mother?

No. If anything, I would threaten him to go back to my mother. If I moved out, he has the fear that one of my sisters wouldn't move in with him. He's afraid of being alone. So he would never say that to me. If he did, I'd say, "Fine."

Do you let that guide your actions? Do you feel as though you should stay at your dad's house just because—

Yes, I do. I would feel bad. That's influenced my decision to live with him. I think about how lonely I would be and I sympathize with him a lot.

He is a hard person to live with in such a small area. It's two bedrooms, a living room, and a kitchen. That's what we live in. So we mainly have one room to live in because the kitchen is just a kitchen. Or you could say that I have two rooms and he has two rooms, but there's only one common room. It's hard to live with anybody in such a close situation, especially a parent. If it weren't for the fact that I was afraid he'd be so lonely, I'd probably be living with my mother right now in the bigger house.

But I wouldn't take it to the point of going to the Midwest with him because I don't want to go out there. Maybe one of my sisters will go. I don't want to live with either parent when I go to college. I would live with him as long as it wouldn't interfere with my plans for the rest of my life.

Do you think he consciously imposes this guilt trip about living with him on you?

It's hard to say. He wants me to live with him badly, but I don't know if it's to the point where he would consciously . . . Yeah, I think he does a little bit, come to think of it. But not a lot. He doesn't say, "I'll be crushed if you don't come and live with me." But to a slight extent I do think he consciously does impose it on me and the rest of the family.

But so does my mother. She says I never see her and things like that. That's one of her defenses. She's a very good martyr. I think that's what you'd call her. She'd volunteer to do something and then she'll start complaining about doing it. And I'll say, "If you didn't want to do it, why did you volunteer?" And she'll say, "It's okay. I don't want to talk about it. I'll do it."

It makes you feel bad, but I can see what she's doing, which makes it not quite so bad. I can see that she is laying a guilt trip on me, so I don't feel as bad as I normally would if I felt they were real, genuine feelings and she wasn't just trying to get some sympathy out of me.

What's your overall opinion about divorce?

It depends on the family situation. For some families it is the best thing that could happen. Sometimes it can tear the kids apart more if the parents don't get divorced. But then, in other situations, it's not the answer. I think a lot of it depends on how the kids were raised and how the kids feel about divorce. That is a great responsibility on the parents.

If I wanted to get divorced, I would consider keeping [the marriage] together just for the kids. But if I felt that it wouldn't permanently harm their lives—it's always hard, but if it's nothing that will hurt them permanently—then I think I would go through with it.

"Everything is mostly stemming from financial things."

MARGARET (18)

Right now I'm the only one home. Everyone else is gone somewhere. My mother is in East Aurora all by herself. She's a great lady. Fantastic. I really like her. She's very quiet. She's small and very easy to talk to, easy to listen to. Right now she's just going through hell. I'm really worried about her.

What kind of hell is she going through?

We're moving out of two houses and moving into a third. She and Dad are fighting and having hassles about all sorts of things in the houses. Everything is mostly stemming from financial things. Mom tells me things he's done and how he's ripped her off, then Dad will tell me how none of this ever happened and that I have no right to say any of the stuff I say.

What sort of stuff do you say to him?

Last night I went to dinner with him and it ended up like it usually does: us not speaking to each other.

He's got a trust for me that he told me about. He had said I would get it when I was eighteen. Then he told me about all these debts that he's got, and these people came over one night to check out the house and when they left, he told me that I don't get the trust for three more years.

How much is in the trust?

I have no idea. I didn't even know I had one. Then he said it's all still in his name.

Last night I asked him if he was taking money out of it and he got mad at me, told me I had no right to accuse him of stealing from me, that everything he did for me was for my benefit.

But from what I can see, my dad hasn't really paid for much of anything, which is what Mom's resented for years. Dad's just lived off her. I don't think he's paid for anything. Mom paid for all the bills in our house out in East Aurora. I don't think Dad did shit. She pays for all the people who work there. When we decided to move into the city, it took us a year to get into that house. Dad ripped it apart, tore down walls, floors, ceilings, stuck all this unnecessary stuff in it, and he still hasn't paid the bills. And Mom is just mortified because you know how it is when people come and say, "Please pay us." They have to kind of beg to be paid and still they don't get paid. It's a bother.

So you are saying that the problems between them are mostly financial?

Yeah. And they can't talk to each other. There's no rapport between them at all. Dad's trying now, he really is; but every time he opens his mouth, Mom just shoots right back at him. It's mostly little things when they're just talking. He'll say something and she'll think he meant something else and tell him to shut up and then he'll get mad about that.

Dad's whole world stems around his business and his work and numbers and figures. He doesn't seem to hook into what people really need, how they need to talk to people. He doesn't understand what other people try and tell him. I don't know what's wrong with him.

The night before my brother left—he was going down to Florida for a job—we had just come back from [a] Bad Company [concert], a

110

really good time. We were tripping that night. He didn't have any money to go to Florida with, so I went in to get a check from Dad. It took me three and a half hours to get a thing out of Dad. He was going through everything. He had me get a pencil and paper to try and figure out all this stuff, all these numbers, and he started talking about stocks. Then he started saying, "You don't seem to realize how much I have to work for all this." And I'm just sitting there thinking, leave me alone.

Are your parents really wealthy?

Mom was. I don't know if she is anymore.

Where did her money come from?

Her mom. Her mom's grandfather was very wealthy, and she got money from that. Dad knew that and he's been living off her. This trust—he says it's to pay for my education, so I'll be paying for my own education instead of him. He hasn't paid for any of my education because all of our schooling has been paid for by trusts that my grandmother gave us.

I go to a boarding school now. I went to Nichols [a Buffalo private school], but they didn't want me to come back. I found out two weeks into the summer and we had to find a school for me really fast. My sister had gone to this place, so I applied there and got in and I'm really glad I went. I loved being away. It's nice to just come back here and visit.

When I'm away at school, I worry about Kate, because she is the littlest.

How old is she?

Fourteen. And she's there all by herself. The other three are down in Florida. I'm away, so she's there and she's kind of caught in the middle.

Kate's birthday was quite a thing, because when Dad knows he's in trouble with his family, he'll start acting abnormally nice. You know that's not the way he normally acts and that it's not going to last that long. I can see it coming. He took me with him to go get Kate's

111

presents. We went to this jeweler and he bought her a ring and a pair of earrings. Nice ring and nice earrings. And Kate can be bought over very easily. She always has been. She'll go with whoever will give her more.

What about you?

Me? I will go with Mom. And James will go with Mom. I couldn't live with Dad.

This sounds like I hate Dad. I really don't. I've got a lot of things to say against him because I've got more things to say against him than I do my mother. But I love Dad. I do. But I resent him a lot.

He's going to be all by himself because no one wants to live with him.

Why were you kicked out of Nichols?

I flunked out. I flunked math, the same math two years in a row. The same with French.

It was kind of my fault. All I did that year was sit and get high every single day. About ten times every day. I didn't want to do anything. I was sick of being home.

You used dope as an escape to forget about what was going on?

Yes.

Did it work? Did it make you feel better?

Not better. It's just after you're not getting along too well, you kind of let go, you get high just to do something different.

Are your parents divorced now?

No. This divorce has just been dragging on and on for so long. Mom won't tell me what's holding everything up.

It's Dad that is holding everything up because he doesn't understand why she wants to get rid of him.

The night that they told us was terrible. All three of us—Kate, James, and I—were sitting in the kitchen, and Dad comes in storming with this very dramatic entrance and goes, "Your mother's got an announcement to make and, frankly, it just makes me sick."

Mom comes in and says, "I want to get a divorce." I started laughing, Kate started to cry, and James just sat there. Then Dad blew up and Mom started laughing.

And then, nothing. I don't know if anything was really done about it besides Mom calling her lawyer and telling him that she wanted a divorce. Mom's got this problem of saying she wants to do something, but then she never gets around to doing it. And Dad's not helping matters.

Where does your dad live?

He lives in the house near the park and Mom is out in the country, in East Aurora, or she stays at her brother's house.

Do you see both your parents often?

I don't see Mom as much as I'd like to. I see Dad. I live in the same house as Dad does, but I don't really see him that often because he works all day. I'll see him for dinner, and then I'll have to go out. Both of them go, "Must you go out every night?" You know how you just have to go. And at times I won't even see Mom for a whole week.

Last week I hadn't seen her for a whole week before and I was supposed to go out with Dad that night, but then Mom came and she was really depressed, and so I wanted to go out with her. I told Dad that I wanted to go out with her because I hadn't seen her for a whole week and I've been with him all summer. Most fathers would go, "Sure, go with your mother." He got so pissed off, and he goes, "If that is the way you feel about me, forget it. Don't even bother coming back. I'm getting sick and tired of being treated like shit. You all say you're going to go out with me and then you don't. I think your mother does this on purpose."

What did you think about that?

I walked out, because he always says that to me. I said, "Dad, you're too sensitive about these things."

So your dad guilt-trips you.

Yeah. I'd say that he tries. It used to work really well. I used to react, "Oh, Dad, I'm sorry." He used to do that to me ever since I was little. I remember one night when I was about four years old and I wouldn't kiss him good night. He got on it; he just made me feel so guilty after that.

Does he guilt-trip your brothers and sisters, too? How about Kate?

Kate is now going through this stage I went through, only she's a year early. The stage is, "Fuck off. I hate you. I don't want to see you. Leave me alone. I'm going to do whatever I want." Kate now is in more trouble than I've ever been in in my entire life.

What kind of trouble?

Mom's caught her so many times with her bong [a device for smoking grass] out and reefer all over her. Dad's caught her before. And her attitude has been really bad toward people. She's been very inconsiderate lately. Which isn't Kate. I think all this is just affecting her really poorly.

Everything is going backwards. James didn't get into this school we thought he was going to get into. He has no school at the moment to get into.

Why does your mother want to divorce your father?

She hates him. She never wants to see him. Mom's got lots of reasons. She resents Dad terribly for the way he's treated Melanie and Peg all their lives. They're my half sisters from Mom's first marriage. Dad told Mom that he would adopt them and take care of them, but he never adopted them; he had no intention of adopting them.

He was married before, too, but he had no kids. Dad is my real father. Mom and Dad are my real parents. Melanie and Peg have a different father, but the same mother. Their father lives in England. My father was married to a Cuban woman. He got a divorce from her and then he met Mom. They got married and had Kate, James, and me.

Do you get along with Melanie and Peg?

They're eight and five years older, so when I was little, I was too little to remember them [at home]. I used to get along with Melanie really well. Peg and I used to fight like hell. Mom always told me that [Peg] was jealous because I was Dad's first kid and Dad treated her and Melanie like shit. And he treated me like normal. Now Melanie has changed; I don't know why. A long time ago her attitude totally changed toward everything. Now Peg is the one I'm really close to.

How did you feel about your father rejecting them?

I don't think I'll ever forgive him for that because they are two great people. I can't understand why he would do that. He's done the same thing with James. James can't stand being in the same room with him.

What do you mean, "He's done the same thing with James"?

He's not proud of James. He tells James he's a stupid idiot. Ever since James was little he's been told he's dumb, and now he has no confidence at all. Absolutely none. He's been in five schools in six years.

Is he smart?

Yes, he's smart. He just doesn't think he can do anything. He looks at something and he says, "This is too hard. I'm going to fuck it up anyway." So he doesn't even bother trying. He can't talk to Dad at all. He stays with Mom when he's here. He'll come over for the day now and he'll stay with me, but he'll leave at five every day just to make sure he's out an hour before Dad gets home. Sometimes when he's there too late and Dad does get home, he sneaks out of the house without saying a word to anyone. He doesn't even tell me he's leaving. He'll just walk out.

Why didn't James ask your mother for the check that time?

She wasn't there. James and I were tripping and when James trips, he totally gets into this state where he's like, "Tell me what to do. I don't know what to do." He can't talk to Dad when he's normal, so I said I'd go do it for him. He came in with me for a little bit, but he didn't know what to do.

For a while there it was fun. Dad and I were really going at it.

Sometimes Dad and I get in these arguments, but they're not really arguments. We've both got our own points to say. He tries to talk me down. I can talk, I can try to get him to be quiet and listen to me, listen to what I have to say. It was fun there for a while, but after about half an hour of battling it out, it got too much and I was just like, "God, I've really got to leave."

Do you do LSD often?

No.

You said you get high sometimes to forget your problems. How do you get high?

Just take a couple of bongs and that's it.

Do you drink to escape, too?

I only drink when I go out. I don't like drinking during the day. I will, but not much. I'll drink if I have a hangover in the morning. I'll drink champagne and orange juice. It's the best thing for a hangover. It's really good.

How does champagne help a hangover?

I don't know, but it does.

I'm worried about Mom. She's drinking a lot, and she's taking tranquilizers all the time and she's in a bad mood all the time. And Dad just sits there and doesn't say anything. He mopes around. Then he'll order you to go do something.

I have to tell him every time I go out what time I'm going to be coming back. I don't go out until ten or eleven and he doesn't think that a girl of my age should be going out alone at ten or eleven at night. He thinks I'm becoming a little barfly.

You want to know what Dad said to me last night? I told him that I never wanted to get married, and at this point in time I never do. He goes, "What are you going to be? A lesbian?" I went, "Nice comment, Dad. Really clean. Thanks a lot." I almost left him. I had the keys and it was my car. I almost got up and left.

I think the divorce was a good thing. I think it should have happened ten years ago. I think it's better for them, because neither one of them is happy at all.

Have you tried to get your mother to stop taking tranquilizers and drinking?

The drinking, yeah, but on the tranquilizers I haven't. I haven't said anything to her because Peg told me not to say anything. She said Mom's going through a really hard time right now. Peg is just as bad. When I was down at her house last summer, I opened one of the cabinets to get a glass out and I've never seen so many bottles of pills in my life. She's got everything, absolutely everything: amphetamines and barbiturates. She went away and took about a hundred hits of speed with her. Didn't leave me any.

Does she do it because she loves to get high, or is she—

She's a derelict.

How old is she?

Twenty-five. You'd like her, you really would. She's great. She's married to this guy and they're having problems. I don't know if she wants to go back to him. And Melanie got pregnant when she was nineteen and got married and now she's twenty-two and has three kids. And now she doesn't want to be with the guy she's with now, which I think sucks because I think he's the most. If I ever do get married, I would want to get married to him or someone like him. He's too good for her.

"It wasn't a good kind of different."

CHRISTINE (15)

I was so little when they got divorced. I'll be sixteen next month and it happened eleven years ago. I actually realized what had happened a couple of years later. I didn't know a lot of kids my age whose parents were divorced and I felt like I was different. But it wasn't a good kind of different.

Did you feel like your father had abandoned you?

Yeah. I felt that way. I felt, here I am with no father to speak of. He was never around, he didn't do anything for us. He lives in Buffalo still. He has a wife and two kids now.

Did you see him often?

No. Not that I remember. All I remember is that he existed and every once in a while we'd see him. He never really made any effort.

Do you know why they got divorced?

They hated each other, I think that's mainly it. They shouldn't have gotten married in the first place.

My mother would tell me things he'd done that weren't really good things: about his bad habits and things I really didn't care about and I really didn't want to hear. Every once in a while when I was around my real father, he'd pop up with a comment about something my mother did. My mother is a little more blunt. She always complained about how my father smelled all the time because he worked really hard during the day, and he'd come home and he'd be really stinky and dirty. She said he was a slob.

Did you want to see your father more often?

There've been times when I've said I really should have a father in my life and I want to see him more. I made an effort for a little while and then it sort of died because he really didn't make any effort himself. Every once in a while he will try. He'll call up maybe twice a year and say, "Do you want to come to dinner with us?" Otherwise, the only other time they call is for something like Thanksgiving or Christmas, or when they need a baby-sitter.

How do you feel about that?

As long as they pay me, I don't mind baby-sitting because they're really not like customers. I can go in their house and I can eat anything I want and do just about anything I want. It's not like I have to watch what I'm doing, as if I was in someone else's house that I didn't know very well. I figure, if they don't want me to baby-sit, they won't call me again. It's not going to break my heart.

There've been times when I've hated him so much. And there've been times when I've really sort of admired him and said, "Yeah, he must love me." But at other times I've felt like, oh, God, he's such an asshole. He's never tried, he only cares about himself, he never puts any effort into seeing me or being interested in what I do.

He's just not a father. He's just someone that I can call my father because of a genetic fault.

They each remarried. My father has a wife and two children by that wife, and my mother has a little son, who is eight, by my stepfather. And I have one real brother; he's eighteen going on two.

My stepmother—she's just there. She's just my real father's wife, that's all she is. She's nice. There've been times when I have spent five hours with her and the only word she said to me was "Good-bye." That was because we didn't get along and I couldn't stand them—the whole family—at that point. But now we're civil to each other. We're nice to each other.

My stepfather—that's another story. He loves me, I know he does—or he says he does. He really cares about me, but he has weird ways of showing it. He's hit me once and that was two weeks ago. He gave me a black eye. But he felt so bad about it that for the past two weeks he's been really nice and he's gone out of his way for me. He's given me everything that I want. He's explained to me that I'm really important to him and that I'm their last hope because my older brother is sort of fucked up and my little brother is a moron. So supposedly I'm their last hope and he really cares about me, and he hates to see me do things that aren't really intelligent. He's cool. He's not really down on smoking pot. He doesn't like to see me in bars, but he knows I'm not going to die from going to a couple of bars. He's pretty cool about that. He likes to keep things in perspective.

Why did he hit you?

We were yelling about something really stupid—I think it was baby-sitting. I was complaining that they didn't give me enough money. I had a friend over and it was a school night and he said, "What is Jenny doing here? This is a school night. You're supposed to be working."

I yelled at him about my grades and I said, "I have a good average in chemistry," and he started bitching back at me. So I yelled at him, and all of a sudden he took off and he hit me. And he kept on hitting me. So I attacked him and then we fought for a while, and he finally pinned me down on the floor and I had no strength left, so I said, "Go ahead and hit me if you're so tough 'cause tomorrow I'm going to go to school and tell everyone what happened to me and why I have a black eye."

At that point I didn't even know if I was going to have a black eye. But I was right. And I didn't tell everyone what happened.

What happened after it was over?

He felt really bad. Immediately after it, he told me to go to my room and [told] Jenny to leave. So we both went up to my room and we packed all my books and clothes, and I left with Jenny out the front door. No one saw me leave. Her mother picked us up on the corner because her mother was coming to pick her up anyway. Jenny explained, "Christine's stepfather hit her and she doesn't want to stay there."

I was really upset; I was in tears. I was saying, "I can't go back." I spent about fifteen minutes at Jenny's before my parents came and got me.

My mother came in and she said, "You have to come home now."

I said, "I don't want to go back to him. I don't want to go back."

She said, "You have to. You have to talk it out and everything will be okay."

So I went. I went for my mother because I knew it would just kill her if I didn't.

How did you feel when he apologized to you?

It was weird. He told me I provoked him into it. But I didn't, really. That was sick for him to take off on me for that. That was just plain sick and he apologized. He said, "It should never have happened." He was very emotional. Really emotional.

What about your older brother? How does he get along with your parents?

Let's see. Last night my stepfather threw him out of the house again. He caught him and his girl friend in the bathroom doing bong hits at twelve o'clock at night. He flew off the handle. He started yelling. He goes, "Call the fucking police. I want you out of here. I don't want my child growing up in this house with you. Get out now."

I was asleep. I had gone to bed at ten o'clock. I was really burned out and I heard all this yelling going on. It was just weird.

Does he go to school?

No. Does he have a job? No. Does he do anything? No.

When did he stop going to school?

Last April or May.

Did he just drop out?

No. He had reasons. He stole a moped and then he ran away. It had nothing to do with school. He just decided. Then he tried to go back. He registered at Bennett. He was going to go with his girl friend; he never ended up going and she never ended up going. She's gone to school a couple of days, I think. I'm not sure how many. But she doesn't go to Bennett anymore; she's in an alternative program. But my brother didn't do shit. He got a job for three days.

Did he get fired?

No, he quit. Couldn't handle it.

How does he get along with your father?

My real father? He doesn't get along with either of them. He constantly fights with my stepfather, and he does fight with my father. He sort of stays away from my father now. I guess he went over there one night to talk to my father and it was around eleven o'clock and my father just said, "Good-bye. Leave. I am going to bed."

So my brother said, "Screw you," and left.

The divorce affected him more than it did me, 'cause he never had a father. He never really had an example to follow, no one to show him what to do or how to act or what he should be like. No one to look up to and say, "Hey, that's my dad."

You mentioned the moped. Had he ever done anything else?

Oh, yeah. He'll be doing things his whole life.

What kinds of things?

Getting kicked out of schools and stealing and things like that.

Why did he get kicked out of school?

Once was for stealing. Once was for setting fire to the school. Once he flunked out and once he dropped out. So now you see why my stepfather hates him.

"He took my brother and threw him through a glass door."

ALEC (18)

They were going to get separated first, but the matter just went through that and it became a divorce case rather than a separation case. That was three years ago.

I have three brothers and three sisters. One's nineteen and they go all the way down to eight years old. I don't know the exact ages of them all.

Basically, my father used to abuse us as children. My mother got pretty fed up with it, so she just went on and got a divorce. He used to beat us for really stupid things.

One time when I was about thirteen, he took my brother and threw him through a glass door. My brother didn't want to go to a Boy Scout meeting and my father wanted him to go. So he pushed him out the door to make him go and my brother slipped and fell through. He had stitches all the way up his arm from it. He's still got a pretty good scar.

A lot of things like that took place, where he would beat us.

We had a dog and it used to shit all over the floor down in the basement. One time my brother wasn't home, so [my father] made me clean it up. I didn't feel like cleaning it up that one time, so he beat the shit out of me. I finally cleaned it up, but he gave me a lot of black-and-blue marks for it.

How did he beat you?

Just with his hands. When we were younger, he'd put us over his knee and slap us on the ass. As we got older, he used to throw us around, throw us against walls and shit like that.

Why do you think he was so violent?

I've gotten together with him now and we're pretty close. A lot of it had to do with my mother threatening to divorce him. It started about seven or eight years before they did get divorced. She would threaten him and he'd get upset about it and take out his anger on us. Then he'd pretty well calm down after a few months and she'd threaten to do it again and it would start all over. It was a cycle like that for a good seven or eight years: he would get really violent and then he'd settle down and then he'd get violent again. I didn't know the reason until just recently when he told me. I can understand a little bit more why he was like that.

How did you feel about it then?

He didn't want to do it, but I guess he had a pretty bad temper and it got the best of him. That's how he took his course of action—to go through us kids.

But how did you feel about that?

Well, it did bother him, but he didn't know how to solve it. He felt bad that he was doing it, but he didn't know how to stop it or what to do.

How did you feel about it? You.

Well, I hated him at the time. It really got me down. The year before, when they were going through the process of getting divorced, when he would actually beat on us, me and my brother

125

would get together and gang up on him. If he came after me and started beating me, my brother would jump in and then we'd both get *him* and beat *him*.

When we'd come home late, he'd be waiting up for us. But he wouldn't say anything until the next day, and then he'd get us during the day. He'd jump on one of us and the other one would get into it. Then he'd have one of my sisters call the cops. The cops came over and they laughed at him. They didn't believe that we were beating on him. They had figured it the other way around.

Did you want your parents to get divorced?

Yes, I did. Like I said, I hated my father. After a while you just get to hate him to a passion because here he is beating on you all the time and you don't know what to do about it. So then we would keep doing more stuff and more stuff that would keep getting him more pissed off, and he'd keep beating on us. We were always trying to get revenge on him one way or another.

Whenever my father would come after me, I'd run to my mother and tell her, and she'd stick up for me. I got really close to my mother after he started beating up on me. She never believed he was doing that to us until one of the neighbors told her. They'd hear him. Finally she found out and it was a shock to her. That's how the divorce started.

When my mother finally went to get divorced, that was one of our key points: to get him away from us. We figured that things would get better. As it turned out in the long run, things got worse after he left.

How did they get worse?

My mother used to take her frustrations out on my dad. I went to Child and Family Services and they agreed with me. They said a lot of times a person like her looks for the next youngest [male] in the family to go after and take her revenge out on.

She had a pretty hard time after [she and] my dad got divorced. Here she was with seven kids and she didn't know what to do. She can't think on her own. She had her father guide her and tell her what

126

to do. It's still that way with her. She was lost at the time, so she started taking it out on my older brother and me, and a little bit on my next youngest brother. But the baby of the family, the fourth brother—she babied him; she never bothered him.

The other three boys, she really went at us. If we'd be sitting down watching TV and she wanted us to take the garbage out right away and we were going to wait for a commercial, she'd come up and pull our hair and start scratching us and shit like that to make us do it right then. She would get really violent at us for little shit like that. It got to be worse and worse; she would threaten to throw us out of the house for little things.

I used to come home at maybe one or two in the morning and she never said anything about it. Right before she threw me out of the house, she started throwing that stuff at me, that I always came in late. I'd say that she never said anything about it before; I didn't know it bothered her until then. A lot of stupid things set [her] off.

There'd be a mess in the basement because all the little kids had gone down and pulled out dolls and trucks and stuff like that. And she'd blame it on me. I'd say, "I don't play with these things. I'm too old to play with these things." But she would blame it on me. So I'd clean it up and then she'd turn around and say something was broken or something else was screwed up and I did it. Or my brother did it.

I could only take so much. After a while I started really hating her.

Then a year ago this past November, I started going out with this girl, seriously going out with her. I'd bring her over and we'd go down in the basement. We didn't do much down there, but [my mother] claimed that we were fucking around and doing all kinds of shit. She got down on me for that; she hasn't seen any other guy since the divorce, and I think she was jealous. She wanted to go out with somebody and she didn't have anybody else to love [other than her children].

My older brother never really went out with any girls. He played the guitar. He was trying to get good at it. He never wanted to have anything to do with girls after a while.

So I was next in line. I was seeing this girl and my mother found that as another thing to use against me. She took me down to this probation officer and told him I was having this girl over every weekend and fucking her. I told the probation officer that we weren't, which was true. I said, "If we were going to do anything like that, we sure wouldn't do it at home where we've got six brothers and sisters running up and down the stairs all the time." There was no room or any closed doors we could get behind. I said, "We'd go out and get a hotel room if we wanted to do that stuff."

He said, "Yeah, that's true, but she's still your mother and you're living under her roof and so long as you're doing that you've got to abide by what she says."

I tried to do it. I listened to his advice. He told me to go see some counselors, which he set up for me and my mother. I went and saw the counselor and I told him what was going on, and he said, "What are you doing here?"

I said, "I was sent here."

He said, "Well, you shouldn't be here. Your mother is the one who needs to be worked on." He talked to her separately and he talked to me separately. He said, "I'll tell you right now. I don't want to tell this to your mother, but she's the one who needs a lot of help." I had a job then and he said, "You're pretty well set, but she doesn't know what she wants yet. I'm going to keep seeing her, but there's no reason for me to see you."

I think a lot of it had to do with the fact that she was seven years younger than my father. Their opinions and their ways of life were different. She was used to having everything handed to her. My dad never had anything handed to him. He always had to go out and work for the things that he had. So between her wanting everything, having everything handed to her, and him trying to earn the stuff that he wanted, it kind of collided and caused a big conflict. They were always arguing.

Do you believe what Child and Family Services told you about her coming down on you because you were the next youngest male?

That's what I told them and they agreed with me. They said it is true that in a lot of cases the mother will take recourse against the next youngest or next two youngest in the family, or any of the males in the family, to take out her frustrations because the father isn't around anymore.

She handed everything to the girls. If they wanted a new pair of shoes or clothing, anything they wanted, they got it. We had old raggy clothes. We'd get pissed off about that because we never had anything that we needed, and when we did ask for it, we never got it. What we got was a big hassle about it. So we learned not to complain after a while because we knew we wouldn't get anywhere.

Things got pretty screwed up. My brother had a bad temper. That was the second year after the divorce. He pretty well became a mama's boy after a while because she was ready to throw him out and he knew it, so he settled down and started kissing her ass, basically, just doing the things she wanted him to do.

That's when I started up, because she started coming after me and my temper was pretty bad, too. I just couldn't handle it. I was used to the freedom that she had given to me. When she started taking it away from me, I didn't want that. When you're used to having so many privileges and they start getting taken away from you, you're going to retaliate. That's what happened there.

Tell me about getting thrown out of the house.

That was pretty wild.

It started last March when I took a road test to get my license. I failed. I used to take off with the car, and so did my brother before he had his license. He used to cruise around and shit, he got away with it, why not me? So I took off with the car one night and I got really blitzed. It was my friend's birthday party and I was doing shots of Southern Comfort and one-fifty-one rum and all kinds of stuff. I took two friends home from the party because it was only four or five houses down from where I was. I went home and got the keys and took [my friends] home. On the way back, this car was coming down the other side of the street and got pretty close to me, so I veered off to the right and I went over a little too far and hit this parked car. Pretty well totaled that car and my mother's car. I drove on home and parked the car at home.

My mom got up the next morning and she was going to work and

129

she shit bricks when she saw her car all smashed up. She got down on me for that.

I was going to fix the car for her. I used to work in a collision shop. I knew what had to be done. The frame wasn't bent. I said, "Get the insurance estimate and I'll take care of it for you."

She was all pissed off about that. She wouldn't let me go near the car to fix it. She didn't trust me after that. Anything I did after that got her mad, and she would use that against me to make me feel bad and try to set me back into doing the things that she wanted me to do.

Guilt-tripping, basically?

Exactly. And I got sick of it after a while. Then the incident that set it off, where I was thrown out of the house, was in the summer.

It was the day before an exam that I had. I was in my backyard with a friend. We were under a tree studying and my little brother was throwing rocks at the dog. I took off after him because I wanted to get him away from the dog. The dog was driving me nuts. I couldn't think. When I was running after him, I slipped and fell in the neighbor's garden. They had cinder blocks in their garden and I wiped out on that and cut my knee right to the kneecap. I had to have it stitched up. The doctor gave me a prescription for pain medicine. It was codeine three, which is two parts Tylenol and one part codeine. And [my mother] wouldn't get it for me because she was afraid that I was going to start popping pills and take more than I should have. She didn't tell me that. She just said she wasn't going to get it for me.

That first night they gave me medicine at the hospital. I lost a lot of sleep, but I pretty well eased the pain with that medicine. But the next couple of nights I woke up and I'd practically cry from all the pain.

It was the third day after it happened, and I just couldn't take the pain anymore. I told her I needed the medicine. She still wouldn't get it.

So I put my hand through the wall. I just lost my head and went nuts. I told her that's how I felt, that's what I wanted to do to her, because that's the anger I had inside me.

130

She went down the next day and put in a petition to family court to have me thrown out of the house. She said I was uncontrollable, that she didn't know what to do with me.

The night of [the Bad Company] concert, when I came back, I saw a note from family court on my bed. I opened it in the morning. It was a summons to go to court. I went.

I went down that day and the judge asked me if I was happy at home. I said no, I wasn't. And he said, "Well, then, we're just going to put you out of the house."

At seventeen?

He said, "Are you staying with anyone right now?" I told him I was staying with my friend Joe. He wrote an order of disposition, which said that if I went near my mother's house, I would be arrested and thrown in jail. It was an order of protection for my mother so I couldn't come back.

She got money from my father for support for me and all the other kids. So before anything else took place in court, I asked the judge to adjourn the case so I could get a lawyer so that I could get the money and stuff that I needed to survive. He agreed with that.

I went to the Bar Association, got myself a lawyer, and then we had another trial on September fifth, the first day of school. My lawyer got me the money I needed to at least help pay for my room and board.

After a couple of weeks with Joe, his mother didn't like the idea of me staying there. She had too many other problems with him and his brother. She couldn't take it. So my other friend's parents took me in. And that's where I've been living ever since.

Since then my mother's been writing me notes to have me come back, but it's written in a way that says she wants me to come back, but the rest of the family don't. I run into my brothers and sisters every so often, and they tell me to fuck off and get lost and shit like that. They won't give me the time of day. She tells me to come back, but there's no reason for me to come back because I'd just come back to the same shit I left. So it's been a real big hassle ever since I got thrown out.

She influenced the kids, she and my grandfather, her father. They would always tell us that my father was no good, that my mother got a shit deal with the divorce, and that she didn't get what she deserved. That [my father] was a crooked bastard. That's what my grandfather used to say. I agreed with him then because I still had anger toward my father.

I didn't have a job when I got thrown out. I had maybe ten dollars to my name. I had to sell a car that I was working on and I only got fifty dollars for it. That was just enough to take care of me until I did get a job, working in a supermarket. That took care of a lot of things that I owed. It's been keeping me going ever since, but it hasn't been very easy, really.

After I got thrown out, maybe the second week, my father had his parents call me and tell me that they wanted to get together with me and help me out. I was pretty well lost then and I didn't know whether I should get together with them or not, but I figured I might as well give it a try because maybe they were sincere. I didn't know whether they were being sincere or not.

As it turned out, they did help me a lot. They took me down and I applied for welfare, food stamps, and Medicaid. They'd have me come over for dinner; they'd talk about my problems and try to help me, try to straighten me out a little bit. Then they told me that my father had called them and asked them to get ahold of me because he knew that if he called me I'd just hang up on him.

This summer I saw him for the first time since the divorce. It had been about two years. When he saw me, he broke into tears and he started telling me that he was sorry for what he had done and that he did want to help me as much as he could. He was apologizing for me having to be put into such a situation as a result of their divorce.

My mother would tell him what was going on with me. He knew what was going on, so he figured that he had failed me, he had failed as a father, that he hadn't been a true father to us. And he wanted to help us.

The first time I saw him he gave me ten or fifteen dollars. I needed a haircut and stuff like that. He said, "Go get a haircut and do whatever you want, whatever you have to pay off." And he's been pretty well broke, too, because he pays half his check to my mother.

And he doesn't make that much. He works for the gas company. He's got to pay for his apartment and his needs, so that was the most he could give me at the time. He gave me as much as he could to help me get along until I could find a job.

That's how we got together, and he's been seeing me ever since. He's been helping me out a lot with any little problems or any needs that I have.

It was really strange that I was hating the guy and then came back to him. We're almost the best of friends now. Now it's my mother that I'm against. I'm not really against her, but I don't want to see her for a while, not until I know that things have settled down at the house and that when I come back I will be accepted. I feel that the time will come, but it will be a while, so I've just got to wait and see what happens.

I wish more people could realize what marriage is about and try to examine things a little bit more before they get into it, because it can be pretty ugly and it does hurt the kids sometimes. It definitely hurts them. It causes ill feelings between them where it shouldn't be like that.

A lot of times you'll see the parents will get along great when they're not together, not living together, but when they're living together they can't get along with each other. I feel that's all right because then they don't hate each other; they can still communicate and still have a relationship.

But when they can't have a relationship with each other, that's when it's hurting both them and their family. I think people should take a better look into what they're getting into, because they've got to realize that they're going to be living with the other person the rest of their lives when they make the commitment to marriage. They shouldn't look at it like they can always get a divorce when they're not getting along. That's not right.

Do you think you'll ever get married?

I don't know. It's hard to say. I've learned a lot through my parents—how not to be and what problems will arise. I would like to get married, but it would have to be to the right girl. I'd have to really think heavily about it. I'm hesitant to get into a situation like my parents were in. It was such a crazy, mixed-up deal that I don't want to put kids through the same stuff I went through.

Divorce screws up a lot of families. I know a lot of other kids [whose parents have divorced]. It creates a different life for them. Sometimes it is for the better, but a lot of times I've found out it's turned worse. It could be pretty ugly, and then again, it could help.

Because of my parents' divorce, I've gotten together with my father and I've learned a lot from him. He's told me a lot of things and he's taught me a lot of things he's learned, and I've taught him a lot of things I've learned from my experience and his experience. From there, we've pretty well helped each other out in [other] ways. He's explained to me how he feels and how he gets depressed about things. He feels good that he can talk to me now. The other kids want nothing to do with him. I will sit down and talk with him and I will tell him what's bothering me or he'll tell me what's bothering him. We'll try to help each other out and make each other feel a little better, straighten each other out a little bit.

I feel to that extent, it's been good because it's brought me and him very close together again. We were never close before like that. We were close when I was younger, but after a while it just got to be shit. I hated him after a while. And now I can talk to him.

The day of the divorce my grandfather said that my mother was going to need a lot of help. I realized that. I was willing to help her. When anything went wrong around the house, I knew more or less what to do because I used to watch my dad fix pipes and faucets and stuff like that if they leaked. I helped him put a lot of electrical work in when I was younger. So I knew what to do if something went wrong. A couple of times some pipes broke and I helped fix them.

Then, after a while, things started getting really screwed up. She found out that I was smoking pot and that I was drinking beer a lot, and she figured that I was really being messed up. She figured I was going to ruin my life. That was another thing she used against me in court.

She didn't know what it was like. She never really had any

134

experience with anybody smoking pot. My brother used to smoke pot, but he didn't admit it to her. And when she asked me, I told her I did, figuring that she would trust me even more. But things turned around the opposite and she didn't trust me. She didn't want anything to do with me after that.

I told her that my brother used to do it all the time, my older brother. She said she didn't believe that, but she did believe I was smoking pot and drinking. She'd find beer bottles lying around. She used to go out and buy me the beer half the time, and then she'd turn around and complain about me drinking. She said I was an alcoholic.

I found out since I was thrown out of the house that she was claiming that I was really off my rocker and that if she would have had me around the house much longer, I would have killed one of the kids. She thought I was totally wacko from smoking pot.

She just didn't understand what it did; that it gave you a good feeling. She felt that it was killing me and that it was making me insane. She would go around telling the neighbors that I was crazy and I was going to kill somebody.

It was a strange situation, 'cause what the hell—I wouldn't hurt a fly. But she claimed that I was going to kill somebody. And she claimed that I beat the kids till they were half dead. She had a knack for exaggerating. She would tell my grandfather this, and naturally he would believe her over me because it was his daughter.

There was one time two summers ago when I had just gotten done making my speakers I had built in school. She didn't like them at all. They threw off a lot of bass and she could feel the vibrations coming through the floor. She couldn't hear the music, but she could feel the vibrations.

She told me to take them outside and play them whenever I wanted to play them. So one time I agreed and I took them out, and then she started complaining that it was too loud. It wasn't loud at all; you couldn't even hear it past our backyard. None of our neighbors complained; nothing was wrong.

We got into a big fight. She came out, she turned it off, and as she left, I turned it on again. I waited till she walked away. I lowered it a little more than what it was so she wouldn't hear it and come out again. She came back out and she snuck up behind me. She grabbed me by the hair. I was sitting in a lawn chair and I had a circle with all my friends around. And she pulled me right out of my chair. I got up and she started scratching me. So I just pushed her away. I didn't push her hard; I just pushed her away to get her away from me.

She was on the edge of the patio and she fell over something behind her. She ran in the house and called my grandfather. This was about three in the afternoon. My grandfather came over that night about seven o'clock. He wanted to fight me and he wanted to fight my friends. He used to be a boxer when he was younger, so he wanted to fight all of us. He's seventy years old and he wanted to fight us all.

I said, "No way." He's got a heart condition and he'd had open-heart surgery. I knew if I hit him in the ribs or if I hit him in the wrong place I could kill him. I said, "I don't want to have anything to do with this. I beat on my father, I felt bad about having to do that; I don't want to have this shit with you. We'll take it in the house."

My friends explained what happened to him, but he wouldn't listen to them. He listened to my mother and he let what we said go in one ear and out the other. He said I was wrong and she was right.

Then I started to be against him, too. He was the copetitioner to have me thrown out of the house. He was always into the affairs at home. He always stepped in as mediator, and he was always siding with my mother. He would never listen to me. Whenever I told him what my mother was doing, he said I was crazy. He said, "You're crazy, you're smoking pot and drinking beer, you're an alcoholic. You're drunk. You're on drugs. You don't know what you're talking about."

Every time I saw him he had a drink in his hand. He didn't think anything of that, but for me to have a beer—I was an alcoholic.

He wouldn't accept anything I told him. So it was him and my mother against me and my brothers and sisters. I mean, him and my mother and my brothers and sisters against me. When I got taken to court, what the hell could I do? It was my word against theirs, and there was nothing I could do about it. So that's how I got thrown out.

A lot of shit like that happened.

136

Did you use dope to escape?

All the time. That's why I smoked it. It was my escape from all the things that were happening to me. I probably would have lost my head, I probably would have been in an institution if I didn't smoke, because I would get so frustrated, because I didn't know what to do.

It was like my family was against me. I wanted to get away from my problems and I tried to stay away from home as much as possible so I wouldn't be there to get involved in all these situations.

I started smoking when I was in eighth grade, which was just before my parents got divorced. I started smoking as a result of my father beating me. A friend of mine said, "I've got some pot. Want to try some?"

I was leery. I didn't know what it was like at first. I thought I'd be really messed up in the head. And I said, "All right, I'll smoke some. What the heck." That was my best friend. He'd already tried it and he said, "It's pretty excellent." So I said all right.

We went out and bought a nickel and we smoked a good quarter of it the first time. I didn't get high or anything. But the next time I really got off on it. We'd start laughing and we'd have a really good time. So I got to like it. Then my brother found out I was smoking pot and he had already been smoking it, too. So [we] would get together and we'd smoke all the time. We got pretty close then.

Then, after a while, he quit and I was still going. He became a mama's boy. He accepted her bullshit after a while because he figured he was going to get nowhere fighting it. And I was the type that was going to fight it to the end, whether it meant me getting thrown out or whatever. I wasn't going to accept it. And he got down on me for that, whereas he used to do the same stuff.

He destroyed my mother's room one time looking for the keys to her car. He didn't have his license, but he broke pictures and mirrors and everything. He went in a rage to find her keys. And he would do crazy stuff. He totaled one of the walls in the house. He just came up and kicked the shit out of it. Then when I started doing stuff like that—there's only that one time when I didn't get my pain medicine

137

and I actually put a hole in the wall—he got down on me for it. He told me I should calm down.

I said, "Well, you were like that, too. You're accepting this shit and I'm not. You shouldn't be getting down on me for it, because you didn't either."

He said, "You're wrong. I learned and I'm just trying to make you learn that you're not going to get anywhere."

I didn't accept it. I just kept on going and he started to side with my mother. So it was like he got all the kids [against me] and all the kids didn't like me because my mother was telling them how crazy I was and shit. That made me even more crazy. I mean, what the hell—all my brothers and sisters are against me; what the hell am I going to do? It used to bum the shit out of me because I tried to be close to them, but they didn't want anything to do with me, and what could I do? I was trapped in the corner. I was looking for a way to get out. The only way I could finally get out was to retaliate and try to fight my way out.

But I didn't get anywhere.

"I never did meet anybody's standards."

JENNY (16), Linda's sister

I was about four years old; it happened thirteen years ago.

Do you have any brothers or sisters?

A lot. I have one real sister, two stepsisters, two half sisters, and three half brothers. I have Linda. She's my only real sister out of the nine of us. Then my mother remarried and had three other kids. And my dad remarried, and he married a woman who already had two kids from a previous marriage and then they had two kids.

My mom used to tell me a lot about my dad. How he had a split personality. She said when they were married, they went to a psychiatrist and the psychiatrist said he had a split personality. I never really believed it. Anytime I've seen him he's been nice to me. He's good with people. But if he gets upset about something, he'll just go nuts. He'll say things that are so cruel and so nasty. I guess it's not his fault, but I think that had a lot to do with my parents getting divorced.

He used to run around on my mother all the time. She'd be home

139

with Linda and me and two little babies. And she had to work when they were married. That had a lot to do with it, too.

I live with my grandmother now.

Does your father live up here?

Yes.

Why didn't you stay with him?

I guess he didn't want me.

They always said—my dad and my stepmother—that I was welcome to come up here whenever I wanted to come up here. I couldn't handle being bitched at all the time [by my mother] down in Florida. After a while it gets to a person. Everything you do, there's something wrong with it. You feel you did something good and you tell them about it, and they always find fault with it. After a while you can't handle that. So I came up here because of that.

I called my dad and explained that I wanted to come up, and he had had a lot of problems with Linda and she had moved out. She got kicked out of his house. I guess he thought I was just like Linda and he didn't want me.

What did he say?

He said, "We'll let you know, we'll talk about it." And he didn't call back. So I had to call them again and say, "What's going on?"

My dad didn't even talk to me. It was my stepmother. She said, "After what happened with Linda, we don't think we could handle another kid in the house."

Is that because of Linda's abortion?

Yes.

Is that why she was kicked out of the house?

Yes.

And how did you feel about your dad and your stepmother not wanting you?

I felt rejected. I still do now, because I never did anything to my

140

dad. I never did anything to him. He never calls me. If I want to see him, I have to go over there and it's hard for me. I don't have a car. Or I have to call him. Sometimes I'll go down to where he works to see him, and he'll leave after ten or fifteen minutes. He doesn't even sit down to talk to me. He'll just go home.

Now I haven't called him or seen him in three weeks. I'm going to wait and see if he calls me. He probably won't.

That's outrageous.

I know. It upsets me. It's like I'm not even his child. It's like my two stepsisters who aren't even part of him are more his kids than I am. I'm his first child, his firstborn.

Do you resent his stepkids for all of that?

I do and I don't. I feel sorry for them because they don't even know who their father is. But then it upsets me because my father is my father. I don't mind if he takes them in; he adopted them, and he supports them. But I don't think he should ignore his other kids because of it.

When my mom first married my stepfather, my dad came down to Pittsburgh, where we were living. Linda, me, my stepfather, and my mother were living in an apartment, and while my stepfather was at work, my dad came with two guys and he kidnapped Linda and me.

One minute he really loves you and another minute I think he doesn't care. I get that impression.

One night, maybe a month ago, I was going to go to his house for dinner. I wasn't feeling too well. I had a stomachache, so I called his house and said I wouldn't come for dinner, but I'd come over later. I talked to my stepmother and I could hear my dad in the background: "Well, if she doesn't want to come over, she doesn't have to come over. She doesn't have any obligations." Then my dad told my uncle that he has no obligation toward Linda and me.

When Linda moved up here about a year and a half ago, all of a sudden I didn't hear from my dad anymore. I thought he didn't give a shit at all. Then, when I wanted to come up here, he didn't want me. And I don't even know why.

How did you get up here? Who paid for it?

My stepgrandfather, my grandmother's husband, who she just married a couple of years ago. My dad said they'd pay back the money for the plane fare and they had to keep going down to his place to get the money. Finally he paid about a month ago.

It's like the child support. He never used to send that. My mom showed me the agreement that they had. My mother wanted to get more money from my father for child support because Linda and I were each getting twenty dollars a week and you can't support a child on that. I eat more than that in food. She wanted to get forty dollars a week for each of us. She tried to take him to court, but he got out of it. I don't know how he got out of it.

He's got so many connections, it's unbelievable. He's a politician, a legislator. He knows so many people. And he lies. He just maneuvers himself.

Like a worm.

Yes. Like a worm.

I like it at my grandmother's. We get along really well and I can talk to her, which I couldn't do with my mother because we just didn't get along. But I can talk to her and she gives Linda and me freedom. I have to be in around twelve on weekends, but if I want to stay out later for a specific reason, she'll let me.

The only thing I don't like is, she's a little too overprotective about certain things, which is understandable because she's my legal guardian. When Linda first moved in with my grandmother, my dad used to drive by and make sure what time Linda got in.

My dad and my grandmother don't talk at all.

Why?

He worked for her awhile at her store. And he's sick, he's really sick. He lies through his teeth. It's unbelievable. He was stealing all this money from her, so she fired him. Then he went out and got his own business. They were still talking then, but not very much.

142

Then Linda moved up. One night at my dad's house, when I was still in Florida, with the abortion and everything with Linda, my dad went crazy and was knocking Linda around. He hit my grandmother. All the other kids were upstairs, so all they could hear was the commotion; they didn't know what was going on. After Linda got kicked out, my dad went upstairs with my stepmother and said it was all my grandmother's fault and Linda's fault. So now my stepsisters don't talk to Linda or to my grandmother. It's like they're not even part of the family.

Do you feel as though you know your dad? Did you ever get a chance to know him?

Yes and no. He's an easy person to get to know, one side of him, because he's so outgoing and he's so friendly. But when you really know him, you realize that he's a liar. He's a huge liar. He's the biggest liar I've ever known. And you realize that he's got a really ugly side to him, which is probably that split personality. I don't know what it is. So I do know him and I don't know him.

Are you glad your parents are divorced?

It's hard to say because I can't imagine them living together. I was so little when it happened that I don't remember when they got divorced. I just remember when we used to go to this hotel and see my stepfather before my mother married him. But I don't remember my parents together at all.

I guess in a way I am and in a way I'm not. I wish I could have one family. Just one. A happy family instead of a split-up family. Because it's hard.

How do you feel about your dad now?

I respect that he went out and got his own business going. As for his personal life—well, I know he used to cheat on my mother all the time. And I know that he calls my mother a whore, which really makes me mad because I love my mother. She and I don't get along now, but I know when I get older, she'll understand me better, and I'll understand her better. I know she loves me and I love her, and it

143

gets me upset when people say things about her. And I know that he's cheated on my stepmother.

How do you know he cheats on your stepmother?

One night Linda and I were in the car with him, and the girl who he was supposedly having an affair with drove by, and they stopped and they talked and then he told us not to tell his wife that we saw her. I know he used to do [the same thing] with my mother. If he's going to do it to one, why not do it to the other one?

How do you get along with your stepfather?

It probably doesn't sound bad when I tell it, because there wasn't any physical abuse [while Linda and I lived in Florida with my mother and stepfather]. It was mental abuse.

I have a best friend in Florida, Katherine, and I don't know why, but my stepfather and my mother couldn't stand her. They hated her. He said I wasn't allowed to associate with her anymore. Katherine and I are sixteen years old; I should be able to hang around with just about anyone I want to. He just didn't like her. Of course, I still hung around with her and he caught me hanging around with her, and it was the same thing with Linda. Linda wasn't allowed to hang around with her either.

Linda and I got put on this unbelievable restriction. I can't even remember how long it lasted, but he took the radio and TV out of our bedroom. Linda and I shared a room. We weren't allowed to be in the same room at the same time. All we were allowed to do is read. One day I would spend in the living room and Linda would spend the day in the bedroom; next day was the other way around. We didn't have radio, TV—nothing. All we had was a book to read.

Why weren't you guys allowed together?

Probably because they figured we would scheme up something, which we probably would have. Linda and I both knew how it was.

When you're under pressure like that, you've got to get out of it. That's insane. Was that all your stepfather's work?

Yes. Then I remember once, when I got caught shoplifting, he was really getting mad at me because I was lying and because I had been shoplifting. Which is understandable, but he went crazy. This is the only time he ever really hurt me. He pushed me on the floor and I fell. I had long hair and he grabbed my hair and he was dragging me across the floor by my hair. Even my mother was flipping out. She couldn't believe it. He took me to my room and he threw me on the bed and banged my head on the wall.

That really got to me. I told him that he's not my real father, he can't do this, and my mother was trying to get him to stop.

I don't know. He's a nice guy, but he doesn't go about things in the right way. Sometimes I'd go in the bathroom and I'd go in the shower and I'd just start crying because of what my parents were doing. Nothing physical, just that I couldn't go out, I couldn't do anything.

Right before I left, I was going out with this boy, Eddie. I remember the first time he came to my house. I was in my room and my mother answers the door and she doesn't even invite him in. He's just standing outside and she closes the door on him. They were always so unfriendly to any of my associates.

And if I would try to talk about college, they would say, "You're too stupid to go to college. Where are you going to get money from?" That's not how you encourage a person to go to college.

Another time I had roaches [partially smoked marijuana cigarettes] in my purse and my parents, my mom especially, were always looking through my purse, looking through my drawers, looking for pot and paraphernalia, and she found the roaches. I didn't even know they were in my purse. So she comes walking in my room when I come home from school and she's got this little bag of roaches.

When she walked out, I got my bag [of dope] and I got my pipe and everything. I was going to go give it to my friend to hold because I did not want it in my room. You never know what my parents are going to do. So I'm holding it and my mom walks in my room, she doesn't knock or anything, she just walks in and they had called the pigs on me. And there I am with a bag and a pipe.

The pigs came over to the house and they would not leave until I told them who the dealer was. I was shaking. I couldn't tell who I got it from. You don't do that. So I'm sitting there, I don't know what to do; I'm just going crazy. I wasn't telling them where I got it from, and my stepfather kept saying, "The police aren't leaving until we find out where you got this and who you got it from." So I made up a bullshit story.

My parents were always saying that I was beyond hope. I never knew what I did. I'm not bad. I'm a typical teenager. I don't go out and I don't do all these drugs and I don't run away from home or stay out all night. It was totally ridiculous. I don't know what I did—that's the thing that really upsets me. But they're always bitching and always getting on my case for nothing. And after a while you can't handle it.

And some of the things that my stepfather would do to Linda and me when we were little, he didn't do to his own kids. He used to hit us with a belt for lying. It hurt. I don't have any scars. But he doesn't lay a hand on his own kids.

Why do you think your mother and stepfather are so negative toward you and Linda?

I don't know. That's the thing. And my father is so negative, too.

Sometimes you get the impression that no one loves you. You know they do. Well, you think you know they do.

I know my mother does, but at times I can't get along with her. My father—I don't know if he loves me or not. I don't know if he gives a damn or not.

Do you love him?

Yeah. He's my father. I do.

It's hard because they're part of you, they're half of you. He's my father, but it's like he doesn't give a damn about me. All my doctor bills, my dentist bills, the orthodontist and everything, my grandmother pays for. She paid for half of the child support when it used to come. There's my dad, spending all this money for my stepmother's two kids, giving them dancing lessons and piano lessons and ski lessons. He could pay our dentist bills or our doctor bills. That's child support. That used to get me mad.

We would come up here to visit, and [my dad and stepmother]

would rave about us. And then when we would leave, we wouldn't ever hear from them.

My two stepsisters are fifteen and seventeen. Linda will be seventeen shortly and I'm almost eighteen. So we're close in age. When we were little, we would come up here and all four of us would go out and we used to have a good time together. Or we'd go to the fair with my stepmother and my dad and we got along really well. It was like one big party.

But as we got older, things changed. The time I really noticed it was two years ago, the last time I was up here before I moved here. Linda and I had just started partying. My stepsisters are pretty ugly, and Linda and I are not ugly. And we're outgoing; we make friends easily. Maybe they were jealous because we could make friends and they couldn't. I don't know what it was, but that's when I noticed a change.

I remember one time we were down at the school and there was a bunch of guys and all those guys were partying. My two stepsisters and Linda and I were playing tennis. The guys asked just Linda and me to come over and party with them. I remember my stepsisters, when we came back, started crying. Maybe they were jealous. Neither one of them has ever had a date and I'm sure that upsets them.

But, then, things they have that I don't have upset me. Like they have my father.

I know one thing the whole experience did to me: I'm not confident about myself, because I was always being cut down. Of my whole life, the past four months is the only time I've never been cut down. Of course, I've been cut down a little, everyone is, but not about every single thing I've done. My grandmother praises me for things I've done which deserve praise or a thank-you or whatever.

I know that my biggest problem is that I'm not confident about myself, about things I do. And I'm afraid to do things because of it. I feel I won't meet everyone's standards. Because I never did meet anyone's standards.

I need a lot of encouragement if I'm going to go out and do something. It's hard to explain, but constantly being bitched at, you don't even want to go in the house. And having them bitch about your friends, [about] every little thing—I know that affected me a lot.

I was never really given a chance to make up my own mind about things because my parents would always do that for me. I was never really given any responsibility. I guess they thought I was too immature. I don't know what they thought. So I'm not used to coping with problems now. Well, I had to cope with my family problems by myself, but those are different from other kinds of problems, like problems you face every day. Right now I face problems that I never had to make decisions for before. But I like it. I like being able to make up my own mind about certain things. Just little things. Everyday things. My grandmother gives Linda and me the freedom to do that; we never had it before.

The only person who I could ever talk to closely was Linda. Linda and I used to be inseparable. We would always know how the other was feeling. I never had anyone who I could talk with about my feelings except for Linda. And then Linda left. Then it was just me, and I couldn't handle it.

Now I can't get close to a person. I don't know. It's funny. I'm sure I'll be able to in a while.

What do you mean, "get close to a person"? You mean get close to a guy or close to Linda again or what?

Linda and I are pretty close, but we're not as close as we were, because this is the first time I've seen her in over a year and we had never been separated for a day until this.

Linda came up in March, and I was going to come up in April to visit. I wasn't ready to leave my mother. It's such a big step—going from Florida to New York, from one family to the other, going to a new school. I wasn't ready to do that, not yet. So I never came up for Easter, I never came up during the summer, and I had always come up during the summer before that. I never came up for Christmas. I never came up the next Easter. And nobody cared.

So Linda and I grew apart. You talk to a person on the phone and it's not nearly the same. So I had to rely on myself. Then I came up here and of course there are going to be changes in the two of us after a year and a half. She's been through so many things that I haven't been through; I've been through things she hasn't been through. And now I can't get close to anyone.

I think before you get married you should know if you're going to be able to handle this person. Maybe you can't tell before you get married, but you should know before you have kids. If there're two people and if they don't get along and they don't have any kids, that's fine. Let them get divorced, let them go their own ways. But when they have kids, they're always going to be tied to each other because of the kids—unless one of the parents totally neglects the kids, which happens. But there is still always going to be a relationship.

I don't believe in divorce.

Do you think parents should stay together and work things out?

They should try to. I know there are times when they can't, when it's impossible.

I know that I'm going to live with a person before I get married. So many people are against that. To me, if you live with a person, you're going to find out how they really are.

After a couple of years.

That's right. If you live with a person two years, you're going to find out how that person is. It's not like you're going out on a date and everything is so lah-de-dah. This way you're going to know how the person is and you're going to see how you deal with problems together.

Twenty years ago, when our parents got married, a lot of people got married for sex.

I think people get married to get married. I think people should wait to get married. It's hard for me to say now when I'm going to get married, but I would prefer to get married when I'm twenty-five.

And you know what is going on.

Right. Know what you're going to do with your life. My mom was married when she was twenty. She had me when she was twenty-one. She had Linda eleven months later. I was two months old when she was pregnant with Linda.

Were you guys intended or were you accidents?

Accidents. My grandmother, who we live with now, wanted my mom to have an abortion with Linda because she said her son was too young to handle two kids.

That's scary. I'm going to be eighteen. My mother was married at twenty and I know a lot of other people that married a lot younger. I know that I surely wouldn't be ready for it.

"There's his side, her side, and the truth."

LINDA (16), Jenny's sister

My father's a spoiled boy, and he's a real bad bullshitter. He's got a good personality, but it's a split personality. The psychiatrist said so. He can be so nice, he gets along with everybody, but if you do something against him, he'll just flip out. Because he's nuts. Like he punched me and then my grandmother. He punched her in the face. His own mother.

Why?

Because she wanted to take me away from him.

He used to beat up my mother. He's a big guy.

When he punched my grandmother, I went into shock. That was after he hit me. I was delirious from that, and then I see him punching my grandmother, right in the face.

Then he went upstairs and told my brothers and sisters, "See how your grandmother is? She doesn't know what she's doing." He just put it out of his mind; it doesn't relate to him anymore.

He used to work for his mother, but she had to fire him because he was ripping her off so badly. He stole money and stuff from her store. She fired him and he got his own place and said that he's either going to bury her in the ground or in business. He said that to her.

I think he's nuts. I don't even want to talk to him. The last time I saw him was on his birthday last summer. He doesn't make a point to see me and I don't make a point to see him.

What's your stepmother like?

She's a bitch. She's real flaky. She puts on a nice act, but she's so jealous and greedy. She's the most greedy person I've ever known in my whole life.

My grandmother took her to Spain. She bought their house for them. Their cars. She did everything for them, and my stepmother wanted more and more and more. My grandmother paid for an addition on their house once and my stepmother added on an extra three feet. On the same bill she bought storm windows for the whole house. She's a real greedy and jealous person.

What do you mean by "jealous"?

She is very jealous for her daughters. Both of them go to our school this year. Alice has curly red hair. You've probably seen her in the halls. She's a real jerk. Real square. She doesn't even walk properly. Never went out with anybody. My stepmother always tried to push her two girls, but they never turned out.

Do you get along with them at all?

With Margie, the younger one, I do. But Alice—she's only a month younger than I am—she can't stand my sister or me.

Why?

I don't know. She doesn't even talk to me in the hall. She'll walk right by me. I guess she agrees with everything she hears about me and against me in the house.

When I first came up here, I got along with my stepmother. But she was putting on a show. Then she made me go to a counselor. It was supposed to be for the three of us {kids} because we didn't get along.

152

I wanted to do my own things. I didn't want to be wild by any standards, but I didn't want to be pushed into the mold that she pushed her stepdaughters into. I mean, her daughters. I'm her stepdaughter. But I don't get along with her.

Are those the only kids that your father and stepmother have?

Those two aren't his kids; they're hers from a previous marriage. From this marriage they have a little girl and a little boy.

Do you get along with them?

No. I never see them now because there's no communication between us. And they're kind of hesitant when I do see them because I'm sure they talk about me around the house, and what's a kid going to believe? You're going to believe what your parents say when you're younger; you don't really have a mind of your own yet.

Does your father ever call you?

No. After all that happened that one night, he said, "I never did any of that stuff you're talking about. I never hit your grandmother. I never hit you. I never abused you."

I went to school and my guidance counselor saw my face. I had a black-and-blue eye.

I remember that.

Do you want me to tell you why I got kicked out of the house?

Yes.

I had an abortion. A week after I had it, they found out about it. This was three days before my birthday and they were sending me back to Florida because I had lied to my father. It was really a messed-up situation.

Did your boyfriend pay for it?

Oh, yeah. Everything was fine. He took care of me.

Why did you move up here from Florida in the first place?

Because my stepfather and my mother are very strict. My mother is

German; she was born in Germany. My grandfather on that side of the family was an officer in Hitler's army. He was real stern. He's got his picture in one of those books, *Life Goes to War with Hitler.* He was a total kraut.

My stepfather used to be my father's best friend. They went to school together. They worked together. Then my mother took off with him. My father hates his guts.

My father was cheating on my mother all along, but he loved her. He really did. I think he still does.

Why do you think so?

Because at one point when I was having problems with my stepmother, we talked about it. My father and I used to get along so well when I first moved up. We were really close. I worked in his store all the time; my sister wasn't up here yet. We had long talks and he said that he still loves my mother, but he hates my stepfather. If he ever could, he would kill him.

Do you know why they got divorced?

My father did go crazy at one point. Not loony-bin crazy, but he had something wrong with his arm, an open wound that wouldn't heal. There's a name for it. They can cure it now, but they couldn't then. And he got a staph infection; he was in pain. So he used to beat my mother up. When she was pregnant with me, he kicked her in the stomach. And he threatened to kill her when he found out about Danny.

Who's Danny?

My stepfather. My father came to my grandmother here, his mother, and said he was going to kill [my mother]. He had a gun. My grandmother hurried up and called my mother and told her to leave. And she did. She took me and my sister and left.

His mother called your mother?

Yeah. Even she knows he's nuts.

We lived in Pittsburgh then for two years. He didn't know where we were. They weren't divorced or anything yet. She just left him totally. Then they got a divorce after that.

So you didn't see your father from the time you were three until the time you were five?

I saw him once in that time period because he found out where we were, and he came and he stole us. He literally took me and my sister and brought us up here. Then my mother's father and her brother came and got us back.

We used to think my father was great because my stepfather used to make us do a lot of jobs and wouldn't let us do a lot of things we wanted to do. So we really idolized [my father]. Then my mother told us some things about him.

Then I would have dreams about my mother and somebody beating her up. I couldn't ever see that person's face, but it was the same thing over and over again. It was real fast. Somebody beating her up. I don't have that dream anymore.

My mother got married when she got her divorce, so I was four or five years old. They went to a justice of the peace.

Was there a battle for custody?

Yes, but of course the mother gets it, especially back then. It was the thing to do. He used to not pay the child support. There were battles about that.

My stepmother used to not send the checks. My father would give her the money and then she wouldn't send them. She wrote the checks out and took care of all that. We were supposed to get twenty dollars each every week, and they wouldn't send that. That's not a lot of money.

Now he doesn't pay anything for me 'cause he doesn't claim any responsibility. He still goes up to school and checks on my attendance. I get mad. I went to see the principal about it.

You should stop him from doing that if your grandmother has legal custody.

She doesn't. My father doesn't either. My mother has it.

When I was getting kicked out, my father was sending me back to Florida. My mother didn't want me to live with my grandmother ever because of the way her son turned out. She didn't want me to turn out like that. He got everything handed to him, and they were all spoiled pisspots. So she kept custody.

How come you didn't go to Florida?

I called my mother to tell her that I got a plane ticket to go the next morning and I told her why I got it. She said I could come back. I didn't leave [Florida] on very good terms. They didn't kick me out, I wanted to leave; but I left on very bad terms. I still haven't seen her, and it's gonna be two years at Christmas.

Do you want to see her?

Yeah. I can't wait. I want to see everybody. Especially my little sister and my little brother because they're so excellent. They're really great. And I've got a little brother that I've never even seen. My mother was pregnant when I moved. He's a year and seven months now.

Do you get along with your grandmother?

It's excellent. She's really understanding. When I moved in here, we made an agreement that if she doesn't like something that I'm doing, all she has to do is tell me and we'll talk about it, and vice versa. And it works out. She lets me be myself. Neither one of my families ever let me do that. It was so restricting. I've got restrictions now, I've got to be home by twelve and things; but it's all right.

You've got to be in by twelve?

It kind of sucks, but I respect it and I do it. If I want to stay out later and there's something in particular I want to do, I just ask her. She's totally cool about it.

Tell me about your mother and your stepfather and your family in Florida.

Me and my sister, my real sister, we used to do a lot of jobs around the house, an awful lot of work, an unusual amount for kids.

156

Then, when I was in third grade, me and my sister were fighting and my mother dropped a casserole out of the oven and it went all over the floor. It was for dinner. My stepfather got really pissed off, so he made us write—literally write on paper—"I will not fight" ten thousand times. And we did it. We had a sentence. We couldn't watch TV or go downstairs after school until we had it done. It took us three months.

Three months?

It sounds like a long time, but I was in the third grade and Jenny was in fourth grade. He used to throw some away and we used to snag them out of the garbage and give them back to him.

My mother wasn't very close to us. Maybe she was but that's just the way she is: cold. She has feelings and loved us and everything, but she just didn't express it. My sister is a lot like her. It affected me more because I'm real sensitive and all that kind of shit. So [my mother and I] got along, but we never talked about things. We never talked about anything.

We weren't allowed to have boyfriends. They let us have this one girl as a friend.

They chose your friends?

Yeah. They thought we were wild. We didn't do anything. We couldn't do anything. We never went out. Nothing. She thought we were so wild. We partied and stuff like that, but you can do that during the day.

How old were you when you were allowed to have boyfriends?

After I moved up here. I was fifteen years old when I moved.

Were you allowed to go out at night?

No. Had to be in the house by dark. We weren't allowed to go shopping by ourselves either, because when my sister was in seventh grade, she got caught shoplifting some little thing. I don't even remember what it was. So they wouldn't let us go to the mall or anywhere. It was terrible.

What about your brothers and sisters there?

My little brother was the youngest and he was their child, their boy, so he got really spoiled. Not bad spoiled. He's excellent. We got the same mother. He was a real cute little boy. And my little sister was excellent, too. She was so cute. We used to come home stoned and she'd say, "You smell like pot." She was really excellent and cool. A good kid. She just turned eleven.

So your father and your stepfather are archenemies now, right?

My stepfather doesn't give a shit about [my father]. He's not worth his time. They're totally different.

My family down there is very down-to-earth, very strict, more like an old-fashioned family. My family up here is real showy, and my father is a bullshitter. And my stepmother is a big show herself. But my parents in Florida are just very nonfalse.

Did you ever wish that your mother and father were still married?

No. The idea never occurred to me, because that's how it always was. We'd come to Buffalo on Christmas and during the summer and that was our life. That's the way it was.

My stepfather used to hit us sometimes, but that was because he was so strict. We were the first teenagers. I don't think he knew how to handle it. His father used to hit him if he got sick and threw up; he was a real jerk. So my stepfather picked that up. He wasn't that bad, but he's very strict and he believed in punishment. He would never go nuts on our face. He used to beat us with a belt. But not on the face.

For what reasons would he beat you?

A lot of unreasonable reasons. That was the reason I left. Like, my sister talks back. If he'd say something to her, she'd say, "Why?" or "How come?" or "I didn't do it." Smash in the face. You couldn't say anything and you couldn't have a dirty look on your face.

We used to get beaten by the belt in the rear end and on the legs for doing stuff, like lying.

What did you lie about?

We went to the mall. Or [about] seeing my friends—I got in trouble for doing that. Once when I was in seventh grade, I had this best friend, her name is Lesley, and my parents didn't like her because she lived with just her father and they thought she was wild. They thought *everybody* was wild. How wild can you be in seventh grade? So I stayed after school once, and I didn't call [my mother] until five o'clock and then I came right home. Lesley and I stayed after school a little while. We were going to have her father pick us up and drive us home, but something was wrong at home, so we had to go over to their house and I didn't get home until later. And my mother and my stepfather really freaked out.

At first I told them the truth, and they didn't believe me. Lesley's mother's new husband was threatening the kids or something; I don't remember. They didn't believe that, so then I said that I fell and I hurt my knee and I went to the nurse's office at school. I took a piece of glass and I cut my leg. Not much, but just enough so it looked like I fell—'cause I was so afraid of them. They kept saying, "You're lying through your teeth." They said that when I told them the truth and I wasn't lying. They wouldn't sit down and listen to you. That was their way and that was it. This is my stepfather and my mother.

My mother and my stepfather used to hit me a lot. My father hit me only that once when I got kicked out of the house. My stepmother would never hit me, because if she ever did, I'd floor her. I really would. At the beginning I wouldn't have, but once she went to hit me and I just grabbed her hand. I wouldn't let her hit me. No way. My stepfather was the one who used to hit us with the belt.

It's confusing, isn't it? All those parents and stepparents.

When I moved, my sister stayed in Florida because she was afraid to move up here. When I moved, they more or less changed. It wasn't a drastic change, but they tried to let her grow up. They wouldn't let us really grow up. You couldn't do anything. They wanted you to stay naive all your life. And we weren't, not by far. We knew what was going on.

Leaving Florida was hard because of leaving my sisters and brothers down there that I loved. But my parents wouldn't let us grow up. I had to leave. I knew I wasn't going to get anywhere staying there. So that was really painful. Leaving my father's house here—that wasn't painful. It wasn't painful as far as leaving them, but it was painful because it was just too much happening at once. It was 'way too much. My parents found out about everything and it caused such a big hassle, and then what happened with my grandmother and [my father] . . . They don't even talk. All because of me. Ridiculous.

Do you think it's your fault?

Not all of it, because it's been going on forever, the rivalry between those two. But, then, if I wasn't getting kicked out of the house, he never would have punched her in the face. But he's done that to her before. He just flipped out.

Do you hold it against your parents for hitting you?

Yeah, oh, yeah. You shouldn't hit your kids like that. I remember getting hit and saying to myself, why are you doing this? This just makes me more against you and more against your principles. It's not like you can beat it into me. This makes me hate and resent.

I could see it if you smartassed your mother and got smacked across the face. But if you had a bad mark on your report card, you shouldn't just get it on the ass.

And if we got a D or an F on our report cards in Florida, we used to be grounded for a period of time. Kept in the house. In the eighth grade I had two Fs in math. So I was grounded for eighteen weeks. Literally. I could go to school, come home from school, and that was it. I couldn't even walk up to the corner store. They stuck to it.

What did the divorce mean to you when you were a little kid?

It was just a way of life; that's the way it was. We just accepted it because it all happened when we were so young, before you can remember.

It was great to come up to Buffalo. I had brothers and sisters up here. It was neat.

160

I could see how if we were seven or eight or older it might have been different. But when you're as little as we were, you don't understand about love between two people. You don't understand man and wife or anything like that. So it wasn't any big, complicated thing. It was just something we didn't know about.

But it upset us when we heard stories about what my father used to do to my mother. She never really bad-mouthed him much, but she made comments. She told us about the gun once. She didn't go into detail or why, she just casually mentioned it. She told us about him hitting her a lot and how she used to follow him at night when he'd be off with women.

I didn't realize a lot of things until I moved up here. There's his side, her side, and the truth.

I love living here because I feel like I've accomplished something as far as being in a place where they love me so much. My grandmother thinks the world of my sister and me. We're the daughters she never had. We get treated like adults. My grandfather—she's only been married to him two years—is really excellent. He'd do anything for us, he really would. It's like a family again.

[But] it's not the same. I don't think I'll be really happy until I see my family in Florida again and get those ties straightened away. As far as the ties I had with my real father and my stepmother, I don't even care about them. Maybe time will heal all. Maybe it will. But right now I don't care about them. I care about them, but not really.

[My Florida family is] coming up here at Christmas. We're going to see them.

I feel like I missed a lot. I was so close to my little sister. She was such a doll. And then there's that little brother I've never seen.

My mother writes me letters, but the letters aren't very friendly. So much has to be caught up between us; I can see why. I imagine my letters are the same. But now we talk on the phone. Before, when I lived at my father's house, when we talked on the phone, she was always very cold to me. We didn't really talk. Just, "What else is new?" and that was it. But now we talk more friendly on the phone. Time heals all. It's the truth.

The way I look at everything now is, I'm going to be a hell of a mother when I have kids. I know what not to do. I know what I want—like being closer to your children and talking to them. I want my kids to tell me everything. What my mother didn't do with me.

The only thing that discourages me is the cost of living now. It's going to be hard to afford a house, especially when you can't get mortgage money anymore.

I'd like to have as many kids as I could afford. To a limit. If I'm a millionaire when I'm older, I don't want a million kids or anything like that. Maybe three. Three would be nice.

I don't think people nowadays, when they get married, think about what would happen if they ever got divorced. They think, okay, let's get married. If it doesn't work out, we can always get divorced. They must, because just look at the rate of divorce nowadays. It's ridiculous.

I think it was good for my parents that they got divorced because it would never have worked. They would have wound up killing each other. But as far as the kids [are concerned], I think it's a terrible thing to have done.

When you get married, you should know, or at least try to know, that it's right. You've got to think about your kids. When I get married, I'm going to think about what will happen if I ever get divorced from this guy and I have kids. I don't want to do that. I think people are very selfish and just think about themselves when they get into a marriage and not about the kids. They think if they're not happy, they'll get a divorce and that's that. If there are kids, it's not that's that.

"She kicked Teddy square in the balls."

ALAN (15)

They brought us up to the room one day—me, my brother and sister—and they told us. They said, "Come up here." It was early on a Sunday morning. "We've got to tell you something." And they told us. It was my father's idea. A month later he married my mother's best friend. My father goes, "We don't want to disrupt you kids, we think it's the best possible thing for us."

My father was just bullshitting us. Totally. One hundred percent. It was because he wanted to marry her. She married him for his money. My mother's best, oldest friend. She's my stepmother now. She's a nice lady.

I was pretty young—eleven. I let it pass for a while and then I thought about it. And then I was fucked up.

What do you mean?

I did what I wanted to. I took advantage of my mother.

No one ever suspected it. No one in the neighborhood. They

fought a lot, but no one ever suspected a divorce. Then everyone laughed because that lady, my mother's best friend, took my father for all his money.

Was there ever any physical violence in your family?

I remember back when I was seven years old. You know those big milk cans that you paint, the big steel ones? They had a replica of one of those, or maybe it was real. My father whipped it at my mother and she flew through one door and right on through another door. Right on her back.

Was she hurt badly?

No. She survived. I don't like to see parents fight like that.

My father's a nutty driver. All my friends, especially when I was little, said, "I don't want to drive with him." One time he really fucked himself and my mother up. Remember that huge rainstorm when everything flooded about five years ago? He ran into a cement viaduct and they both rolled out of the car, and my mother had to have all this shit done to her mouth. My father was home that night. We said, "Where's Mom?" and he said, "She's in the hospital. I fucked her up."

It was strange. I didn't know what to do. I was worried. I didn't know if she was dying or if she was all right. Then he said she would be all right, so I felt better.

I've moved back and forth four times. Now I live with my mother during the summer and with my father during school. He wants me to go to private school and she can't pay for it. He'll pay for everything. I said I'd go to that school only if I can live at my mother's during the summer.

My father is a lawyer, and he can pull whatever shit he wants in court. His wife is a nice lady. When you don't do anything to her, she doesn't do anything to you, unless she is on the rag. Then she bitches. But she won't bitch to me. She'll bitch at her own kids. She can be an asshole to other people, but she doesn't bother me at all. She's cool to me.

She doesn't like it when I get in trouble, though. Like when I stole the Valiums from my grandmother. That was pretty sick. Nutso.

What happened?

I only took a few Vs from her. Not too many. But I dropped one on the floor because I was flipping out. I got careless and I got busted. I got out of it because I said, "I need money, I was going to sell them. I don't *do* them."

My dad knows I don't trip or anything anymore. He's known that for quite a while. He knows I party. I tell him I won't quit. There's nothing he can do about it. But he still doesn't want [drugs] in his house and I won't bring [any] in his house. For a while, for about six months, I had him thinking that I don't smoke pot anymore; then I couldn't let it fly by. I had to tell him. So I told him.

My mother gets on my case about it. "You use it for a crutch." She keeps saying that to me. And I say, "Yeah, Mom. I'm so depressed every night I just want to go out and smoke a joint by myself in a corner, tucked away, tripping on LSD." Then I get her mad.

What's your mother like?

My real mother? She used to be normal, but then my father totally fucked her up. I don't have command over her, but she doesn't have command over me. We're more friends than we are mother and son.

I get along with my father fine. I don't mind him at all. He's pretty cool, but don't ever fuck him over. He's into grounding.

This year I've been grounded a lot. I got busted for [caught] smoking pot at school; that was pretty bad. Then I got busted for stealing Vs. Then I got busted for taking out my father's car, a Seville.

I've got two stepsisters and one stepbrother, a half brother which my father and my mother's best friend had, a real brother, and a real sister. The only one I don't get along with is Bobbie, my sister. Bobbie is a loser. I don't think about her anymore. Never even bother.

Why?

She fucks me up too much every time I live with her. She parties,

165

she trips, she does everything else, but she's such a loser. She lies to herself. She makes herself think her lies are true. She lies to herself and she believes it. And she just fucks me over all the time.

She tells on me. Tells my father when I live with my mother that I do acid and shit. And she tells my mother when I'm smoking pot downstairs in the basement or in my room. I used to live down there and I would smoke down there. I had a bong just like this one. Then I'd get busted. Bobbie would say, "They're partying down there." She'd come home from work in the summer and the whole house would be in a cloud.

When she wanted to move in with my father and my mother wouldn't let her, my mother got a grip on her leg and my sister was dragging her down the street. They were both screaming and yelling and scratching each other. Then my sister came running in the house and she kicked [my brother] Teddy square in the balls as hard as she could 'cause he was going to hold her. He would have killed her if he could have, but she killed him. Right in the balls.

She's very attractive, I can say that. She's got a lot going for her, but she has no brain at all. My father's totally given up on her. She gets a lot of places with her looks, like her job and shit like that, but she's still fucked up in the head. She just totally rags and bitches. She tells herself lies and she tells everyone else lies. She'll steal dimes off a counter. She'll tell lies just to tell people things.

My brother has pulled some stunts. When he took off from home, he said he was going to school. He hid behind the fence and he called the moving van and they came and took all of his furniture. A fucking moving van.

My mother said, "Go get Teddy for dinner." I went upstairs. I was little. I didn't get high then and I'm going, "Something is weird. There's no furniture around." And I'm going, "Teddy's not here and none of his furniture is here either." She starts crying.

The only reason I moved in with my father was because my mother couldn't pay for my school. I wasn't about to go to that school where she lives.

When they got divorced, I first lived with my mother in Williamsville. Then Teddy moved out for good; he's been with my father. Then Bobbie moved out once, and me and my mother moved into an apartment. Then Bobbie moved back in. I took off and my mother moved into a smaller apartment. I moved back again when I was in the eighth grade.

Then we got kicked out because I had so many parties. The guy who owned it was cool, though. I partied with him. But all the neighbors complained too much. They're townhouses there.

Now I'm with my father for school and my mother for all vacations. I might go to boarding school next year. I don't know yet. I wouldn't mind it. I know a lot of kids where I would go. All they do is party. They get out of school at one o'clock and they still have fine grades. Grades are no problem for me anyway. It's not like I would ever fail. I could never get under an eighty in anything.

You do well in school now?

Yeah. I don't get ninety-six averages, shit like that. I stay in the eighty-five to eighty-nine range, then I blow it off. Homework and all that shit.

Do you think your mother will get remarried?

By the summer. She's seen Craig for about six years now. I know Craig's kid. I've been over to his house for parties and I've seen Craig there. I don't say anything to him and he doesn't say anything to me. Then he comes over and he gives me a ten-dollar bill. He does that all the time when he sees me, so I have some extra money. He's a cool guy.

I wouldn't mind if she married Craig. We'd live in a nice big house and I wouldn't have to live with my father. He laughs at my mother now. He looks down on her.

She thinks he's an asshole because of what he did. He totally screwed up the marriage, screwed us up. She just wanted to live. She's off the wall because of that. I've been fine, though. Nothing ever emotionally hurt me. Not like my mother [was hurt].

What was the hardest part of it for you?

The moving. All of the moves that took place. They're all pretty hard. You can't just say, "I want to come back and move in with you," and move on in. You've already done it. I can with my mother, but I can't with my father. I've got to talk to him each time and say why I want to move back and all this other shit. An application you have to fill out.

Do you think you'll get married?

Yeah, but I don't plan on having a lot of kids. Because if anything ever did happen, I wouldn't want to fuck up a lot of kids.

I wouldn't marry somebody fucked up. I wouldn't marry somebody if she's good-looking but she's an airhead or just rich. That doesn't matter. Just as long as she's cool.

Wouldn't want to have a lot of kids anyway—they cost a lot of money.

"I think divorce is dumb."

JOE (16)

I remember my mother came home really drunk and I was trying to help. I didn't know what was going on. That was a long time ago. My father had my mother in a headlock and he was choking her. I could never hit my father or anything like that, but I tried to help her. She was too drunk.

She never listened to me. She would just go her own way, like normal people do.

When they were married, they went to gin mills, they went out drinking, and they came home drunk. That's when they usually got in the fights. They'd call each other "fuckers" and things like that.

At first I cried. I didn't know what was going on. I tried to calm my sisters down. One time my older sister left and I went after her, and then my father came after me.

There were a lot of fights. And money problems. We had this house when we were all together and we didn't have enough money to pay the bills. My father wasn't making enough money. He took two jobs and he tried to make it, but I guess he couldn't do it.

So they got divorced four years ago. For the first year I lived with my father. I didn't want to live with my mother and my four sisters. But it didn't work out, so I went back with my mother.

He's still living in Buffalo. I don't see him that much. I see him on Christmas and New Year's.

Do you want to see him?

Yeah. I get along with him well.

Why don't you want to live with your mother?

I guess it was the age I was. I just wanted to be with my father. I didn't want to live with my mother and the four sisters. You know how that goes.

I lived with my mother for about a month at my aunt's house and I got in a fight with my aunt and uncle and they kicked me out of the house. So I went and lived with my father for about a year. Then I just couldn't hack it anymore, so I went back to my mother.

Now I'm living with my mother and I get along with her. I try to help her any way I can. I stick up for my sisters and all that crap. My father—we don't see much of each other.

I lived with him for a week and we got along real well then. He's really a father, real nice. He was trying to help me learn some things.

My sisters, if he says that he'll take them shopping, will call him. I'll call him just to talk to him. But I haven't talked to him for a few months now.

How do you think the divorce changed you?

I didn't drink as much before, and I didn't smoke pot as much as I do now. I like to forget what's going on.

Do you think it was a good or bad thing that your parents got divorced?

I think it was good for them, but not for us, not for the kids. I think divorce is dumb. If two people love each other, I think they should stick it out, they should talk over their problems, they should try to work it out. If they have kids, [divorce] is the worst thing they can do. It's pretty bad for the kids. It is. If I get married, I don't think I'd go through it. It's pretty bad from what I've seen, what I've gone through.

"My mother never told us she was divorced."

MARYANNE (21)

I was five the first time they got divorced. The first time I never heard about until later. The second time I knew. It was one of those things you just felt coming.

How long were they divorced the first time?

About a year and a half. It started when I was just going into kindergarten. I lived with my mother, my sister, April, and my older sister. My mother never told us she was divorced. She just told us that my father was living at the other house until he sold it, and then he'd come and live with us. We always thought that. The other house was only about two miles away from where we were living, so we never questioned what my mother told us.

I didn't find out about it until I was fourteen. I was snooping through my mother's papers and I found a marriage certificate for 1964. I went, what? I was born in 1957. How did they get married in 1964 and I didn't know about it? I asked my mother and she said, "Yes, we were divorced and remarried."

The second time I was about nineteen.

How did you feel when it happened?

Pretty shitty. I guess nobody likes to see their parents get divorced. You just feel, there goes my family. And in a sense that was true.

My mother left my father. She'd just had enough. They were living on a lakeshore then, in a big house that needed a mother to take care of it, and after my mother left the whole place went downhill. My father wound up selling the house about nine months later. And he moved into Buffalo, along with my mother. Not in the same house. At that time I was living in Buffalo with my husband-to-be in an apartment.

When my mother first left, she didn't tell anybody where she went. She just disappeared for about two weeks. Nobody heard anything from her.

My father was a raving maniac. He couldn't believe that my mother would leave him. It was like the great indignation: How could she do this to me? And he was crying. I had never seen my father cry before. Ever. He was always in tears. So when I finally did find out where my mother had been hiding out, I was very hostile toward her. I was like, "How could you do this, Mom? How could you leave? It couldn't be that bad. God, Dad's getting old. You could have stuck it out a few years longer."

She said, "I couldn't. My sanity was on the verge of departing and I had to leave."

"Mom, Dad's crying. He's a wreck. He's talking about . . ."

He was talking about suicide. I think he just wanted people to feel sorry for him. But it just made me feel terrible to see my father going through such mental anguish. He was really a basket case.

We are a family of many divorced parents. I have six sisters. Only two of them are whole sisters. I have four half sisters from other marriages. My father had been married twice before he was married to my mother. And my mother had been married and divorced once before.

Do you get along with your half sisters?

For the most part. I don't see them very often. My oldest sister, Katie, is considerably older. She's fourteen years older, and I was just five when she moved out of the house. She went on and had her own life-style. And two of my other sisters grew up in New York City, where they went to boarding school and away to college. Then another sister ran away from home when she was fifteen and I was about eight. She ran away and got married and got pregnant. So it was just basically me and my two younger sisters at home. And we got along relatively well, considering everything. There was a little bit of rivalry, but I suppose that's normal in a big family.

How did your younger sisters take the divorce?

April, who is twenty now, took the divorce very hard. She felt abandoned by my mother. She chose to stay with my father, I think partially because my father is the softy in the family. April knew she would get some emotional support from him, where my mother is more cold about things. When she left it was like she said, "I'm sick of kids, I'm sick of being married, I'm sick of having a house and a husband. And you can stay with your father. I want him to see what it's like." It was like she was just abandoning all her responsibilities as a mother. So April was really very upset.

And Linda, who was fourteen then, didn't show any emotion toward it. It was, "Mom's gone. Big deal. So what?" Linda went on to get into a series of bad events, and it was just because after my mother left, my father provided no supervision whatsoever. He stayed overnight in the city a lot. He didn't come home. Linda was free to do as she pleased. As the youngest, she was always a brat anyway, but she just went wild.

For about three months after my mother left, she never even called my sisters to see if they were all right. Not even to say, "How are you? What are you doing?" She never called. I'd call her up and say, "Mom, I think you have some responsibility toward April and Linda. Call them. They feel so bad."

She'd say, "Well, I can't call."

She just felt that [at that time] she had to go through a period of healing, and I guess leaving them out was part of it. I'm not quite sure.

Where was she staying?

For a while she stayed with a girl friend, and then she moved in with another friend of hers and she's still living there, but now she's rented another place. This friend of hers lives in a huge home, and he's got an apartment on the end of his house which would have been servants' quarters at one time. This friend of my mother's is gay. That's my mother's new hangout: gay men. She probably feels safe with them.

What kinds of things did Linda do?

Oh, God. Linda started throwing wild parties and the word would get out and there'd be fifty kids at our house having beer parties and smoking pot. And she used to take my father's station wagon for little jaunts down to her friend's house.

Right after my mother left and made it clear that she wasn't coming back, my father went out and bought a brand-new Jaguar. I think he felt that he needed a bachelor car to impress all the girls. Linda borrowed it one day and smashed it up. A twenty-seven-thousand-dollar car. After she did that, my father got so furious he literally pounded the hell out of her.

Two days later Linda moved to Atlanta to live with one of my sisters. That was the end of Linda until last November, when my father convinced her to come back home and try living here again. Since then she's been shuffled back and forth between my mother's house, my father's house, and friends of the parents. She hasn't really lived anywhere since she came back from Georgia.

How does she get along with her mother now?

She has absolutely no respect for my mother. But my father has told her that that's okay. He said, "Your mother abandoned us. You don't have to listen to her. I'm in charge. And what I say goes. You can just tell your mother to go to hell if she tells you to do anything. You don't have to listen to her."

I think Linda, deep down inside, knows that she really should listen to my mother, but she doesn't do it. She figures, Dad says that I don't have to, so therefore I'm not going to.

Did your mother ask her to leave her house?

No. Linda left my mother's of her own free will because she decided that she didn't like my mother's friends. She didn't like my mother's apartment.

Linda was under lock and key at my mother's. She couldn't get away with anything. She had to live by the rules, which is something Linda never had to live by before, and she figured, well, I'd better go live with Dad because I can do whatever I want if I live at Dad's house. Which is true.

So she lived with my father for a while, but then he'd come home in a shitty mood and he'd scream at her and say, "Linda, get the hell out of here. Go back to your mother's house. I don't want you."

This went on at least once a week. Finally, Linda felt like a pawn, moving between both parents. My mother didn't want her, my father didn't want her. So Linda moved back out to the lake and lived with some friends of my parents and finished out her school year there. Then, during the summer, she came to live with me, which didn't work out because she couldn't follow my rules and orders. She totally took advantage of me.

Too many kids wind up really fucked up because they don't know how to handle their parents' divorce. And their parents can't help them because they are going through a trauma at the same time. And nobody else really knows what they're going through. A friend's parents might have been divorced, but that doesn't help because every divorce is different. There are no two identical divorces.

Do you think your parents will remarry?

I doubt that my mother will ever remarry. I think she's taken a very bitter attitude toward men. I think she feels that marriage isn't necessarily the answer anymore. My father, on the other hand, is the type of person who needs to have a wife who is home cooking and cleaning and making his environment pleasant for him. At the moment he's got a twenty-seven-year-old girl friend; if anybody is going to become his next wife, it will probably be her. My father is thirty years older than she is. I can't see where any attraction comes in, but I suppose that if he gets remarried, she'd probably be the next one.

Do you still talk to them a lot?

I talk to both of my parents on a regular basis.

Do they bad-mouth each other to you?

My mother has always had a policy of not talking about my father, not saying anything nasty about my father. My mother does not talk about my father. She never has.

My father, on the other hand, whenever he is upset, has been known to say things about my mother. I think it's because he's the less secure of the two. Deep down inside, he still loves my mother. Whenever he is around my mother, he begs her to go back. I think there have been times when my mother was half ready to say, "All right, let's try it again," but her psychologist told her that my father would only take it out on her, that she left him in the first place, that he didn't think it would be a good idea for my mother to go back, and that my mother should just try to construct some kind of new life.

What sort of things would he say about her?

He used to basically justify the reason my mother left him.

My mother left my father because he had a severe drinking problem and because he had been caught sleeping with one of their friends' wives. My father would say, "When your mother was in Europe for a month three years ago, I know she was screwing around." Now, he has absolutely no proof of that at all, but he's the type of guy that justifies everything. He can rationalize when he has no basis for it. It's just like when they got divorced before, my father said, "It was because your mother was carrying on with some lawyer."

That wasn't the case at all. It was probably more my father's fault, and just because my mother had a boyfriend after they split up, my father was all flipped out about it.

177

After my mother left this time, my father made a point to follow her everywhere she went to see who she was with, to see if she had any boyfriends. He had his friends keep their eyes open, he had them literally spy on her, which I thought was not right at all on his part.

My mother never said, after they split up, "Are you sleeping with anybody?" She didn't care. She hoped he'd meet somebody that he'd like.

But my father is a martyr. He's got it in his mind that he's got to have my mother back. It's been a year and a half and she'll never go back to him. He should know that by now. But he claims that they were married for twenty-two years, not including their first divorce, so what could have been so bad about their marriage if it lasted that long? He's just an old stick-in-the-mud. He likes things a certain way and that's the only way he likes them. He's not willing to see anybody else's point. He says, "Oh, I'll change. You come back to me and I'll change." He might change for six months and then he'd be right back to his old self again.

He really made my sisters feel betrayed, that my mother had shafted everyone. For a short time my sisters really did feel that my mother didn't love them at all, that she was just a selfish bitch that left. I felt like that at times. There were times I would call my mother up and I would beg her. I'd say, "Please call Dad. Try to work things out." I was forever the one trying to mend the marriage, trying to get them back together. For my own reasons. It probably wasn't fair, but it was just that nobody likes to see their parents split up. Even if they have a terrible relationship, nobody likes to see their parents divorced.

The important thing in my parents' case is that my parents now are really good friends. They see each other a lot. My mother works for my father. They get along better now than they did when they were married. They seem to have a mutual respect for each other. My father knows that if he ever needed my mother, she'd be there to help him. And he'd be there to help her. But as far as any type of romantic adventures, there won't be any more with them. They're friends now and they'll always consider each other members of their family—but that's all.

I always said that if my parents got divorced, I'd be really happy. That was when I was younger, when I was fourteen or fifteen, and it was because they did not get along well together. I always felt the best thing that could happen would be if they got a divorce. But then, when I was confronted with the divorce, I thought it was terrible.

I've seen some of my friends' parents divorced when they were younger and I always felt sorry for them. And when my parents decided to split up, I felt sorry for myself.

Actually, my mother decided. My father had no choice in it.

My father wasn't outwardly mean to my mother. He'd leave for work at nine o'clock in the morning and he'd come home at nine o'clock at night—bombed. In the meantime, my mother would have made dinner, she'd wait for my father, then he'd come home and pass out. That was the way he was abusive. He never hit her. They didn't get into outward fights that we ever heard of. They did a few [times], but they were rare.

What would you say to a kid whose parents were getting divorced?

I think the best thing is to seek some kind of counseling. I felt for a little while that I should have gone. There were a lot of things I just couldn't deal with. I couldn't deal with my father breaking down and crying. I couldn't deal with my mother's cold attitude about the whole thing.

Since my mother and father have split up, I have not gone over to her house once for dinner. I haven't had that much to do with her. Not that I've had that much to do with my father, but I think you sort of expect something of the tie with the mother. I've probably been closer to my father, even though I really like both of my parents a lot.

I am sidetracking. Back to your question: I would suggest that if my friend was having severe problems handling the parents' divorce, they seek counseling. There are a lot of places they can go for it. School. They can go to a federation. There are county services available. I think that's one of the only ways to deal with it.

Everybody always thinks it will never happen to them, their parents will never split up. And it is a very saddening event when it does happen.

You just have to realize that both your parents do love you and they are very upset, too. They may say things about the other one to slant your opinion, but I don't believe they mean it. I think they're going through a tough time and they put a lot of it on you.

In my case the kids stayed with my father instead of my mother. Usually the kids go to the mother, but in my case my mother didn't want anybody. She wanted her own independence. And my father has done a pretty good job, considering that he was dumped with two kids and two dogs and four cats and a house. He did pretty well.

I still feel bad to this day and I still wish that they were married. But they're not.

"Michael, I don't want to remember."

DIANE (17), Ellen's sister

I don't know if they will go through the whole procedure of it. I don't know the details of the whole thing. All I know is, they're not the same. They used to love each other.

I remember going to Washington a year ago last summer. They were just so much in love and they did everything together. My dad always used to kiss my mother good-bye. He used to kiss her hello. He used to be home on time.

All that's changed. It's all so different. He's never home anymore. She bitches constantly. I don't know. It's so weird.

What does she bitch about?

You name it, she bitches. My little brothers. She likes my little brothers more than anybody else in the family; that's because they're little and she can control them and manipulate them. But she yells at them all the time, and it upsets me when she yells at them. I don't like to hear people yelling at six o'clock in the morning. If they do the slightest thing wrong or don't snap when she tells them to, she'll yell at them. And that bugs me. You shouldn't yell at people like that. She's very high-strung.

Do you stick up for them?

Yes, I do. And that shuts her up immediately. I wish she'd fight back, 'cause then I'd know what's going on inside her head. She's always so damned sweet to me that it kills me. She's just too sweet to me. And too mean to everybody else. She'll say some real bitchy things. We're not close. She's closer to my two sisters, but she's bitchy to them. I'm never there.

She'll call my little brother to set the table or [to do] something that he has to do. She'll yell for him and he'll say, "I'm coming," and he won't be there for the next five seconds because he's putting away a toy or something like that. And she'll come in there and she'll yell at him and yell at him and yell at him. I'll say, "Will you shut up?"

I try to talk to her about it and she doesn't listen. She just automatically agrees with me and won't tell me her opinions 'cause she's really hard to communicate with.

I remember when she used to yell at me when I was little; I didn't like it. She yelled about everything that she yells at my little brothers about. Everything that they do in their lives, they get yelled at for. She doesn't hit them. She just yells at them.

My mom puts everybody down and she is always making you feel like you're the lowest thing that ever lived. But my dad always tells you that you're good and he always builds you up and tells you everything is all right. And you don't get in trouble with my dad. You know you're in trouble with him, but he doesn't yell at you.

They're just two different people and they disagree about how to raise us. I think that's really a lot of their problem. Plus my dad can't handle my mom anymore. He used to be able to. And he comes to me to talk about it and I don't know what to say to him. I don't know what to do.

What does he say to you?

Stuff like my mother gets on his nerves so much and she doesn't talk to him. He can't talk to her about anything really relevant. All she does is complain, and all he can do is react to what she says. But he can't initiate something and talk to her about problems. My dad comes to me with these unreal problems that he should be coming to my mom about.

Like my grandmother. She's getting real old and senile and stuff, and the problem is up to my dad [to decide] what to do with her, but he should talk about it with my mom and he should get her ideas and have her help and stuff. But it's not her. It's me and my sister that have to do it. I don't know how much he goes to Ellen because I'm not around that much. And when she and I talk, it sounds like he comes to both of us a lot about the same things, but you never know, you never know. He can't talk to my mother.

How do you feel about that?

Bad. 'Cause he used to be with her. They used to be so close.

She complains about everything. It could be sunny out, it could be the most beautiful day in the world, and she'd find something wrong with it. Something. That the wind was blowing too hard or something. She's like that. Her personality is very unstable.

Has it always been that way?

I've begun to realize it more lately. My dad says that it's become a lot worse lately. I've just become old enough right now to start noticing stuff like that.

It's not money. It's a personality conflict. I mean, once in a while my mom will spend too much and my dad will say, "Hey, look," but he does not bitch at her. He doesn't argue with her. But she'll sit there and she'll complain and she'll argue with him without him saying anything, and finally he'll say, "Goddamn it, shut up" or something like that.

When I come home from work, it's lying in bed at night and hearing them fight that's the worst. My bedroom is in the back. I hate to see what my little brothers think. They hear it. They hear all that. They hear everything that they say.

I remember when we were little and they had fights like that, but it stopped. It stopped for a good ten or twelve years. Then all of a sudden it started all over again.

Do your parents drink?

Yes. Too much.

Would you say they're alcoholics?

What's an alcoholic?

Someone that needs to drink.

How many times a day?

How often do they drink?

Put it this way: my dad has a few beers at night to relax him so that he can try to handle my mother. My mother is either high on some type of medicine or coming down and using alcohol to come down. She's doped up all the time. And when she's not doped up, that's when she's really bad. When she gets doped up, she's tolerable.

Do they do anything irrational?

When they're drinking?

Yes.

They fight. It could be because they're drinking. I'm not sure. I think it's because my mother is drinking. My dad does it just to handle her. He doesn't get drunk. I don't see my dad get that wasted. If they go out to a party or something he does, but not just sitting home.

Whose side are you on? Are you on a side?

What side does it sound like I'm on?

It sounds like you're on your father's side.

I don't like to say I'm on anybody's side because I love them both. And that's what's the worst. Some people can say, "My mom's at fault and my dad's right," and that's the way it is. But it's not that way for me. My sister sides with my dad completely. I can't do that. I love them both and I just don't know what to do about them.

I try to run away from it. I was talking to [my friend] Connie today because I was afraid to talk to you. I don't know what to say to you. She said that I seem like the typical person who doesn't know what to do in the situation because I run away. And she's right: I do run away. I don't face it very often. I run away from it.

I go out with my friends a lot, as much as I can, and I work and I don't go home very much, 'cause when you go home and have dinner at our house, they sit at the table and they pick at each other. You try to prevent it. You try to talk rationally. And no matter if you're sitting there having a conversation about nuclear energy, they'll take opposite sides and that will get them into a fight. You can't win. I just don't want to be there anymore.

Do you ever get wasted to forget about what is going on at home?

I tried to figure that out because I don't get wasted during the week. I do on the weekend and I have a feeling it is because of that. I think so. I don't think I'd get as wasted as I do if it wasn't for that, if I didn't know that I had to go home and probably listen to them.

One night the weekend before last, I was sitting at Mary's house and Bob walked in after we were talking for a while and said, "You want to go for a cruise?" and I said, "Sure." We just sat out and talked about bullshit until three in the morning. I went home at three in the morning. I told him I was scared to go home. When he dropped me off, the lights were on. I knew it. They were fighting. At three o'clock in the morning! You just can't go home anytime. And it's my house.

What do you think they should do? Do you think it would be better if they were divorced or separated?

I think it would kill my mother and I think it would be better for my father.

Which parent filed for divorce; your dad?

They haven't really filed yet. They're thinking about it. I don't think they've filed yet.

Your sister told me they have filed.

See: she knows. I think she knows a little more than I do because she's around more. If they file, it would be my dad. I'm pretty sure my dad would do it. But it would kill my mother and he knows it would. It would.

Have you ever talked to him about it?

Yeah.

He knows it would hurt her and he doesn't know what to do. He's stuck. I mean, look at it: he's stuck. He's the finest guy I ever met. If I was old enough, I would marry my dad. I would. He's the kind of guy I want to marry. He's perfect.

Why is your mother so sweet to you?

I don't know. When I was in there today with Connie, my mom walked in and said, "Oh, you look so nice" and stuff like that. I felt like saying, "What act are you putting on now?" Because I heard her yelling at my brother before she came upstairs. She turns on and off like that. It's really weird. It's like she's scared to get me mad because she thinks I'm going to run to my dad or something. Maybe that's the reason they are so against each other: because I would run to my dad all the time when my mom would be obnoxious to me. She used to be so obnoxious. When we were little, she used to hit us. I can remember my sister being beaten. I mean really beaten. I can't remember it happening to me, but my sister told me that it has happened to me. You know how you block that stuff out of your mind?

My youngest sister sees a psychiatrist because she's really screwed up. It's all because of what happened to her when she was little with my mom. My sister cannot block that kind of stuff out of her mind. She remembers when Ellen and I got beaten by my mother. Really badly. I was sent to the hospital once and Ellen got beaten with a lead pipe.

We didn't know we weren't supposed to tell my dad about that kind of stuff because it would get him mad at my mom. We would

186

tell him what she did. I don't know how he reacted because I can't remember that, but I know they had some pretty bad fights.

You have no idea what your dad did when you and your sister used to go to him?

No. I can't remember. I block that stuff. I don't want to remember, to tell you the truth. But I know that if you talk to my little sister, she could tell you the most intimate details about everything because she remembers. She had to watch it.

Did Ellen tell you what Melissa did when Ellen got hit with the lead pipe?

I don't think so. Why don't you tell me?

I don't want to. Not if she didn't tell you. She should tell you.

You can tell me. She told me about the lead pipe.

Melissa was just a little kid. She must have been about four. And she just took off and ran and ran and ran in circles around the backyard screaming, just screaming, because her mother, who she was supposed to love, was beating her sister.

I remember coming home from camp after that happened. I never remembered this until Melissa brought this up and told us, but I remember it now. I remember how Ellen looked. She looked almost deformed.

She was that badly beaten?

She was that badly beaten. I don't remember what my dad did about it. That's what bothers me. And I don't want to ask him. No, God, not now. I don't want to ask him. Nothing like opening up old wounds.

How old is your sister Melissa now?

Fourteen. She's the one who's probably been messed up the most. It's not because of the divorce, though. That's not hurting her now. She'd like to see that, I think. It's the way my mom treated her and us when we were little.

Do you hold that against {your mother}, that she hit you and your sister?

I don't know. I never thought about it. I guess I sort of do. Maybe that's why I'm not close to her, I mean as close as some people are to their mothers.

Why were you sent to the hospital?

Which time? I've been in the hospital a lot of times. What time are you talking about?

The time your mother put you in the hospital.

Oh, I was just in for stitches.

Where?

Children's Hospital. Why?

No, not the hospital. Where on you? Was it because she'd hit you? That's why you got them?

Yeah.

Where?

When I fell.

Because when she hit you, you fell?

Yes. Michael, why do you want to know this?

It's relevant.

I got stitches in my shoulder. There's a spot right there from it. I fell on a blade.

Do you remember what you did?

Michael, I don't want to remember.
I didn't think much about this kind of stuff before, but I know what was happening to my friend Lois, and I used to tell her to do stuff that now I know is impossible. Her mother used to sit there and cry about it all the time and I would tell Lois, "Get out, just go away.

Get out of the house and let your mother solve her problems for herself." Lois couldn't do that because she's close to her mom. Now I know that if that ever happened to my dad, I couldn't just leave my dad. I couldn't even leave my mom either, if she was just sitting there crying. I could not detach myself that much.

I have.

Why did she cry? To have you stay home?

Because I was going out. She'd start crying.

My mother's done that so many times I don't even listen to her anymore. I'd always take off because I couldn't stand her. I guess I've never really been able to stand her.

How long ago was this?

Eighth, ninth, tenth grade. In tenth grade, when I first started going out with Jack, she used to cry a lot. Her first little girl, et cetera, et cetera. She had a hard time with it. She used to say a lot of bad stuff, demeaning stuff, very demeaning. She tried to manipulate me. At first I let her. At first I'd do what she asked me to do. Then, finally, I just said, "See you," and took off.

Does she guilt-trip you anymore?

All the time. She always guilt-trips me. Since Jack left she hasn't done it very much, but she'd do it when he called.

I don't come home sometimes until two or three in the morning. Even if I just have to take the car somewhere, I'll sit and just talk to somebody, or just sit by myself and try to think things out. But I won't come in the house until a lot later, and she thinks that I've been out with a guy or drinking too much or something. And she'll guilt-trip me about that. She'll say, "I don't want you to become an alcoholic. God knows, I've tried." She gets into guys: "I don't want you running around like a little slut."

When she says something like that and you're not even doing it . . . It's bad enough if you are doing it, but when you're not even

189

doing it, you can't say to her, "I'm not," because anybody's going to say that even if they are doing it.

How do you feel about your mother favoring your two little brothers?

It's never really bugged me because I've never been favored, so I haven't lost anything. It bothered me about Melissa, because she was babied for six years and then all of a sudden, *wham,* two little brothers. Two new people to be favored. Ellen always got more attention than me because she was smarter. Melissa got it because she was cuter. I haven't lost anything because I didn't have it, so it doesn't really matter.

I get jealous, yeah. But I figure they deserve [the attention], they need it. They're littler.

If you were faced with a decision, who would you want to stay with?

I don't know. It would depend on who would want me to stay with them. How can you say?

I would probably want to stay with my dad because he's better with teenagers than my mother. My mother is better with younger kids.

Our family is two families, if you want to know. It's not one family. It's my mother and the little boys and my dad and the older kids, the three girls.

[My parents] disagree about everything. My mom will say things; she gets mad at my dad over the stupidest little things, like if he doesn't want to eat. When he comes home from work, he likes to have a beer, sit down, read the evening paper, and then eat dinner. That's the way he is. She gets all huffy about that. She gets huffy about everything he does. She'll say to my little brother, "Eat your dinner," and she'll yell at him about it, and my dad will say something like, "Don't put the boy down like that. Joey, just eat as much as you can." And she'll yell at him about it. I've seen times when he's gotten up and whipped a plate of food away and walked out because he's gotten so mad.

How old is he?

Forty-three. Why, does he sound like a little kid? No. He just gets

190

really pissed off at her. They're both immature when it comes to their fighting.

It bothers me. Otherwise I'd stay around more. I've told them to grow up.

Have you ever had plans in your mind to make things better at home?

Not really a plan, but sort of a dream or a wish or a hope. There's nothing that I can do.

I don't play them against each other. I probably used to do that when I was little without knowing it, because they are so different. They have such different views. But I never meant to do it. When you get married, you should have the same views about how to raise children. They've got totally opposite views.

When I was in the seventh grade, my mom had a nervous breakdown, a real bad one. She was in the hospital for a couple of months. And my dad had a breakdown because of her breakdown. It wasn't his own, it was hers; it just played back on him. Maybe that's why my mom's on so many pills.

She'll say things like, "I know you're all against me." This is her favorite line. And, "I know what you're all trying to do." And she'll hallucinate sometimes. God, how she'll hallucinate. She thinks we're all out to get her, that we're all against her. I mean the four of us— my dad and the three older girls.

She knows it's her fault and she feels guilty, but she doesn't know what to do about it. She can't change her personality. That's just her.

I don't know how he ever fell in love with her. I think maybe because she was helpless or something. How can he tolerate her for as long as he has? I block the bad things out of my mind, but now that I'm recalling some of them, I think, how could he have ever stood her?

I've often wondered that myself. My dad and my mother were married fifteen years, and it's amazing how different they are. They are two completely different people. My dad hasn't changed; my mother has adapted. She's like an amoeba. She changes to fit the surroundings. She smoked dope ten years ago

191

and she won't admit it now. She's gotten religious. She won't recall anything of her past.

I talk to my little brothers a lot. I tell them everything is okay and that both Mommy and Daddy love them. I go in sometimes when I get home from work and my little brothers will be crying because my parents are fighting. I'll talk to them and tell them as much as I can. I try to be rational with them. They're still young. You can't tell them the ins and the outs of the whole thing, but you can explain it a little.

I always listen to both sides. Form my own opinion.

That is what I try to do, but I get in trouble doing that. You can get in a lot of trouble doing that.

How do you mean?

Not in *trouble* trouble. In trouble in your own head because you confuse yourself so much when you do that. And when you don't have your own opinion to put in, you get confused. Especially if you can see that both people are right or both people are wrong. It just doesn't work sometimes.

That's why I was so messed up in fifth grade. My mom was putting down my dad and my dad was constantly putting down my mom. I didn't know what the hell was going on. I didn't know and I had to find out. It fucked me up for a long time.

It sure did. I don't mean that meanly. I could tell. It did.

But I've got my shit together now.

You're lucky. A lot of people wouldn't. So you're strong mentally.

Do you think you'll be stronger mentally when this is over?

Yes, but I don't know how. The only thing that's good about this right now is, I'm so much closer to each of my parents than I was before. I can talk to them more now. We're closer. But that's a terrible way. It's how it's got to be, how it's got to come.

192

I don't know how I'll be stronger. I just have this feeling that if I can make it through this . . . That's what I always say when they're fighting. I'm lying in bed and I think, if I can make it through this and still have my sanity, I can probably live through anything.

"She took the lead pipe and hit me with it."

ELLEN (16), Diane's sister

I can't even remember crying or the last time I cried. I don't cry. I just think about things and get all worked up and upset, but I don't cry. I'm not emotional that way.

Have you ever, because of the situation at home, gone out with the intention of getting really wasted to forget about what was going on?

A lot of times. Like on a Friday night, me and my sister'll want to go out. We'll say, "Can we go out, Mom?" and she'll say, "No. You have to wait till everyone's done with dinner." No phone calls during dinner, nothing like that. My dad will get pissed and they'll fight, and when we finally get out of there, me and Diane take off and get totally loaded to forget about it. And sometimes we just sit and talk about it.

Does getting wasted make you feel better about it?

No. It just eases the pain of it. It doesn't help and it doesn't hurt. I don't think it hurts.

194

My father went away for a while, then they went away together and they reconciled, and now they're back together. But things aren't the way they used to be.

They went to Toronto. They very often go away together to get away from the children and spend some time together and give the marriage another chance. So they tried it again. I guess they reached an agreement of some kind. They haven't explained it to us.

They haven't actually come out and said they're getting divorced, but they've implied it in different ways. Just through their attitudes toward each other. They're putting up with each other for now, a temporary thing. I can see it in the way my father acts. You can tell that he's just putting up with her.

What he doesn't like about her is the way she doesn't know how to handle people. He's a lawyer, and he's really hung up on handling people the right way and saying the right things. She doesn't know how to do that. It really upsets him when she puts down my little brothers. He makes faces and sighs and lets us know that he doesn't like it and [that] he doesn't approve of it. It's not so bad now because my dad is all up on his big thing about relating to people in the right way and trying not to get them upset.

They fight over small things. My sister says that when she comes home from work the door is always closed. That's how we know they're having a disagreement: the door is closed. You can hear them fighting.

My dad never really loses his temper anymore. First time I've seen him do it in six or seven years was a couple of months ago at dinner. He threw a plate across the table and said, "Fuck you," and took off.

Why did he get so upset?

Because my mother was bitching at everybody. She picks on everybody all the time.

What was she saying?

I don't remember. My little sister and her hate each other. They do, they really do. You can tell that right away. They don't get along. They can't say anything to each other without fighting. My mother was saying something to her like, "You're not doing anything right." She says that to Melissa a lot. "You don't do anything right."

Melissa is now seeing a psychiatrist 'cause she's all hung up on this stuff. She has a lot of problems.

How is she hung up? You mean on the divorce that's coming?

No. I don't think she really sees it because she is so wrapped up in her own conflict with my mother. They really don't like each other. It's because Melissa picks on the boys. Melissa does that because she hates my mother, but my mother hates Melissa because she does it.

How many children are there?

I have two little brothers, a younger sister, and an older sister. Diane is seventeen, Melissa is fourteen, and my brothers are six and five.

My parents have been having marital problems for as long as I can remember. I remember being really little and being taken away by my mother to live with my grandmother. That was because my dad used to drink a lot; he used to be the violent one. But now he's learned to control his violence. I used to see him beat my mother. I remember one time she had this huge thing on her neck.

A neck brace?

Yeah. But now it's changed around. They used to have real fights then. I guess the nervous breakdowns happened about six years ago. Both were about the same time.

My mother's not a very strong person psychologically. I think she's heading for another one. She said to me, "I can't stand any more. I think that pretty soon I'll be back in Buffalo General." Man, when she says that to you, you feel kind of guilty. You feel it's you doing it.

The reason they have the conflicts is my mother. A lot of times I have the feeling she really doesn't like us, the older girls. It seems like her whole life is my younger brothers. She works better with younger children and has control over them. Now that she's lost control over us, I feel that she doesn't really care about us, that she doesn't like us.

What do you mean by "lost control"?

Being able to tell us what to do.

How did you feel about your dad hitting your mother?

That was so long ago. That was when I was really young. Things like that, I try to forget the emotions and I just remember the facts. I was scared at the time because I thought he was going to come after us. He used to pound on the door and say stuff like, "Do you like all the nice things I buy you? You'd better appreciate everything I do for you." He said that to me and my older sister, pounding on the door. He used to be, now that I think about it, like my mother is.

When we were little, seeing my mother [get] hit, it was scary to think that maybe something was wrong. We were so young we didn't realize what was going on. I remember the alcohol and the violence.

Is your dad an alcoholic?

I don't know. I was too young then to know. He isn't now. He's really off that stuff. He's on vitamins now.

My father left about two weeks ago. When he came back he said, "I'm sorry that I left." He said it on the phone because he was staying at my grandmother's, his mother's. He said, "I'm sorry to have left like that, but I just need some time away." I could understand it because I see what he puts up with around my mother.

In some ways I think it might be better if they did get divorced, but then I think about my little brothers. Maybe it won't be better for them. Maybe they do need my dad.

Do you think it would affect you?

I've been thinking about that. Not really, not unless he moves far away where I won't get to see him. Generally I don't get to see my mother and father at the same time except at the dinner table, where all the conflict occurs.

I love them both, I love them both a lot. There's never been an incident where I don't like my father. I respect him because he is always trying to do what's best for everyone. I always respect him. A lot of times my mother does stupid things. I know it's human and all that, but you'd just like to kill her. A lot of times she doesn't see what she does to other people.

She's always doing really good things, like all this charity work. She's better off when she doesn't try to tell people what to do and how to live their lives. It doesn't really bother me that she tries to do it so much; it's that she does it in the wrong way. She says, "You're doing it all wrong. This is not the way to do it." She could be subtle about it.

If they got a divorce and they lived apart permanently, I think we'd have a choice of who we'd want to live with. That would probably be the hardest thing for me to decide, where to stay and who to stay with.

I'd probably go with my dad. If my mom needs me around, I'd stay with her, because I can see how hurt she is already. You can see the hurt in her, and you can tell that she sits around and cries a lot. I feel really sorry for her. I do. Because her whole life is my father, just about. But if I had a choice and there weren't any pressures, I'd stay with my dad.

Sometimes [when] we can see something starting, like with my mother picking on something, we change the subject real fast and get her to talk about something else so that my dad won't get mad and there won't be any problems.

What's really weird is how my dad feels he can't talk to my mother and he comes to us, to Diane and me. He always talks to us about things you wouldn't think your dad would talk to you about. Like about Mom. It's kind of weird for him to come and say stuff about her like he can't talk to her. He doesn't tell her how his day was; he tells us.

My sister works and he goes to where she works and talks to her all the time instead of staying home with my mom and talking to her at the end of the day. Normal conversation—he doesn't have that with my mother. He only talks to her about the facts of daily life, like the economy side of marriage. Bills and what's got to be paid.

Then there's a side where they always go out to dinner together, and I wonder what they talk about then. I wonder if they just go out and fight because sometimes they come home and they're really loaded and in bad moods.

Do they take that out on you kids?

My mother does. My dad would never do that. He's really tuned in to psychology stuff. My mom does it a lot. If one of the girls gets her mad, she'll directly take it out on the boys, or vice versa.

Or we'll say, "Forget it, I'm not going to stay home." And we'll get out of there. Then one of the boys might start shouting in the other room, something that you should just go and say, "Stop shouting." She'll go in, and she'll use violence. That's something about my mother: she is totally violent.

She's improved a lot since she's been going to the psychiatrist. Both of [my parents] see psychiatrists.

Do they see the same one? Do they go together?

No. They go together to see my little sister's psychiatrist. They don't see the same one for themselves. My dad only goes twice a year because he's a lot better. They both had nervous breakdowns and that's what started them seeing a psychiatrist.

But my mom is totally violent. When I was little, she used to do stuff like hit me with lead pipes. They were child-abuse-type things.

When was this?

I was in third grade. It was for something totally minor. We were having an addition put on our house and I stepped on a floor where I wasn't supposed to be. She took a lead pipe and hit me with it. She always used to threaten us with knives. She would hold one right up to my neck and say, "You do this" or "Don't do that anymore or I'll cut off your head."

That's crazy.

Yeah. But I don't hate her for it the way my little sister does, because I understand. It's not really her so much as it's a sickness she has. It's got to be. She's really a loving person who tries to do right. It's just that she has a lot of hang-ups from when she was a kid. You can't really blame her. It's like alcoholism, the way I look at it.

But things like that, like being hit with that lead pipe, I didn't even think of until my sister brought them up. I just blocked them out. Maybe that's not the most healthy thing to do.

Did you or do you ever feel that it's partly your fault your parents are getting divorced?

Yeah. It's got to be, because when we go away and they're alone together, they're fine. But when we're around, that's when the problem starts. So it's got to be us.

Do you feel guilty about that?

Yeah. You have to. Your parents are breaking up because of you. But then, if you totally engulf yourself with guilt, I don't know what happens.

I just try and find a solution. I don't know if there is a solution to it, so instead of feeling totally guilty and hiding in a corner, I try to do something.

I try to avoid the conflict. When something is coming up and I can see it coming, like a fight or something, I step in and change the subject. You can do that. Last night I did that. I heard them starting to talk about the boys.

Get this: it was about whether or not my mother should cut my little brother's hair or let a barber do it. I just walked up there and said something. If I ever walk up there and say, "Are you having a discussion about something? Can I interrupt?" they'll go, "Sure, come on in." My dad will; my mother will get teed off at it. But my dad always makes a point of having time with us. So I just went up and asked him about going to Florida.

A better way of thinking about it, I would think, is, it's not your fault your parents had you. It's not your fault that you're there. It's their fault. You shouldn't feel guilty.

But if I had been a different person, if I had turned out differently . . .

You shouldn't feel guilty about it, though. A lot of kids do. Even if parents do break up because of kids, the kids shouldn't feel bad about it.

That's true. You shouldn't. But it's hard not to.

Does your older sister feel guilty?

I don't think we ever talked about that. I think she does in a way. I'm sure she does. But she's not around much anymore. She doesn't see a lot of things that I see because she works and she is away. She's hardly ever at home.

When did you first think your parents were going to get divorced?

It's been in my mind as long as I can remember. They've always had fights and there've always been times when they've walked out on each other. They wouldn't stay away, but they would go out and stay gone for a few hours when a fight started. I've always thought about it since I first learned about divorce. I learned about it from people at school who had parents that were divorced.

There's always a chance that they won't get divorced. They believe so much in the Catholic church. It's really stupid. I don't know if my dad would go against [the church]. He was raised in Catholic schools and so was my mother. They're really strong on that stuff.

Do you think it would be better or worse if they got divorced?

I think it would be better for both of them. Then I think, maybe if they're apart, they'd realize how much they need each other. Because I think they really do need each other. My father's totally helpless, even to the point of getting dressed in the morning. My mother lays out his clothes. He'd have to live with my grandmother, and my grandmother is getting senile. I don't know what he'd do. And my mother needs somebody strong. She's not a strong person. They need each other, but it's just that the kids get in the way.

Maybe if we left, maybe that would help.

They haven't said to me that they're getting divorced. I think what they're afraid of is, they couldn't very well tell me and Diane without telling Melissa, my younger sister, and if they told her, they're afraid that they would have a very bad thing [on their hands]. I think they've talked to my sister's psychiatrist and she said, "I wouldn't say it now," because my sister is going through a rough time. She is really psychotic.

It's because of my mother. She hates my mother. Because she was the youngest and then the boys came along and my mother wasn't there when Melissa needed her, or ever since then. So she takes it out in different ways that are totally abnormal.

Do your parents show any love for each other?

My mother does. My father doesn't. She comes running down the stairs when he comes home. She's always done that. She's always made [it] a point—when he walks in the door, she's there. That's always a ritual at our house. When he leaves in the morning, she stands in the window and waves good-bye. I think now she's happy to see him come home because I think she's afraid that one of these days he's not going to.

If your parents were to get a divorce, who do you think would get the house and all that?

My mother. My dad would say, "I'll pay you whatever you want. You can have the house, the car." I know he would. He'd want the best for her. They wouldn't break up hating each other. I would like to think that it's not really going to happen, that they're going to change their minds. But then, if you look at it logically, they probably will [divorce]. They've made their minds up.

I mean, they have filed [for a separation agreement].

My dad told me. I don't know if he's told anybody else, but he told me the night before last, that they decided it would be better for the kids so the kids wouldn't see them fighting all the time, because that's not the atmosphere to grow up in.

I said, "If you guys think that's best." I didn't really say anything for a while. I just sat there. Then I said, "If that's what you think is right . . ."

Do you want them to get divorced?

Yes. It's so complicated. There are so many aspects that you have to look at. I'd like to see them get divorced because then they wouldn't fight so much. And I wouldn't feel so guilty if they just went and got it done instead of fighting all the time. It would ease a lot of the tension. But, then, I don't know how it would be for my little brothers.

Did you and Diane ever talk about them getting divorced before they did?

Yes. We talked about it. We talked about the problems. We could see it and we used to discuss what we should do to stop the problems. We never came up with anything [that would] do any good.

What sort of plans did you have?

Nothing, really. Just to keep Melissa away from my mother, to keep Melissa away from my little brothers.

The really hard thing is to guess my mother's moods 'cause she is always taking tranquilizers and shit. You walk in the house and the first thing we do, me and my older sister, is look at her eyes, and if they're dilated, you know you can get anything out of her. If they're not, you'll have trouble because she'll be totally upset and irrational.

How long has she been taking tranquilizers?

As long as I can remember. She took pills for a while right after she had my youngest brother because she had so much pain. I don't know; they said it was rheumatism. I don't understand it. Then she stopped for a while and everything was okay and the marriage was going great. Then she started again. I can't even remember when it started again and what it started over.

Do your parents ever drink a lot?

Depends on what you mean by a lot.

Do they go out and get crocked often?

Often enough. Maybe once a week. Every night my dad can have two beers before dinner. My mom won't drink until after she has my brothers in bed, and then she just drinks and she gets bombed.

Once a week or so?

No. That's every night.

Your mom gets bombed every night?

Yeah. It's not really bombed. It's the combination of the tranquilizers and the wine she drinks. She just kind of lies there. She'll drink all the time that they're fighting. She'll just sit there and drink and drink and finally she will pass out and that's what ends the fight. How can you get anything accomplished if you're fighting when you're drunk? She's not thinking. Maybe it would be better if she took one tranquilizer and then she would be calm enough to sit down and have a discussion with him. But either she doesn't do it at all or she overdoes it completely. And my dad gets pissed at her for doing it.

Do your parents give you money?

The system we have is we borrow it. You either make it or you can borrow it and pay it back. He keeps a running tally on how much you owe him. My dad just wants us to learn how to make [money] and how to keep track of it and stuff. If it was up to my mom, she wouldn't give us any money.

My dad has us at the point now where we've learned how to keep track of money, and so he's willing to buy us really expensive things, like pay for a plane ticket or something like that. My mother doesn't want him to give us anything because she feels that he's favoring us.

As opposed to?

As opposed to I don't know what, because he shells out money all the time to my little brothers.

In a way I kind of feel like slugging them because I think if they hadn't been born, I don't know what would have happened, but things would have been an awful lot different.

Do you ever wish they hadn't been born?

Yes. But then it would be terrible if they weren't here and I knew what I was missing, because I have really good times when they're around. They're great kids. But when they start doing asshole things, you think, my mother would be totally different. Maybe she would be worse, maybe she would be better. I don't know. I know that Melissa would not be fucked up at all. Her problem is the boys.

I thought her problem was your mother.

The reason that my mother changed is because of the boys.

But, then again, my mother might be twice as violent as she is now. She was really violent when we were little. She doesn't do anything to my brothers like she used to do to us. If she didn't like something, you'd had it.

I don't remember anything about being hit. I just always had this feeling that I was bruised from being hit by her. I block it out because I don't want to remember it. Because I might end up hating her. I don't want to hate her.

Did they hit Diane?

Dad doesn't hit.

Ever?

No. He has never touched me. He's hit my little brothers, but that's because I think he thinks that boys need their father to show discipline more than girls do. I think he thinks that. Because the girl is the father's favorite. That's the way I've always heard it.

But, yeah, Diane got hit. Everyone did. All three of us got hit— [with] the brush over the head so hard it broke. She used to have this big metal ruler in her drawer. We used to have to take naps. If she heard any noise in our room while we were supposed to be taking a nap, she'd come in with that and hit us with it.

Really hard?

Yes.

Did you cry?

Yes. Cry—you better believe it!

Or we'd be downstairs goofing around and making too much noise and she'd get a book and *wham!* She was totally violent.

What I don't understand is why my dad never did anything about it. He never did anything when she hit me with that lead pipe and I had the welt on my back. Maybe it was at the time that he was drinking a lot so he just forgot about it and let it go.

I was talking to him about it last Sunday and he said, "Yeah, that must really have affected the way you are now." Because now I'm totally intimidated by anybody. An authority or not an authority. My dad said that he remembered the time that she took my face and rubbed it in the ground. You don't do that to your kid. That's why I am the way I am. Anybody can intimidate me by saying anything. Just anything. I used to not be able to walk down the street and face somebody. I would cross the street. I've come a long way.

That's because of your mother?

Yeah. Because she'd just intimidate us so much. You do anything. Anything. You'd get out of line in any way and she'd hit you. I would flinch when I'd get near her.

Do you hold that against her?

No. Because like I said before, I think it's just a sickness or something. It's not her.

Do you think you'll ever get married?

No, I don't want to get married. I never want to make that commitment. I don't want to have any kids. I'm afraid that I'll end up too much like my mother. I can see the tendencies now. I baby-sit a lot, and so many times I would just like to hit the kid.

You're only sixteen years old. Kids aren't a part of your life. So when you have to put up with them, they're a pain in the ass.

My baby-sitting job is just about every day. So it's like I am their mother because their mother works all the time. And I can just see so many of my mother's characteristics coming out in me. I don't want to fuck up my kids the way she's done.

"Something happened along the way."

CHARLIE (16)

About a year ago my father asked my brother and me whether [my parents] should separate or divorce. We both thought that maybe a temporary separation would be all right because they were brawling. I never thought a divorce should happen, but I thought maybe a temporary separation would help.

Why did he ask you?

He just sat down, gave us a beer, and asked us.

What are your parents like?

My father was kind of conservative, but my mother was a high-flying liberal. My father was an attorney and my mother was just a housewife. Now she's working for an old folks' home. She's director of the place.

Can you tell me what happened to him?

He had manic depression.

What's that?

It's like you'll be at a party and you'll be feeling great, and then the next day you'll want to kill yourself. And that's what he did.

His closest friend, a lawyer in his firm, had said, "Fred, you'd better see a psychiatrist." He saw a psychiatrist two times and then he said it was all a crock. He thought he didn't have it. He wanted to think that he didn't have it, that he wasn't sick. He was.

When he killed himself, did he leave a note?

Yeah, a six-page note. I haven't read it yet. It's almost a year now.

How come you haven't read it?

I think I'm afraid to.

How did the rest of your family take it when your father jumped?

Both my sisters resented him for it. He lost communication with them when he left the house, so they didn't talk to him for about half a year. They resented him first of all for the divorce and they said they never wanted to see him again. But after he jumped, they were upset, but in a way—how can I put this?—they were kind of relieved. They didn't want him to die, but it brought a mess of relief for them. They can finally breathe now.

My older brother was suffering from a nervous breakdown. Not because of my father. It was because of a lot of drugs he had taken.

How old are your brothers and sisters?

Jane is twelve or thirteen, Ricki is nineteen, and Bob is going to be twenty-one.

How did your mother feel about the separation?

She didn't want it. My father was the one who wanted it. She'd say, "He's acting like an ass" and shit like that.

He had a lady friend that he was going to marry, just for someone that he could hang onto, someone that would understand what he's doing. She comforted him and said, "Oh, Fred, you're doing just the right thing." Which is understandable.

Of the whole family, I was the only one that really had communication with both of them. Bob had a little, but he wasn't in much shape.

Were there scenes between your parents? Did they fight a lot?

Not really. They'd argue a lot, but it shouldn't have ended up the way it did. It shouldn't have ended up in divorce. Just a temporary separation.

My father was on this power trip where he thought everything was at his disposal. He figured he could "later" us and take off. And he thought my mother was holding him back from what he wanted to do.

What did he want to do?

He wanted to go on trips all across the U.S. and talk about law. He wanted to quit the law firm. He was writing pamphlets and books and he was speaking at graduations across the country and my mom didn't like that. She wanted him to slow down. He was living at such a pace that all the pressures broke down and he got manic depression. At least that's the way I saw it. The doctor diagnosed it that way.

Were there hassles about child support or money?

Yeah, oh, yeah. My father wanted us out of the house because he couldn't afford it. He couldn't afford to pay the mortgage. So he took away our car, which was leased in his name. And he took away all Mom's credit; all the credit was in his name. And he threatened to shut off the heat and not pay the mortgage so we'd be out in the street.

That's when my sisters really got pissed off and started to rebel against him and not to talk to him. He went about it in a really lousy way.

Did it ever get to court?

My mom had a really good lawyer. My father said, "Danvers is a great lawyer. Have him for the divorce." And by the first week he was saying, "Oh, your mother's lawyer. Damn it." By about the third month he was saying, "Goddamn Jack Danvers." And right before he committed suicide he was saying, "Fucking Jack Danvers." Because [Danvers] was really screwing him to the wall. I think they had one court appearance. I don't remember what happened at it.

How did the divorce affect you?

It made me grow up faster.

How?

I don't know. Just all the bullshit. All the responsibility that I had to take with Bob. And then explaining to Jane and Ricki about Dad. And listening to my mother because I was the only one that my mother ever talked to about my father. Because I was the one that really felt sorry for him and knew there was something wrong. My mom tried to prove me wrong, saying, "Your father is really acting like an ass" and crap like that. I had to listen to that, plus listen to Jane and Ricki, and then help out with Bob.

What did you tell Jane and Ricki?

That he was going through some rough times. Crap like that.

They didn't understand what was wrong with him?

Right. They didn't understand at the time of his death or before it.
I lost communication with my dad in the last month of his life because he caught me in bed with a girl. I was living in an apartment with him while he was living with his girl friend. I brought home a date and he caught me. That's when he got really mad. He never talked to me after that.

Never? Not once?

No. He'd call up and try to talk to Jane and Ricki, but they wouldn't talk to him, and I'd answer the phone and he wouldn't want to talk to me. I think he was afraid to talk about what happened.

Why do you think he was so upset about that?

I don't know. That's what I couldn't understand. He was turning around and doing the same thing.

211

What is it you were taking care of with Bob? What was that about?

I was helping him out with his sickness. I was trying to discourage him from going back to school where his friends were feeding him all these drugs. He was doing a lot of heroin and shit like that. And I was the mediator from Mom to Bob, because Bob wouldn't talk to my mother. My mom would say, "Try and talk to Bob about this," and she'd talk to me, and then I'd turn around and talk to Bob.

He was having a lot of pressures there. He went to a tougher school than he could handle; it was the wrong college for him. And he was having a lot of problems. So he got into the drugs too heavily, a little more than he could handle. And that's when he went kaput.

Did he do it for an escape?

Probably, but not from the divorce. I don't think so. It was more from the pressure of the school.

What other kind of responsibilities did you have around the house after your dad left?

Just a lot more listening to my mother and being a mediator between the two of them.

When he took away the car, my father wouldn't listen to my mother. So I went to his house and said, "Listen, you can't do that. You've got to give us back the car."

He goes, "No way. Your mother is being a real asshole about this whole thing."

Another time he threatened to [not pay] the gas bill or the mortgage. I'd have to sit there and tell him not to do it.

Did he listen to you?

He did with the gas and the mortgage, but not with the car. But my mother's lawyer got us a leased car.

How did you feel about being a mediator?

I didn't mind it just as long as I knew I was doing the right thing.

212

Did you feel as though your parents used you to do it?

No. I put myself into that position because I was tired of listening to my mother say, "Oh, your father's gone nuts."

What did he say about her?

He would say, "Why won't she move out of the house?" He'd get forceful. He'd say, "Your mother is just a cold-hearted bitch," which is wrong. He wanted it done like that, really fast. He just went about it too quickly.

When your father left, did you feel abandoned?

No, but my mother did. We still had my mother, but my mother had nothing except for us kids. She had no financial support. She's doing all right now.

Divorce is good when the marriage is harming the children, but it wasn't harming us. My dad just got tired of it, of my mother. My mother and father weren't harming us at all.

When they first separated, how were your relationships with them?

Pretty good, although I used my mother a lot. I would say, "Well, I can move in with Dad any day."

When would you do that?

If I wanted to go out really late, or if I'd be out all night and she got mad 'cause I didn't call her or anything.

What would you do when one parent said you couldn't do something? Did you ever go to the other one?

No, I never did that. I just threatened I'd move in with the other one.

But you never carried through?

I did it once. That was the time he caught me in bed with the girl. I was just over there for a week when that happened. I hadn't seen him in a long time then.

I feel I've lived more of a problem life than many other kids. I look at some people I've been growing up with, like Irwin Dole—he used to be my best friend, but he seems really immature to me now. I look at him and then I look at me, and I think something happened along the way. I don't know what it was.

"I'm happiest when I'm out of the house."

MARY (17)

I was fourteen or fifteen when I found out my parents were getting divorced. My mother was messing around behind my dad's back, and my dad found out and served my mother papers.

I was at my stepfather's apartment. He wasn't my stepfather yet. We were there and my mother came in all hysterical and she was crying. And she showed everybody the papers. That's when I found out.

I thought it was great.

Did you dislike your father?

I did then, but now he's okay. I like him a lot better. I live with my mother now and we fight a lot. My dad and I get along great.

I used to live with my dad last year. In November my mom kicked me out of the house for a dumb reason. My stepsister stole some money and she blamed it on me. So I went to live with my dad.

Now I get along good with my father and I get along bad with my mother. Before, I got along bad with my father and good with my mother.

It's all her fault.

Because she was fooling around?

Yeah. He might have been fooling around before, but nobody knew about it. She started telling us all this horrible stuff about him, about bad things he had done in previous years. It didn't matter, because he wasn't doing it then.

So she was trying to make your dad look like the bad guy?

Yes. She still does. My dad never does it to my mother and my mother does it all the time to my father. She'll just say anything about him, what a horrible person he is, that he's crazy and he's been fucked up for as long as he's been alive. I don't think it's fair.

When I was living with my dad, she invited me over for Thanksgiving dinner but not my dad. She said she didn't want him in the house. It was my birthday. All these steprelatives were over, and they made me feel really guilty that I wanted my dad there.

My dad wrote me this letter recently about how I should be happy and that I'm beautiful when I'm happy and things like that. That I should be happy no matter what anybody says to me. I believe it and I think it is very important. But my mom doesn't believe that. She read the letter and she said it was an attack on her. She said that my father was crazy. I think my mom is a little bit wacko.

Every time I get pissed off at my mother, I call my father and they sit there and yell on the phone. I'll call my dad and talk to him. He doesn't pick a side, he just tells me what's best for me and that I should calm down and that I shouldn't get emotional. He says I should walk away from a fight when I get mad at her instead of causing both of us to lose.

My dad makes it hard for me by telling me to hang in there and live with my mother till I graduate. He knows it's hard. I don't like to live with her and I don't want to stay with her.

216

Why don't you move to your father's?

You have to be eighteen to live in the apartments he lives in now.

Did you ever feel you were responsible for the divorce at all?

Sort of. I introduced my mother to my stepfather. I met him when I was in fourth grade [through] the girl I hung around with. [He and my mother] got married a week after the divorce.

I used to like him, but now I don't like him. I hate him. He's a real bitch.

Does he give you a hard time?

All the time. About everything. You can't do anything right.

He was nice before they were married. It was great before they were married. We used to go to the beach all the time. We had picnics and we went horseback riding. We used to do a whole bunch of stuff. Now that they're married, they don't do anything but sit around the house and bitch about the mess.

Did you know your mother was having the affair before your father did?

Yes. We used to hang around.

Spying?

No. They'd bring us places. It was right out in front of us. I thought it was really good then, but I'm sort of sorry now.

My stepfather causes a lot of hassles with me and so does my mother. And it affects my sisters and it affects me. And it is not good. They make me feel bad and they tell me that I don't do things right. I don't know. I'm happiest when I'm out of the house.

Maybe it was good for them. It might have been good for my mother. I don't know if she's happy. I don't think she is, [judging] by the way she treats us. But maybe she's with someone she loves now. I'm not sure; I can't make that kind of judgment.

I think divorce stinks. [My parents] shouldn't have gotten married if they didn't love each other.

They probably loved each other when they got married, but they didn't know each other too well or something.

No. It's just that it wasn't their divorce. It was *our* divorce. She just rips us apart. I think a family should be a loving unit.

"I've learned to swallow my pride."

ANN (16)

They had a big argument one night and my father left. He went and stayed with my aunt. That was around Easter. I went to camp that summer and that was when they got their final divorce. Alimony and all that stuff was cleared up that summer at court. My mother [had] told me [that the divorce was coming] when they separated. She said, "Your father and I are separated and we're getting a divorce."

It didn't hit me. I was twelve then. It hit me when my father was gone. I cried that night when I was sleeping. On Sundays I'd go and see my father. He lived way down in the city and that's when it really hit me. Not when she first said it, but when I visited him.

They were always fighting. My father had a bad temper. My mother is a bitch. We had financial problems because we moved into this big, huge house and my father didn't have the money. He did it because he wanted to make my mother happy. They fought a lot.

[In] one argument my father was just furious and my mother was crying. He left instead of getting really mad. He just left. They had been running around the dining-room table.

I was close to my mother and I was close to my father. My father always liked me. I'm closer to both my parents than my brother or my sister [is]. I've inherited equal things from both of them. And my mother doesn't really get along with my brother and my father doesn't get along with my sister.

After my parents separated, my father would tell me things about my mother and my mother would tell me things about my father. Things like when my brother was born, my father wasn't around. He was off. He said he was going to be somewhere and he wasn't there. He was at a bar. And my father would tell me about how my mother's father was an alcoholic, and when he called to congratulate my mother and father the night of their wedding, she wouldn't talk to him. He says she was a real spoiled brat and she always had to get everything she wanted. He'd say that she'd say he didn't have any friends 'cause he was a real obnoxious person.

My father and my brother moved out of the house and my mother got remarried to my father's best friend. It'll be three years next month.

The way they met was, my father's mother used to live on Lamark and my father was never around, so she filed for someone who was on scholarship at the university to come and help her work at the house in exchange for room and board. My stepfather was on a football scholarship and he came and lived with her. There's maybe seven years' age difference between him and my father, but they got along and they were close. My father got him a job at the same plant. This was when my father was going to school, too. My father and his friends had a cottage and my stepfather was invited up there. My stepfather got married and my father got married. My mother said they always got along. Jake used to idolize my father.

My father had a good job and my family had a lot of money. The only thing was, my father was an obnoxious person. That's the way he is.

Then Jake divorced his wife. When my mother was divorced, he'd have business to do in Buffalo and he'd come and see my mother. He came more and more often. He'd stay at our house, and then you-know-what started happening. Then, when it was our birthdays and stuff, my mother would tell us he was coming for dinner. I wouldn't want him there, but he'd have to come anyway just because she wanted him there. Then she said that they were getting married.

How long was this after your parents got divorced?

Not even a year. They got divorced in the summer and my mother and Jake got married in May.

Did you like him?

No.

Do you like him now?

Yes.
But I held grudges against him. My mother would make him come to my birthday, and I didn't want him to be there. I didn't like him. I felt like he was intruding. My parents had just gotten divorced and I didn't want some guy coming in there. But my mother couldn't handle that.

I'd call her up and say, "Mom, can you come pick me up? I'm at a party. Will you give me a ride home? I've got a couple of friends." And I'd say, "Mom, don't bring Jake with you because I don't want to have to introduce him." I used to hate to introduce him. I still hate to introduce him. That's why I'm never downstairs when anyone comes because then my mother can do it.

Was he nicer to you when he first started seeing your mother? Did he put on an act?

He'd say things like, "Oh, let's go throw the football around." That was so I would say, "Gee, Mom, wow, that Jake is really a great guy. Great if you two got married." That's why he'd do it.

Okay, so back to when I'd say, "Mom, will you come pick me up?" Who would come pick me up but Jake and my mother, and I'd have friends with me and I'd get in the car and my mother would go, "Oh, this is a friend of mine."

I'd say, "Mom, you know I hate this." So it started even before they were ever married.

I remember my thirteenth birthday. "Ann, Jake is coming up for your birthday."

"Mom, I don't want him here. It's *my* birthday."

"Ann, that's too goddamned bad. He's coming."

And there he'd be. Happy birthday, Ann.

Once they got married, he started telling me what to do. He'd tell me when to be home and everything. He still does, but he's a nice guy. He means well.

Has your father remarried?

No. He has a girl friend. She's fun. She moved to Cleveland because of her job. I don't know if he'll get married.

He was married once before. I have a twenty-year-old half sister in Buffalo. I don't know her. I don't even know her name. My father left his first wife when the baby was about three months old and he didn't give her any money or support. That poor lady. He's a very hard person to get along with.

We lived in this big, huge house. It was great having this big, huge house and you could have all your friends over. Then the money was tighter and we moved.

I had to be more responsible. I had to help my mother in a lot of ways 'cause my brother didn't help her at all. Once she got married, I lost a lot of respect for her because I didn't respect my stepfather. I still don't. He's a nice guy, he'd do anything for me, and he has a lot of respect for me. There's just something there. It's still there. When I'm mad, I still look at him, and I could never love him. I don't think I could ever love him. It's just a grudge, a personal grudge.

When we were moving, it was hard. It was really hard. And when my mother got married, that was hard, too. I'd have to listen to what my stepfather said and I couldn't stand it. I hated him. I hated him so much. And my mother would say, "Jake will make the decision."

My father used to live down by the river, and I didn't see him very often. Maybe on Sundays. But now he lives near us and I see him a lot more often. He calls me all the time—a couple of times a week.

Do you get along with him well?

Yes, I do. I can talk to him. He's very intelligent. He's so smart.

He's just got a big mouth and people don't like him 'cause he's always making obnoxious statements because he knows everything. He knows what he's talking about. He won't get mad at me, 'cause I'll just say, "Dad, don't yell. I'm right here. You don't have to yell at me." And he won't. He'll get in massive fights with my brother, but he won't with me.

I stayed with my mother because I couldn't stay with my father and I can't now until I'm sixteen. I wouldn't want to, anyway.

My father lived in Buffalo and I couldn't live with him and keep going to school at Amherst. He had an extra room, I could have it if worse came to worse. But things are going a lot better than they were as far as my relationship with my mother and my father.

My mother really fucked my brother up. And she realizes it now and she helps him, like [when he broke] his arm. My father works and she took [my brother] to the hospital because he can't drive.

How did she fuck him up?

Well, he got in this fight with my stepfather, and my stepfather beat the shit out of him, practically. Well, he didn't really. But my stepfather is a big guy. He's not a big, tall, goony guy, but he's short and stout and he's muscular. He played football. And my brother's not a big kid, and he's not muscular either. So that started it. Then my mother wanted my brother to go to Washington with her and he didn't want to go. He couldn't go 'cause he was taking driver ed at school and he couldn't miss the days. So they got in this big fight and he left. She told him never to come back. I was standing right there. She called her attorney and made plans right there for him to go live with his father.

And my father is hard to live with. I don't think I could live with him. I really don't. So I wouldn't [take] it upon myself. I've learned to swallow my pride. There're a lot of times when I've gotten in arguments with my mother and stepfather, and I just won't say anything 'cause I know that it will all get thrown back in my face. It was only a year ago that they didn't think that a child should have an opinion, that a fourteen-year-old should have an opinion. What I said just got me in trouble. So I just kept my mouth shut, which is what my brother didn't do. I learned to do that. Which is good. My father told me that.

There were a lot of times when my mother said, "Go live with your father. Go ahead. Go live with your father down in the city." And then I'd shut up because I didn't want to go live down there.

My mother always gets jealous because my father buys me really nice things. She gets mad. She says, "You're so goddamned materialistic. Your father is trying to buy love." She goes on and on.

Did you ever feel abandoned? Like when your father left?

My mother has a lot of friends and they helped us. I never felt deprived or anything. Did you?

Yeah. I thought my father had abandoned me.

My mother used to say he abandoned us, left us. He did. We didn't have a car. We had one, but it was broken, and there were all these mortgage payments due on the house. We had no food, and he didn't care. He wasn't sending us any money, and my mother's job was only paying her two-sixty an hour.

Would you be with your dad if he had a big house?

Yes, I think I would. He's a hard person to live with because he's got fixed ways of doing things, and I'm his daughter so I'm supposed to do what he wants me to do. He's cool, though. If I wanted to go out, I could go out. If I wanted to borrow the car, I could borrow the car. But as far as, "Ann, clean the house; do it," I'd have to do it. And he has a really bad temper and so do I. But we never argue because most of the time, if I have something to say, I think about it and I'm right, so he can't argue. So then we don't get in an argument. I think if he did have a big house I would live with him.

There was an incident on my brother's birthday. I had been at my father's. I came home and [my mother] was all pissed off. Really angry. She was in her room and she said, "Ann, come into my room. I'd like to talk to you." I walked in there and she was crying and she said, "I hope you know that you ruined my second marriage, Ann."

I said, "What?"

She said, "Jake left the house tonight and it was all because of you."

I said, "Mom, I wasn't even here."

She said, "You treat Jake like a piece of furniture. You know he lives in this house, too, and you don't even talk to him."

I said, "I talk to him, Mom. Come on, be serious. If you had an argument with him, it was between you and him. I wasn't even here for any of it."

I left and she said, "Get in here. I want to talk to you. I'm not finished. Sit down. Do you know that you ruined my second marriage? Do you know that you did that?" Then I don't remember what she did, but she got mad all over again and she told me, "Do you want to go to live with your father, Ann?"

If I had said yes, I would have been out right there and then. She would have called my father. He would have had to come pick me up. I can't stay with him.

Why?

Because he lives in that two-bedroom apartment. There's not enough room for both of us there. And I have learned from past experience to say, "No, it's great here." I kind of mumbled the answer and I said, "Come on, Mom, get off my back. I'm going to go in my room. I'm going to close the door. I'm going to lock it. Don't ask to come in, okay?"

"All right, Ann. Go upstairs. Close the door. Lock it."

So then she keeps on bitching and keeps on bitching and then I said, "Mom, I'm going to leave. I'm going out, okay?"

"Ann, you're not going to go anywhere until you tell me where you're going."

"Mom, I'm leaving. Come on. I just want to go, all right?"

"No, you can't go."

So again I said to myself, blow this off. I went upstairs.

The next morning she was real bitchy to me. Then in the afternoon the truth comes out. My stepfather's old wife is moving back to Erie, and that's going to cause some problems. My stepfather's son [will] not be able to come to Buffalo because he saw my brother getting high and he told his mother. She thinks it's a bad environment. So [my mother and my stepfather] got in this big argument, and she blamed it all on me. I couldn't stand it. It sucked. It was such a pain.

And that was it. Then she was real nice to me. It was a phase. She gets in these phases, Mike, and she just goes schizo.

Has she had any more schizo phases?

Not lately. But it'll come again. It'll happen again. Before your book's over with, it'll happen again. Probably about three times.

In my freshman year I was always stoned. I got in a lot of trouble, too. My father smokes grass. I can go over to his apartment and sit and do bongs and he won't care. I can do it right in front of him.

My mother would have a fit. At my party I had two half kegs and that was okay. I wasn't even sixteen. But I couldn't walk upstairs with a joint. My mom would fall over. I went through such hassles with her. One day she was raging about how nervous she was and I said, "I know something you can do to get unnervous." She goes, "What? Smoke marijuana?" And I said, "Yeah, Mom. Why don't you just try it?" Oh, she got so mad. I told her I smoked it and she was so disappointed in me. It was terrible. That was a year ago last spring.

Do you think it's better that your parents separated?

I still to this day don't know. Neither of them is very well off as it stands. Both of my parents are sick, they're troubled people. And maybe they're better off not being together.

For my sake, I was old enough that it didn't affect me. For my little sister's sake, no way. She doesn't need that. It affected her a lot. Her grades went down and she had other problems. For my sake, oh, it was fine.

Did you ever blame yourself for your parents' troubles?

No way. I was a good girl.

Which parent was it that really wanted the divorce?

They both wanted it, but what happened was, my father filed for

226

the separation, which was a big mistake because then my mother got the house and all the belongings, all the furniture. They both wanted the divorce; they both felt they needed it.

When they were going through the divorce, I wasn't at home. I was at camp for two weeks. My mother wrote and told me what was going on and my father sent me candy and stuff. It was great.

How did you feel about what was going on while you were at camp?

I was oblivious to it. I didn't really know. It didn't faze me.

Did your parents ever use you against each other?

Yes. We always have hassles on Christmas and Easter over who's going to have the kids for dinner. My mother would tell me all the bad things about my father, trying to get me against him. She'd tell me how he galavanted around with his buddies when she was in labor with my little sister, how he wasn't around when she was born. She told me how he'd never pay the bills, how she'd go with her credit card to buy something and they would call the credit office and they'd say she had five hundred dollars worth of bills to pay. It would be very embarrassing. And she'd say how he'd always put people down, her friends, so that they wouldn't even want to come to the house anymore.

My father's more rational. He faces the facts. He wouldn't sit there and tell me all bad things about my mother. He'd tell me good things, too.

When your parents told you those things, how did you feel? Did it make you dislike either one?

No. I felt glad they were telling me. I like to see the good and the bad points about them; they are my parents. What's them is a part of me, and that could be why I'm the way I am.

Tell me what happened last weekend.

The incident with the window? Okay. There was an assembly at school on energy. I didn't go. I rode my bike home to get some papers for English, and the house was locked up and I couldn't get in. I lifted

227

up the garage door and it was locked. I went to the back door and that wouldn't open either. So I went to bang on the window. I had these big gloves on. [I didn't bang] hard, and the window broke. It was pouring rain and I was really pissed off to begin with that no one was home and not even a door was open. You should be able to get into your own house.

You don't have a key?

I had a key, but it wasn't with me. It was inside.

So I left. I broke the window and I left. I went to my brother's and I sat around for a while.

Your brother's?

My father's place. I finally said, "Joe, you know what I did?" And I told him.

He said, "Don't tell her and she won't find out. She won't suspect that you did it and it will all blow over."

I figured, yeah. If I tell her, she'll be really pissed off and she'll make me pay for it. And I'll have to sit down with her and Jake and have a discussion about why I broke the window.

Then I made another wrong move. I didn't go in and clean it up. I got home that night and all the glass was out. I walk in the door and my mother says, "Ann, we had an attempted robbery."

I go, "Oh, *really?* Tell me more about it."

She said, "I was only gone from ten to twelve-thirty and someone broke the window, attempting to get in the house. Poolie [the dog] scared him away."

Hah! Poolie scared him away.

I didn't say anything. I figured, they're not going to make a big deal out of it. My stepfather was putting a board over the windows. Then she got in one of her little phases.

Since she's been married, she drinks so much more. She never used to drink at all. My father's a conservative, he'll drink a glass of wine. But every night since they've been married, she has a couple of Manhattans. She never gets incoherent. She never falls over, but she gets—you know, what's the word?

228

Silly?

Not laughy. She gets buzzed.

She says, when I was asking her to help me with some word, "You know, Ann, how would you feel if all these possessions that you've had ever since you've grown up were stolen?"

They had this gallon of wine. My mother was drunk. When she gets like that, I don't say anything because she'll just ramble on and ramble on. So she called her mother in Florida. She always calls her mother in Florida and cries to her mother. Her mother is about sixty-five years old and she doesn't need it. She doesn't need to hear my mother bawl about all her little problems.

Then she was bitchy to me all night and the next morning. So I went to my brother's the next day. It was a Friday, the day before my birthday. He said, "Ann, Mom called me this morning and asked me if I knew if you broke the window."

I said, "What?"

And he said, "Mom called me and asked if you broke the window."

I said, "What did you say?"

He said, "I didn't know anything about it."

I said, "Oh, Jesus, what should I do?"

He said, "Tell her you did it. Call her and tell her. Get yourself out of it now, Ann, 'cause she's going to question you when you get home tonight and you're not going to be able to keep a straight face. You want me to? I'm going to go over there anyway. You want me to tell her something?" And we planned out this whole speech and he'd say, "Well, she really didn't mean it."

So I called her after school and my brother hadn't gone over there. I said, "Mom, I was at gymnastics."

She goes, "Anny, did you come home yesterday?"

I said, "Yeah."

And she said, "Did you break the window?"

And I said, "Yeah."

And she goes, "Why didn't you tell me? Why didn't you tell us both last night when we were both worrying about it?"

"'Cause I thought you'd be mad."

"Not half as mad as I am now. I'll see you when you get home."

"Okay, Mom. 'Bye."

So I walk in the door and she's sitting in the kitchen. My stepfather is downstairs in the basement and the TV is on and the door to the basement is closed. I walk in the living room.

"Ann, sit down. I want to talk to you." It's my mother. So I sit down. "Ann, why didn't you tell us that you broke the window? Why did you have us worry?"

I said, "Mom, I don't get in trouble a lot. I haven't gotten in trouble in so long. I never get in trouble in school. I always do as you tell me to do. Why are you making such a big thing out of such a little thing?"

Right then my stepfather begins yelling, "What? Making a big thing out of a little thing? No way!" He's yelling and screaming. Who the hell is he to yell at me?

I didn't even want to look at him, so I looked at his reflection on the table and I was really getting sick.

He says, "We're not making a big thing out of a little thing. You saw me and your mother, and how we were worried last night. You knew it all the time. You couldn't even face up to it."

I said, "Well, I thought she'd be mad."

And he goes, "Well, that's too bad. You have to face up to it." And he's going on and on. And he said, "Why couldn't you call your mother then? You can call her for rides and to come pick you up at school or bring things up to school, but you can't call her and tell her you broke the window, could you?"

I'm just sitting there and I was clenching my fists. I was really pissed off. I just said, "I don't know."

He goes, "You apologize to your mother right now."

So I said, "I'm sorry, Mom, for breaking the window."

"No, you're not sorry for breaking the window. You're sorry for lying."

"Okay. Mom, I'm sorry for lying."

"That's it. I don't want to hear another word. This is the end of the discussion." So he goes downstairs.

"Ann"—this is my mother talking to me now—"Ann, come and eat some dinner."

"Mom, I don't want to eat dinner. I had a big fish lunch." I had it at Brunner's Bar, but I didn't say that.

"Ann, you're going to eat your dinner."

I went upstairs and I was ready; if he was standing in front of me, I would have belted him one. I was so pissed. I had all this anxiety built up in me and I was really tense and I was really pissed off. I went downstairs. I was kind of crying, too. I don't like to cry because I don't like to let them make me cry.

So I went downstairs, and he was in the basement; the door was closed. I said in a nice, calm voice, "Mom, it wouldn't be half as bad if it would be you who'd do the lecturing."

Wham! opens the door and in comes my stepfather. "What did she say to you, Margaret? What did she say to you? I told her not to say another word."

"She didn't say anything, Jake."

"What did she say to you, Margaret?"

"She said that she thinks that I should do the lecturing, not you."

"What? She thinks you should do the lecturing? Sit down, Ann. I pay the bills in this house. You live in this house. You listen to what I have to say. I can lecture you."

I go, "You're my stepfather and she's my mother. You're no direct relation to me. Why should I have to listen to you?" I didn't yell. Nice calm voice, and he's getting all blue in the face and everything.

"What? That's too bad! You live under this roof, I pay the bills."

I said, "What if I pay room and board?"

He said, "You pay your room and board, you still have to listen to the rules and regulations. If you go to college, you listen to the rules and regulations. You live in a hotel, you listen to the rules and regulations."

I'm just playing with my soup. By then I was *really* pissed off. And he goes, "You want to pay room and board?"

"No."

"Let that be the end of it, Ann. I don't want to hear another word out of you."

So that was it. I threw my soup down the drain after my mother went downstairs. I went upstairs. I got my grandmother's key. I said, "Mom, I'm going to Gram's."

"Ann, what time are you going to be home?"

"I don't know, Mom."

"Ann, tell me what time you're going to be home."

"Okay, Mom. What time is it?"

"It's quarter after seven."

"Okay. I'll be home at nine-thirty."

I had the SAT on Saturday morning. All day I didn't even want to open my presents from them. I didn't even want them. I said to my friend, "I don't even want the card. You know what it's going to say? It's going to say, 'Love, Mom and Jake' in my mother's writing. I don't want any of the things from either of them." I was so pissed; I was so pissed off.

I swear, when I get like that if I could I would take off. I don't have the nerve, but I would. I get so mad. I wonder if sometimes when it's all built up if I'll explode or something. I'll just have a huge fit.

I used to be like that. I used to have a lot of anger in me. I think it was because of what was going on with my parents. I used to blow off and I'd slam doors and knock things over and scream and beat the shit out of Jessie. I used to say, "Fuck you" to anybody, especially my mother. And I used to get kicked out of the house all the time.

I can't do that. If I yell, it's ten times as bad. It does no good to yell, first of all. You can talk. You can handle it. You can talk in a normal voice. Yelling is no good. So I talk, they yell. They yell, I listen. I sit there. I suffer the consequences. It's always me who suffers the consequences, Mike, always. They never get shit. They never feel like I do. They never cry or anything. It's always me.

You know what I said to her? I said, "Mom, when I'm eighteen, you have a big surprise coming." I was so pissed that night I said to myself, Ann, when you're eighteen, damn, tell them to fuck off. I was so pissed.

I went to my grandmother's again and I was just terrible. It was terrible.

I didn't see my stepfather until that night. I was just wandering in and out of the house and I wouldn't open any of my presents. Finally, when I walked in the house from gymnastics, it was, "Ann, come on, open your presents." So we all sat down. Big, happy family, right? And we opened Ann's presents.

She wonders why I treat him like a piece of shit. Mike, I hate him. I hate him.

When I said that about eighteen, she said, "Nothing will surprise me, Ann." She's going to have an attack. She will. 'Cause then I can say it. I can tell them whatever I want. If I was to say, "Fuck you" now, my stepfather would—

Hit you?

He hit me once. He did something and I said, "I'll take you to family court." I trucked up the stairs and he was running after me. He was over me, he was yelling at me. Oh, it was so gross. My father contacted his lawyer and said if Jake ever touched one of his kids again there'd be a summons to family court.

That was years ago. It was something about my brother. I was sticking up for him or I was sticking up for my father. My mother gets so pissed when I stick up for my father. When that starts, she'll be mad for the rest of the night. She'll give me dirty looks. She's a forty-two-year-old woman and she'll sit at the dinner table and glare at me like, "You're such a little beast." I'm not that bad.

You said you treat your stepfather like a piece of shit. What do you mean?

I'll say, "Hi. How are you? 'Bye. I'm leaving."
"Where are you going, Ann?"
"I'm going to such-and-such."
"Okay, see you later."
Walk in the house. "Hi. What are you doing? Oh, okay." Go upstairs. "'Bye, I'm leaving."

That's it. It's not like you ever sit down and have an intellectual conversation with your stepfather.

You said that since your mother has been married to Jake she's been drinking a lot more.

I said to her once, "Mom, why don't you try to stay off the Manhattans?" She talks about how she wants to lose weight.

Manhattans are four hundred calories. I said, "Why don't you just try and not have one?"

It's the same old thing every night. They get out the glasses and the ice. Liquor. I don't know if she's an alcoholic.

I feel bad when I say that. I feel sorry for my mother. She's not happy. I know she's not happy.

The thing that really killed me was that time when he asked her, "What did she say?" and she said, "Ann said she thinks I should do the lecturing." It showed whose side she was on.

I don't see why they force the relationship, and then she wonders why I don't kiss him. I was opening my presents and I got a purse. I was going to give a kiss to my mother and say, "Thanks," and then I sat back down and didn't do anything because then I'd feel weird. I might have to kiss him. I could never. Ugh.

I don't like to hate people, but I think I hate him.

Nowadays people are living together, which is against church rules and stuff, but it's better than getting a divorce, I think. Don't you?

Yeah. Definitely.

I wouldn't marry someone if I didn't want to spend the rest of my life with him. If I knew him well and I loved him and I knew that he loved me, I wouldn't get married. I wouldn't even think about it. I don't think about getting married. I'm not saying, "I'll get out of high school and I'll get married." It's not like that. I'm going to get out of high school and I'm going to college and if I find someone, I find someone. But it's not in my plans.

234

"Then he attacked my dog."

PETER (15)

I was one when they were divorced. I don't remember anything about it. They've been divorced for fourteen years and I haven't seen or talked to him for a year or two. Maybe [I spoke with him] once when I got in trouble. He comes over about twice a year. I don't care to see him.

I was always scared of having a father. I got away with a lot more not having one. [My mother] had a boyfriend one time, and it dawned on me what could happen because they were going out, or whatever you want to call it, for quite a while, two or three years.

My brother is a dropout and my mother knows nothing around the house. Whenever something happens, I fix it. You wouldn't believe some of the things I fix. And they give me crap that I never do anything. They'd be lost without me. Nobody does the shoveling.

I don't remember my father ever being with us.

He came over once when I was in seventh grade and he was drunk. He was being a real asshole. He was telling us how much he loved us

235

and stuff, and this was thirteen years after the divorce. He's a bowling fan and he said he was going to take my brother to Chicago on a bowling trip with him. Garbage like that.

Then he attacked my dog.

She was sitting in the chair and she was looking at me. She didn't like him, obviously. But he came up to her and grabbed her by the neck. It wasn't really hard, but it was hard enough because she was a little dog, and she started growling because he was choking her. He got a little madder and my mother made him let go. I was in seventh grade so I couldn't do anything. He's been over twice since then.

What for?

I don't know. My mother was never home. She was at work and my brother was out, so I just sat there and watched him through the rec-room window. I was going to open the window and throw some hot water on him and tell him to hit the road, but then I couldn't do that to him. Then I wanted to go down there and bash his head in, but I decided not to do that either.

Why did you want to do that?

Because he's a fool and he was making all kinds of noises. It's really late when he comes over, around one in the morning. And he'll be wobbling back and forth on the outside stairs 'cause he's drunk.

"My father would take me to the zoo every Sunday."

CAROL (17)

They were divorced twelve years ago, when I was five. This is weird because it's the first thing I remember. You know how when you're a kid you remember something as far back as you can remember? This is the first thing I can remember.

My father was sitting upstairs in this big chair and he said, "Come here." Then I was sitting on his lap and he told me that he wasn't going to live at our house anymore, and he promised that he'd take us out every weekend, which he did until about four years ago.

I didn't know what divorce meant.

My little sister never even knew they were married until three years ago. My father was at our house and he was talking to the neighbor and she goes, "Oh, how do you know him?"

"I used to live here."

And she goes, "Oh. Before we did?"

Do you know why your parents got divorced?

My father started getting into therapy, and he just decided he didn't want to be married anymore. They never fought. I don't remember one fight. There was no other woman. There was no conflict.

How do you think not having a father in your house for most of your life affected you?

I know me, and I can see this in my sister, too—I'm always looking for some guy that I can confide in. Maybe a teacher. Not so much a teacher, but like this couple I worked for this summer. I'm really close with them. They're young and the guy couldn't be my father because he's too young, but I can confide in him. It seems he's more of a father than mine would be. It's like another person to give you advice and a second opinion about the way things should be.

My older sister—I don't know if you remember that she was pretty wild when she was in high school. Don't you remember how she was? Really into drugs. I don't know if the divorce had anything to do with it. She didn't get along with my mother; she didn't get along with my father. She'd go out and get wasted, and she started skipping school a lot. Then my mother kicked her out of the house when she was fourteen. She said she couldn't handle living with her anymore. So my father, instead of having her live with him, sent her to Mexico with his friends for a year. He paid for her to live at their house for a while, and then when they were going to Mexico, she decided to go with them.

I don't think she likes [my father] very much. She's pretty bitter because she had to take out loans for school. He should have thought about that.

My little sister falls in love with her teachers. She finds reasons to stay after school. If I were her, if I really wanted to see my father, I'd get mad and call him up. But I don't think she ever does.

And the reason she stays after school and sees her teachers—

Father figures, definitely. When you're around that age—twelve, thirteen, fourteen—that's when you're really changing, you're becoming an adult. I think it would have done her a lot of good, it still would do her a lot of good, to spend more time with [my father].

238

It seems like he's totally blown us off. My little sister loves him a lot. She always used to talk about him. In the past couple of years she could have used his companionship. But it's like, if he thinks of it, he'll call us on Christmas and he'll call us on our birthdays.

I'm mad at him. Two weeks ago he took my sisters out to some art festival or something, but I didn't want to go. So I didn't go. I never talked to him.

This summer I hadn't talked to him all summer, and one night I was sitting around drunk with a good friend and we were talking about what went wrong in our lives. We started talking about my father and my friend said, "Well, just call him tomorrow. That's the best thing to do."

So I called him. I invited him to come out and have dinner with me. He said, "Oh, yeah, all right. I'm going away but I'll call you when I get back." He never called.

And he was supposed to pay for our college education and he's not going to.

Why not?

He's saying that it's a luxury. And *he* went to MIT.

He owes his shrink thousands and thousands of dollars. And he has a boat. My mom was talking to him and he was saying that he wanted her to take out a mortgage on our house for him. You know what it is when you take out a mortgage on a house? Like you can remortgage it. Did you ever play Monopoly? You go to the bank and they give you money and they own part of it again. It's called a second mortgage. He wanted her to do that and then give him the money.

What did she tell him?

"Go to hell."

I don't really care about the money. It's just that he could make himself available more.

He got remarried three years ago. I like this lady a lot. I thought she was really nice, but then they were totally nutso. They started to make us have these family discussions. There would be her three kids, me and my sisters and my father. They'd say, "We know you hate

239

your stepmother." They're telling us this while we're saying, "No, we like her." They were totally off the wall, just totally weird. The lady brainwashed him. It was, "We know you have all this hate inside you."

I said, "No, I honestly do not hate my stepmother."

Then he got her on the track of saying that the money he gave my mother she would buy clothes with, which is a bunch of shit. She pays the bills with it. I think he gives us something like sixty dollars a week for me and my little sister. He won't give my mother any money for my older sister because she's twenty-one. My mother is supporting her and paying for her college. He's supposed to pay for the college, so we could go to court about it. But I don't know if I want to. I'd rather pay for it myself.

Do you resent him for it?

Yeah. I resent him calling it a luxury.

It goes 'way back with him. He hated his parents. All of a sudden he turned against them. I think that was partly because of the shrink. He's been going to this shrink for nine years. Maybe more.

He disowned his parents and says he's adopted, which I don't think is true. [When] his father [was on his] deathbed he went back and said good-bye, and that was that for him. His mother is still alive, but he never calls her. He says they did all these things to him, but what is he doing to his own kids now? He's really nuts.

The way I am, it sounds like I hate him, but I really don't. I just think he's sort of an asshole.

He doesn't want to accept any responsibility. He gets crazy. I've seen him throw things to express his anger. He threw a chair at my sister, and a lamp and a suitcase before that.

Did he ever hit you?

No. He tried to one night. He wanted me to go to his house for dinner, but I didn't want to. I was going to have a friend come over and stay overnight because my mother was away. We just wanted to hang out. So I called him up and told him I didn't want to go. He said, "You're going." So he comes over and picks me up over his shoulder.

Do you remember that night I took off and was hysterical and I ran around the block?

Yes. Very well.

How do you remember?

Because it was my street you came running down.

I ran into Joe Barber. "Joe, Joe, don't let him take me away."
I was in seventh grade. I was twelve or thirteen. I got really hysterical. And I was mad. I was so mad.
Do you know Tammy Walsh?

Yes.

She was talking on the phone to Toby Barber when I ran into [the Barbers'] house, and years later she was talking about some crazy chick that she heard screaming over the phone. That was me.
But I was so mad at him. He couldn't accept the fact that if he called me I might say, "I don't feel like going anywhere."

What became of that?

I didn't go to his house. I got my way.

Did he catch you?

Yeah, he caught me. I think that [incident] really hurt him a lot. We ended up talking. I used to be really close with my father. I used to like him better than my mother for a long time. But just lately he's been really bad.

How did he blow you off? Did he stop calling or what?

I think a lot of it is my fault. It seems like when we were kids, we were always ready for it, for the Saturday afternoon go-out with Dad. Then you get older and you either want to go out with your friends or you have to work. And we just drifted apart.

Do you want to have relations with him?

Right now I don't. I think it's better if we didn't right now.
He left when my little sister was two, so he's missed a lot of things.

I feel sorry for him. But he could make more of an effort. I'm not bitter toward him at all. It's not like he took off and left town. If I called him up and said, "I'm really [dis]stressed, I want to see you right away," I'm sure he'd come over.

I don't really know him. I don't know how he's affected my life. Most of the time I don't think about it.

Tonight I sound bitter about my father, but I'm really not. If I had talked to you a year ago, I'd have said, "My father is really cool." It's just that right now I probably have the lowest attitude about him I've ever had. Something is going to change.

My stepmother is really weird. Her name was Shirley and she decided it should be Daphne, so she changed her name to Daphne. They had this massage room and they had a room where you could go beat up the walls. It was a—

Frustration room?

Yes. Exactly. A frustration room. They were off the wall.

At one time I wanted to live with him. My mother—now I know how to handle her, but she used to be sort of hyper. My father is easy going, things don't faze him. So at one time I thought it would be cool to live with him. But when I saw how strict he was with my stepbrothers and stepsisters, I decided against that. I never wanted to live with him after that. I would never want to see my parents live together. I can't even picture it. They are so totally different, I can hardly believe they were married.

It's funny with my father. I think when we were little—little kids are easy to be with. Then we started being adults and I don't think he could handle it. We used to do a lot of things with him. We went on trips, and he'd rent a cottage every summer. But now it seems he's all into himself. It's weird.

I think he feels rejected, that's why he's been like he has the past couple of months. When he first got married to this wife, he did want us to live with him. He thought he could have the whole family there. But I didn't want to go just because all of a sudden he wants us. That was no reason to pack up and move. I guess he was really hurt. And if I had moved in with him, I would have had to [change schools]. It's like at that point in his life, he felt like he wanted to be head of a household. Now that he and his wife have broken up, would he have sent me back?

What do you think of your stepmother?

They're separated, so I don't think she's my stepmother. He decided one day he didn't want to be married to her. I feel so sorry for her. She's in love with this guy, and all of a sudden he decides, well, that was that. He kicked her out of the house and told her to leave.

I feel so sorry for her because she got married when she was seventeen. She had three kids by the time she was twenty, then got divorced at twenty-one. She raised her kids all herself, and then she meets my father and everything is rosy. And now he just decided he didn't want to be married anymore.

Are they getting divorced now?

He can't afford to be divorced, so he's got a girl friend named Betty. I met her a couple of times. She seems pretty nice. I don't know her very well.

What do you mean, "He can't afford to be divorced"?

Alimony to another wife. Well, he never did pay my mother alimony. She didn't want it. She works. But there is child support. But you get divorced and it costs money.

His wife was nice. Young, pretty, cool. I think they partied occasionally. But she was into this therapy, always trying to analyze everything. It was really weird.

Did you get to know her kids?

A little bit. I felt sorry for them because they were constantly being analyzed. Constantly. I never could have stood living in that house. The oldest one got kicked out because he was dealing, I think. They're all really nice. One was twenty; then there's another boy that was eighteen and a girl that was seventeen. I got along with them pretty well. I liked them. But the two parents were always trying to bring this stuff into it, like, "We know that you hate your stepmother." Stupid.

My mother's going to pay for my college. She inherited some money from my grandfather. She works at the library and I think she does okay. My father makes more, but she has degrees, too. I'm going to pay her back. I'm saving money for college.

My mom's cool, but she works too hard. She works all the time. I'm pretty sure she's an alcoholic. She's lonely. She only went out with one guy that I know of, and that was years ago. She has a lot of friends, but she'll come home at night from work and she'll be tired and she'll just pass out.

My mom has treated me like an adult for as long as I can remember. I used to make her dinner when I was eight years old. She'd come home and there'd be dinner on the table.

I have responsibility. Whatever I'm going to do, just about, she lets me do. I'm not outrageous. She doesn't say, "You have to be home at this time." I went to Washington for that anti-nuclear rally. Most mothers would say, "No, you can't go," but she respects what I think is right. She doesn't make me do anything.

We've gone through times when I didn't get along with her, but most of the time I have. I remember around eighth grade when she found out I smoked pot and we had big confrontations. She confronted me with that. But I think everyone goes through that with their parents. I'm sure you did. But besides that stupid stuff, nothing major. She gets on my nerves sometimes, of course.

She hasn't disciplined me for a long time. I do it myself. When I do something I know isn't right, like if I go out one night and I stay out pretty late, even though she doesn't know that I got home at four, I'll think, wow, tonight I should take it easy. It's automatic.

I sort of feel bad about my mother. She's happy; if she wasn't I'm sure she wouldn't be the way she is. But I always feel like if it wasn't for us she might travel or whatever. I always feel she should go out more. I always try to take her out to places.

When I say stuff about my father, she always says, "Oh, don't say that about him." He never has said anything bad about her. I think my parents' divorce is more practical than most.

My mother is happy. She has a career. I can't see her being a housewife at all. She just doesn't fit the part. I don't think there was much pain involved in their divorce. It was just like, "Well, it was fun."

She never tried to fit me into a mold, and that I appreciate. And my father hasn't contributed very much [to our lives]. She has done a really good job of being both parents. I don't feel affected by it in any way.

I used to get mad in school when people would say, "Your parents are divorced. That's too bad." But I don't care to hell. My father would take me to the zoo every Sunday. He used to take us to some really neat places. Then we'd go sit in his apartment and eat McDonald's food. I never regretted anything.

I have made most of my decisions on my own. If something in the house breaks, I know how to fix it. I think I'm just the way I am; I don't think their divorce had much to do with it.

I could say, "The reason I got a C-minus on my test is because my parents are divorced." I hate kids who do that. They have this image of being a screwed-up kid with divorced parents.

A lot of kids are.

I've been screwed up and I've had my head together. Right now I have my head together.

Would you get married?

I plan on having a career. I would never, ever get married and have someone support me. I plan on having a career and being independent. But if I met a guy that I loved and I really wanted to marry, I would. I haven't condemned the institution of marriage or anything like that. But it's not like I am dying to get married and have kids.

Do you think divorce is a good or a bad thing?

I don't know if it's good or bad, but it's necessary. Can you imagine if there was no divorce? Then your father would really have to take off. This way it's legal.

The one thing that I miss—this has something to do with my boyfriend. He's got this big Italian family. There's all these aunts and uncles and they're all close and they all live in Buffalo. I sort of like that. I get into that because they all get together. If there's a funeral, they're all there. But in my family, I met my father's parents only once and that was when I was a baby. I don't remember them at all. I don't have any relatives at all that live in Buffalo. My father is totally cut off from his parents. I've talked to his brothers a couple of times on the phone, the couple of uncles that I have, but I never met them.

I'm not bitter about the divorce. I know, I said that before. It sounds like I am, when I talk about my father. But that's just recently. For most of my life it's been, "I've got a good father." It just seems like he should take a few responsibilities right now that he's not taking.

I always say my mother's crazy, and she is, but she's done a lot for me. So I have nothing against my parents. I'm glad they're divorced. I can't see them married. Nothing would be the same if they had been married. Doesn't that make sense?

"She wants an abortion sixteen years too late."

FRED (16)

[The divorce] was better for them, but I don't think it was better for me. It was better for my sister because she never liked my father. I didn't like it. I didn't like him leaving. I would rather my mother had left 'cause I like my father more.

They wanted a divorce ever since my sister and I were born. I didn't think they should be divorced. He didn't want the divorce, but my mother did, so he divorced her.

The divorce made the relationship between my father and me a lot better than it was before, though, because I get to see him as much as I used to, but it's more meaningful because he's separated, because he doesn't live with us.

I wish I didn't have to live with my mother. I did not have one word to say about who I would live with. The court said it. My mother is the legal guardian even if my father would want us.

How did you feel about that when she told you?

Mad. I wasn't angry at first, but then I got uptight after a while in the house.

Were there fights?

Yes. A lot of them. Still are. Some are about drugs. She busted me a lot and I didn't like it and she didn't like it. Now I have a car and she doesn't like it. Anything I do, she doesn't like it. It seems my sister has gotten to her and I don't get anything around the house.

Do you work?

No.

How did you get your car?

I've got money.

What did your mother say about drugs?

She found my stash. Then she found other things in my wallet. And she was wondering where I was getting all this money. She wanted to keep track of my money, where it went, 'cause she thought it was going for drugs. Sometimes it was and sometimes it wasn't. But I don't see why she should care. It's my money.

Were you dealing?

A little. Not much.

What did your mother do when she found these things?

She held them there and she questioned me. I told her some were mine and some weren't; some belonged to my friends. I tried to get away from her as much as possible.

Did she punish you?

She can't. I'm bigger than she is. I don't stay in. I'm grounded right now.

Did you ever feel like you had been deserted?

No. My mother wants to desert me. She just wants to leave. She wants an abortion sixteen years too late.

My dad is thinking about remarrying now. He asked the lady already. She's a nice lady. My sister thinks she's a nice lady, too.

How did your sister feel during the divorce?

She didn't want my father. She didn't like him at all, so she really had no feelings about it. She wanted the divorce anyway. She thought he was doing bad things to the house.

Like what?

My father used to yell at her. My father and I are a lot closer than my father and my sister. She feels that she was always the one that was hated in the family, and she decided that it was only my father that hated her. But my father doesn't hate her. But that's the way she thought it was. She didn't feel good about that.

Does she ever see him now?

Every once in a while. When she's out shopping or when he comes over to the house to pick up his mail.

My mother won't let me get my license. And I'm almost seventeen now.

Why?

I'm a bad boy. She says I'll flunk. She thinks my grades will go down. My grades are pretty bad now. My dad doesn't hassle me about my grades, but my mom does. I have a C-minus, D average now. She thinks when I get my car on the road my grades are going to go to an F because I'll be in school less and be out more.

Do you ever go to your father when she says no about something?

Yeah. Once I lived with him for about a week when she was really mad at me. I don't remember what it was for. I know it was bad. I can't remember. Something about alcohol or drugs. She found everything I had.

What did she do?

She tried to ground me for a month and I got real pissed at her. I threw her and she got real mad at me, so I said, "I'm going." She said, "Start walking to your father's." My dad called and he came and picked me up.

You have physical fights with your mother?

I don't think I could ever hit my mother, or my father, for that matter. But I use force as a means of getting my way. My mother is heavyset and I will lift her up and squeeze her until she says yes. If she doesn't say yes, I'll squeeze harder.

I think divorce is a way for people to find some reality. If something is not going right, people should find out what's going wrong with their marriage. And if it's beyond repair or hope, they should get a divorce. It would probably be much better—if there's no hard feelings after it about money or child support or that sort of thing. You can find out what your real life would be like if you weren't married.

"I was in the way."

ED (18)

One night I went to bed and I was sleeping. It was real late at night, and my mother comes flying into the room. She jumps around like my father's ready to punch her or something. They had already had a fight, I guess, while I was sleeping. She came in the room and she was lying on top of me. She woke me up and I got up and my father ran into the bedroom and she got all hysterical. She goes, "I'm going to kill him! I'm going to kill him!" She got a knife. I go, "No, Mom." I was grabbing her, trying to get her back. The house was a shambles. Her face was kind of battered.

Ever since, I've tried to hurt him for that one time. I hated him for that, to tell you the truth. It's my mother. Nobody touches my mother, not even my father. Not like that.

That one really stands out in my mind because it was so bad. The whole house was torn up. She was right at the time, because my father was having another lady on the side and she found out about it. That's what caused the whole thing. So she was right. But he went crazy and started punching her.

When did you change your mind about hating him?

I never did. What he did—that was really cruel, I think.

My mother told me they were getting divorced. She said it was hard for her to tell me. She thought I would feel really bad, which I did.

Did you know it was coming?

Oh, yeah. The way they were acting. Never talk to each other. Things like that.

She just told me, "Me and your father aren't getting along anymore. [We] are different from each other now, and he's wandering off. He's just not a part of the family anymore."

At first I didn't really care, but then I felt kind of down and out. It was bad because I couldn't go to my father and ask him some of these questions that I had. I was thirteen years old, and I had questions about the facts of life. No way I can ask my mother that.

My father wanted me to go with him at first. My mother made him look like the bad one. I was younger, so I went with my mother instead. I believed her.

Did you ever feel you were responsible?

Sort of. I was in the way. They wanted to do things and I was too young. They wanted to go on trips and they had to baby-sit me or get a baby-sitter.

Did your parents ever use you against each other?

Like I said, my father wanted me and my mother wanted me. My father would give me things and take me somewhere to get me on his side. When I came back home, my mother would do things for me and try to get me on her side.

If you had a kid your age and you were getting divorced, what would you tell him?

I'd sit down with him and tell him the reasons why we're doing it. That's about it. And I'd hope he takes it well, naturally. But that's about it.

252

They decided to tell me they were going to break up. They told me why. That they're just not right for each other, so, *bam*: divorce. At first I started crying. Wow, they're breaking up. But then I got used to it after a while, without the father being home.

Did you get away with more because your father wasn't around?

Definitely. My mother couldn't hit me. When she did hit me, it didn't hurt me. I was the man of the house, I'd do anything I wanted. But now she's married again and things are definitely changed.

"I used to think it was all my fault."

SALLY (14)

They're not divorced. They're separated, but it seems like they're divorced, only we don't have to go through all that other shit. They didn't tell us until they decided they weren't going to live together anymore. Then my mom said she was going to live somewhere else for a while, that she had to get away from my father. That was when I was eleven.

She moved out in Williamsville to an apartment. It was about a half-hour drive from here. It wasn't that far to ride a bike out there.

I saw her more than my sister did. I got along better with my mother than with my father, so I slept over at her house once in a while. And I go out to dinner with her sometimes. I'd go shopping with her and bullshit like that. I saw her less than once a week.

Did you have a choice about who you were going to live with?

Not at first. My dad was really stubborn. He didn't want to leave the house. He wanted to live with us. Since nothing was really legal, my mom didn't want any hassle, so she just moved out. We didn't have a choice who we were going to live with. My dad just lived there, and we were going to stay in this house. But later on, me and my dad got in a huge fight and my dad moved out.

What was the huge fight about?

It was really stupid. My dad was really strict and he used to ground me for a month for coming in five minutes late. I thought it was really ridiculous. So I ran away once for about a week. I stayed at my friend's house. I stayed at my mother's house a couple of nights, too. She brought me home.

Then a week after that, I went to Fun and Games Park. I came home a half hour late, and my dad was hitting me. We were screaming at each other and he was hitting me, so I called my mother and I had her come pick me up. I stayed at her house for a couple of days and then they started switching. My mom moved back in and my dad moved out to my grandfather's house.

Where's that?

About an hour away.

Did you ever see him?

At first we didn't see him often because he didn't want to see my mother. They're not even friends now. Every once in a while he'd come, but only when my mom wasn't home. He wouldn't talk to her.

And he was mad at me for a while. He wouldn't even talk to me because it was because of me that he'd had to move out.

But now we see him. He comes over once a week and he gives us five dollars a week and he takes us out to dinner. So everything's cool now.

How did you feel about it when he wouldn't talk to you?

At first I didn't mind because I was really mad at him for what he did. Then I started getting upset about it because he was my father and I loved him. I was hoping he would understand why I didn't want to live with him.

Did you talk to him about it?

No, I never talked to him about it. I talked to my mother about it.

She said that he was stubborn and it wasn't worth talking to him about, so I never really talked to him.

My father says bad things about my mother, like about her going out, and he thinks she's kind of an idiot. He calls her a "bitch" and a "shit" sometimes. But my mother doesn't really say anything bad about my father, except something like, "He's really stubborn." Sometimes when they get in a fight, she'll call him a bastard or something. She doesn't do that often, but my dad does it a lot. A lot of times he just shakes his head at my mother.

Does it bother you when they do that?

Yeah. When my mother says bad things about my father, I say something to her. I say, "Don't say it in front of me." But when my dad does it, I just get upset. I don't say anything to him. He doesn't really try to make me hate my mother, but he'll say things about her that will make me think less of her.

I remember one fight they had. It was really stupid. Most of their fights were really stupid. I remember two of them now.

One fight was about putting the Christmas tree lights on the Christmas tree. My dad was mad 'cause he thought he had to do everything. They got in this huge argument and they were yelling and screaming, yelling and screaming. Me and my sister were upstairs crying.

Another one was when my dad lived with us. My mother came over one day and my dad wouldn't give her one of the hot dogs he was cooking. She went to take one anyway, and he came and pushed her and my mom threw the hot dogs at him. And they got in a fight. My dad hit my mother and I was hitting my father. It was a huge fight and it was just awful. Everybody was crying.

Did you ever go to one of your parents when the other said no?

Before the divorce I did. Before the separation, I mean. If my father would say no, I'd always go to my mother because my mom was really sympathetic. She'd always say yes. I got in trouble every once in a while for doing that. But I haven't done it since they separated.

If you had a friend whose parents were getting divorced and your friend asked you for advice on how to handle it, what would you say?

That it wasn't their fault. I used to think it was all my fault that they weren't going to live together anymore. I thought it was all because of me they weren't getting along. I thought that everything I did affected [their relationship].

So I would tell a friend, "It wasn't because of you. It was because your parents didn't get along. It would be better if they did get separated rather than have them home fighting all the time."

Did they ever fight about you?

Not really. They'd fight about who was going to live with who, who wanted the kids, who was going to get us, who was going to get the house. But they never really got us into their arguments too much.

How did you feel when they were fighting about who was going to get the kids?

I was upset because I didn't want to say, "I want to live with Mom," because I would hurt my dad's feelings. And I didn't want to say, "Well, I'll live with Dad," because I would hurt my mom's feelings. And I really didn't know who I wanted to live with. So I was confused. I didn't know what to think. I wanted to live with both of them.

I think things have been a lot better since they got separated. There's not the arguing. And they kind of get along better because they don't really talk to each other, which is better than them arguing all the time. And I get along with my father a lot better now that he doesn't live with us. He's hard to get along with.

"It was better for all of us all around."

ANGELO (17)

I was about fifteen when they separated.

It's had its good points and its bad points. I lived with my mother and I could stay out as late as I wanted—as long as she knew where I was. So I didn't mind telling her where I was going. But then I had all the responsibilities that my father had, like taking care of the house and the cars.

Ever since I can remember, my parents never really got along. They didn't even sleep in the same room together for about five years before [the separation]. They slept in different bedrooms. I figured eventually it would happen. But they were planning on waiting till after I was eighteen; they said that maybe it wouldn't be so much of a hassle if they waited. But then it came to a head one day and they decided to do it. My parents always threatened to do it, but they never went and did it. They never got a divorce; they just got a separation.

It didn't bother me much because I got along better with my parents after they did it. I'd go see my father on Sundays and I'd spend the day with him. I never got along so well with my father until after they got separated. I never liked my father that much before. It was better for all of us all around because then those two were happier and I got along better with them. So it was good.

My mother told me everything that was going on, like when they were getting their lawyers and stuff like that. She even took me down to see her lawyer one time. He didn't want me to come to court. He said it might leave mental scars or some bullshit like that.

It didn't really change anything. It's just that I had more work to do around the house.

They were never really divorced because they didn't want to go out of their way. They just wanted to see what it would be like.

My father got an apartment. Between what he paid us and what my mother made working, we got along okay, but it wasn't that good. My father couldn't afford to keep his own apartment. He had to buy a refrigerator and a stove and everything. Got too expensive for him, so they settled their problems and they got back together. Now they're starting to drop off a little bit. If one of them's tired and he starts bitching, they'll both start bitching, start battling.

I've got three older brothers. When it happened, they were just worried about me. They realized that it was better for them, too, but they were just worried that I'd be upset about it. They all talked to me and they all came around to make sure everything was okay. One brother was working for the FBI at the time; he was in Washington, D.C. Another was down in New York City. The oldest lives downtown, here in Buffalo. He came over on weekends to make sure everything was okay. If I had some job around here that I couldn't do, he'd do it.

I never really talked about anything. I never really talked about [my parents] getting separated, what it was like. I never really talked like we are right now except when I saw that social worker. My mother thought it was going to be really bad for me. She was worried about me. My brothers were worried. But it didn't bother me that much. If I'd been younger, it would have bothered me a lot more.

Did you think they were going to get a divorce?

No. My mother wouldn't go for divorce because she knew there was no way she would get married again. My father knew he wouldn't get married again. There was no sense getting divorced if they weren't planning on getting married again, so why bother?

How long after the separation did they start getting along again?

Ten or eleven months. Pretty long. Almost a year. My mother called up my father to fix the car one time. He came over and fixed it, which was cool. He just charged her for the parts. Then I guess he called her back for something, and they started calling each other once in a while, and I guess they got their problems ironed out and he went back.

And you had more authority while they were separated.

I could do just about whatever I wanted to as long as my mother knew where I was. She didn't like the idea of me staying out super-late, but she didn't bitch about it as long as she knew where I was and who I was with. One time I came in about five o'clock in the afternoon totally drunk. I couldn't walk. I'd walk about two houses and fall over and start puking. She was just worried. She didn't get mad and she didn't try and ground me or punish me.

Did you lose some of your authority when your father came back?

Definitely. While he was gone, I was "the man of the house." When he came back, I couldn't stay out as late anymore. I had to do my homework all the time. Stuff like that. My old lady didn't hassle me very much about schoolwork. I didn't do too well, but she didn't hassle me about it. As soon as my old man came back, I had to hit the books again when school started.

My mother, when she started working, would get home late. My father liked to have his dinner on the table at five o'clock, when he got home. And she couldn't get home that early 'cause she didn't get out until four-thirty and she had to take a bus. And he always used to get really pissed off. If she put something in the oven and [set] the [stove timer] and it didn't go off and the stuff wouldn't be cooked, it would still be raw when he got home. Then he'd get all pissed off.

Then my mother would say that he never did anything around the house. He'd be bitching; he'd go, "I do all the stuff that you're supposed to do, like clean the house and wash the dishes and cook." She goes, "Well, you could at least help out somehow." She didn't want him doing everything around here, but since she was working, too, she figured he could do some of the things around here, like help with dinner.

What else did they battle about? Stupid things.

My father slipped in the bathtub one time, and he smacked his head. Ever since then, he's been really excitable. His temper is real short. Anything would set him off. They'd just start bitching. Nothing that was worth arguing about. They just liked arguing with each other. They never really got violent. One time my old man started pushing her around. I remember I came up and I told him to knock it off.

What were they arguing about?

I don't know. I was downstairs and I heard them arguing. Not enough that I could hear what they were saying, but I knew that they were fighting. Then I heard this shuffling around and I came upstairs and my father was pushing her. I told him to knock it off because my mother was scared. She thought he was going to start beating her up. But he never did.

They didn't really have anything to argue about. My mother would start nagging my father and he'd start bitching at her. Nothing, really, no big hassle that they had to fight about. It was just nagging. Stuff like that. Minor things.

Did you side with either of them?

I was more on my mother's side. I always got along with her. Before they separated, I used to hate my old man; I didn't like him worth shit. So I wanted my mother to get the better end of the deal, which in a way we did: we got the house and she got one of the cars, the newer one. And my father had to pay for the house taxes and shit like that. We didn't get too bad a deal. (I wanted my mother to get the better half.)

When did you stop being biased?

After I started going to visit my father. He wasn't such a pain in the ass. He wasn't always bitching about everything. He was in a better mood, so I started getting along better with him. In a way I hoped they would get back together, but I wasn't going to press it.

Did you have any plots to get them back together?

No. I figured both of them were happier apart. It was working out well for me; the only problem was not having too much money to spend.

My mother always had big plans, like going down to Florida. But we only got fifty dollars a week from him, and with the money she makes—she doesn't make a lot of money—we were just making enough to get by. We never got to buy much. All we really bought during that time was that stereo over there. She paid for half and I paid for half. If I wanted to go out, I paid for that kind of stuff. If I needed clothes, my mother paid for some of it and my father paid for some of it.

Did you get an allowance?

I did before [the separation], but then I didn't ask my mother for one because I knew she was having a hard enough time trying to make ends meet. I had a paper route at the time and that usually covered my expenses, like if I wanted to go out drinking or something.

Did either of them have boyfriends or girlfriends?

Never. They didn't want to get stuck again. That's the way they figured it. They didn't want to take the chance of getting stuck with somebody like they have now. They used to hate each other.

How did you take it when you first found out?

At first, when I was younger, around eleven, I realized that eventually they'd end up getting divorced. It used to hurt me. Every time they'd start battling, I'd start crying. And that usually stopped it. But after I got older, I realized [divorce] was much better for them and it didn't bother me that much anymore.

When you were older, did it affect your schoolwork? Did you tell your friends about it?

No. I didn't mention it to anybody. I kept it to myself. It didn't bother my schoolwork or anything. It didn't bother my social life. It was just something that every once in a while would bring me down, but it wasn't that big a thing; it wasn't something that scarred my life.

Did you learn anything from it?

I realized [that] when I get married, if I get married, I'm going to do a lot of things differently with my kids. I'm going to make sure that when I get married it's [to] somebody I really want to spend the rest of my life with, not somebody I'm going to end up splitting the family over after it's already started. I won't want to be battling and stuff in front of my kids. You've got to learn to control your temper. Nothing's worth battling about. Usually you can talk about it and settle things.

Is there anything that stands out in your mind about it?

It's just that I think I was the happiest in my life when they were separated, because I definitely got along a lot better with my old man when they were.

The only thing I felt bad about was, I was the only thing that was holding them together. I was the only reason they didn't get the divorce or the separation sooner, because they wanted to wait until I was eighteen. They wanted to wait until I could move out so they could sell the house and split the money. My mother didn't want me to have to go to a different school.

"The judge—you wouldn't believe . . ."

GINA (16)

They started arguing all the time. My mom finally got her head together and started to quit catering to my dad all the time. My dad always wanted my mom to serve him. She got sick of that shit. She started becoming more independent.

The arguments were mainly about money, then just about everything. After a while every little thing would agitate the other person, and then they'd get in arguments over the stupidest things and it would just blow up. They'd start fighting and throwing things.

After they separated, my dad moved to live with my grandmother, about a block away. It was in the agreement that he would only come in the house to do his laundry or something like that. He came over one night and he was just sitting in the living room. My mom wasn't home. She got home and my dad was there watching TV and my mom didn't want him there. She started getting all excited because just his presence there would bug her. She was really uptight through the whole thing.

So my mom called her parents, who live right across the street, to

264

come over because my dad wouldn't leave. He goes, "No, no. I'm doing my laundry. Don't get all excited."

My grandparents came over and me and my brother and sister were all sitting around watching TV. My mom's sitting here saying, "Will you please leave?" And he wouldn't leave.

My grandfather said, "Would you just get out of here and leave her alone?" My mom kept getting more and more hysterical. It doesn't sound like much, but after all they've been through, all the fighting, she couldn't stand to have him in the house. So my grandfather, after my mom was getting all excited and hysterical, goes over and he starts shaking my father. He says, "Would you just get out of this house?"

So my dad gets up and they both started fighting. Physically fighting.

My sister was about seven and I was in eighth grade, about twelve, and we're all sitting there, and my little sister starts crying. I'm sitting there hugging her. My father and my grandfather are still fighting. My dad got a bloody lip. Then my mother starts getting in, trying to pull them apart. And then my grandmother—she's about five feet tall and weighs ninety-nine pounds—she starts getting in there, too. And the four of them are in it, rolling all around, and the lamps are falling over.

All I remember is just sitting there holding my sister, trying to calm her down while this is going on.

My mom screams, "Call the police! Call the police!" So my brother calls the police and gets them to come over, and meanwhile they're all still rolling around.

Finally they stopped and the police came. All the policeman could do was talk to each one of them and try to work things out because there was no law that applied. It was in the agreement that he couldn't be there except to do laundry, but supposedly he was doing his laundry. So all the policeman did was talk to my grandfather, and then he talked to my dad and advised my dad to leave. Told him to leave. So he left.

One time they were up in the bedroom and they were fighting because my mom wouldn't sleep with him. The police came over and my grandmother came over from across the street. I guess they were fighting really badly then, physically, so the police had to come to break it up.

I remember once my mom got so mad at him she kicked him in the balls as hard as she could. She said, "Oh, I was just so mad at him, I just wanted to kill him." So she did that to him. She thought she'd never do that to anybody.

I remember when I was little always seeing them on the stairs throwing punches. I couldn't believe it. I hated it. I wanted to get my dad out of there. I tried a couple of times, but he'd just fling me, too, and I'd go flying. There's no way. When my dad loses his temper, he's so strong, there's nothing you can do. There's nothing you can do except try and get someone bigger or call the police.

Once we were eating dinner. I was in the dining room eating, and all of a sudden they started arguing about something really stupid, and my dad threw this plate of hot spaghetti at my mom. We were sitting [in the dining room] eating and my dad and my mom were in the kitchen, and all of a sudden we hear my mom scream. We go in there, and there's spaghetti all over the whole kitchen. It was in my mom's hair. She got so mad she threw some back at him.

That was before the separation. The time he had the fight with my grandfather was at the very beginning, when my mom filed for divorce and they were just starting to separate. My dad was going to stay at my grandmother's for a while to see how things could be worked out.

Things kept getting worse. After [the separation], it wasn't physical anymore. It was through the lawyers.

It was really hard because neither one of them wanted us kids to get in the middle, but it was impossible for them not to put us there. My dad would always talk about my mom to us. He'd ask us what she'd been doing when he was not around. He'd talk about what a bad person she was [in order] to get us to say stuff against her in court. And that's what my mom was trying to get us to do, too.

She had me go to court to testify. I said I would because my dad was trying to prove that she was an unfit mother, that she had all these psychological problems. I said that I'd go and defend my mom in court.

266

I went, and the judge—you wouldn't believe. They had waited months to get me to court and finally they get in there and they have all this stuff ready to present to the judge, all the witnesses and stuff. The judge heard about fifteen or twenty minutes of it and he said, "I'm sorry, I'm not going to give you a divorce because I don't believe in divorces. You can go back and work it out with yourselves."

He was a real asshole.

The judge wouldn't give them a divorce. He said, "No, I don't want to hear anybody's testimony. I don't want to talk to any of the defendants, or to any of the witnesses."

He was some asshole judge from some hick town somewhere that they'd brought in. I don't know who he was. He just said, "I don't see that you should get a divorce." He couldn't even have said [whether] he thought we needed one or not, because he didn't hear any of the testimony.

There was so much shit going back and forth between the lawyers and everything, it was such a mess for so long. One lawyer would put everything off. Every little thing took months and months to solve. Finally they worked out these agreements, and they ended up getting the divorce outside of court. We didn't have to testify.

I remember when my parents got divorced, they didn't have to go to court. It just got written up in the paper. What do you know about the agreement?

There're all these clauses. My dad got to keep the house and my mom got to keep us. But we had a choice of who we wanted to live with; even though my mom got custody, my parents allowed us to choose who we wanted to live with.

My brother didn't want to live outside of Derby, so he lived with my dad. My mom had to get out of Derby because you know everyone there and everyone knows about everybody's business. She didn't want to live there. I wanted to live with my mom. There was no way I could live with my dad. My brother lived with my dad for about a year and a half. He moved in with us last September. So we can live with whomever we want, even though my mom has custody, but my mom can't move outside of Erie County with us. Otherwise we'd probably be living in California or something.

And my dad has to pay a hundred and fifty dollars a week child support as long as the three of us are living with my mom. As soon as I turn eighteen, my mom won't get any more child support for me. My dad pays all the medical expenses. They worked out who was going to get what in the house. My dad was getting down to every nitty-gritty pen and pencil. And my mom was getting really frustrated with that because it was just the littlest things he wanted written up in the agreement.

Why didn't you want to stay with your dad?

'Cause there's no way I could have lived with him. He's got a very, very bad temper. And he's kind of a chauvinist pig, so I'd have to always be doing the cleaning and everything. I still love him, but he's like this: he'll sit there and he'll say, "Hand me the book, hand me the book, hand me the book," before you can even catch your breath. Then he gets all excited about things like that. I'm not that close to him. He's really conservative. If I ever got caught drinking or even if I smoked cigarettes, it would be the worst thing in the world.

How come your brother moved?

Because he couldn't stand living with my dad. He finally said, "I don't care if I have to move or not." He was afraid to move because he wouldn't know anybody. All his friends were in Derby and he thought he could just work it out. But he couldn't live with my dad anymore.

My brother was turning into like my dad. I notice when I'm around my dad on a weekend or something, I start acting like him. He's really sarcastic. I notice with my friends I would end up being really bitchy, and that's the way he was.

My brother has changed a lot since he moved in with us. I couldn't even stand living with him when he first moved in. He'd sit there and punch walls. When he'd lose his temper, he'd destroy things. My mom always thought [the divorce] had the worst effect on him.

He's in the middle. My sister was too young to really know what was going on. I pretty much understood. I don't really let it have an

268

effect on me. It did, but I figured [the divorce] was all for the better, because they had been fighting for years.

I remember when I was little and they'd fight and I'd ask, "Are you guys going to get divorced?" and my mom would always say, "No, we're never going to get a divorce." I remember I'd be trying to get to sleep and I'd hear them fighting. I'd think to myself, I'd hear her saying, "No, no, I'm never going to get a divorce."

I'm really glad that they waited. I have good memories of growing up like a regular family. I would have missed out on a lot of stuff. I can see it with my little sister. She's been pretty much on her own since she was eight because my mom had to work and my dad wasn't around. Ever since they got divorced, my mom has had to work.

I had a girl friend, my best friend, whose parents were going through the exact same thing at the time. And we pretty much went through the whole thing together and it was good that I had her. We'd always be one of us telling the other person about the latest big fight that they had.

Do you think it's a good or bad thing that they got divorced?

I think it's great. I could never stand living with my dad. Whatever my dad said, that's what my mom would go along with. So I grew up with really strict parents because of that. My dad was a lot more strict than my mom. I couldn't even wear pants to school, jeans to school, until I was in the seventh grade. I used to sneak out of the house with my jeans on because my dad wouldn't let me [wear them]. And you could never swear or anything like that. It's not that big a deal, but now I can be myself at home, too.

How did you first find out your parents were going to get separated?

I think they just told me. It was a year before they decided to get divorced. Really, my dad would still be married to my mom if my mom hadn't filed for a divorce.

A year before they decided to do it, my dad went to stay with my grandmother for a good two weeks, and my parents told us kids that he was going over there because my grandmother wasn't feeling too well and he had to keep her company. Just some excuse. And they didn't say why until later; then they told us that was why.

I think my mom told me. It wasn't much of a shock at all because by the time they told us, it was pretty obvious that they were going to do something, and if they weren't, they'd better. By that time I hoped they would do it because it was long overdue.

What was the hardest or most painful part for you?

All the abuse they went through. And seeing my dad hit my mom. And thinking that my parents would actually fight physically with each other, that they would throw things and destroy things so the police would have to come. That was the main thing.

Did your parents ever hit you?

My dad would—for being bad. My mom used to spank me when I was little, but my dad, when he gets mad, he just throws you against the woodwork. I've gotten bruises from him. That's another reason why my brother can't stand living with him—because my dad would just take it out on him. He'd be the only one there and he couldn't fight against him.

My dad will skip a week paying the support because of some stupid reason. One of the most recent things was, my mom agreed to pay for my brother's bus ticket home from Boston. That was if my dad told my mom how much it was. My mom had the money last June, but then she didn't have an income because she switched jobs; she hadn't had any income all summer. So when my dad asked my mom to pay him back, she didn't have the money at that time. She said, "I don't have it right now. You should have told me a long time ago." So my dad didn't pay her support. My mom got all excited and called him up. I guess finally they worked it out.

And then every once in a while, like when my dad gets a dentist bill and he doesn't think it's valid, he'll skip a week.

The arguments now are mainly just over the money.

How do you feel about that?

I think my dad is an asshole because he has so much money. My dad is a lawyer. He's got all this property and all these stocks, and he is the biggest tightwad. It makes you sick. I swear, money is like a disease with him.

That's another reason why I could never live with him. Just to go to the store to pick up a few things you need, he has to look through all the papers and see where he can get the coupons. So he'll end up going to about five stores to pick up five different things because they're on sale at these stores.

It gets me so mad when he does that because he's got so much money. And we don't have any money. My mom is trying to get started here pulling some money in, but it's hard for her to do because she's got three kids. Not that she has to take care of me now, but, you know . . .

Would you like to see your dad or mother get remarried?

I wouldn't really care. I think it would be good for my dad to get remarried. I think he'd be happier if he was married again. I think if my mom found the right guy, I'd want her to get married. But it won't have much effect on me because I won't be around too much longer.

Do you see your dad often?

We try and do something at least once a week. Like last night, he took me out to dinner—with his coupon book.

Does he contribute to your welfare? Does he buy you clothes?

Never. Everything is a big production. It's got to be on sale. Last night I was getting so pissed at him. It was about last year when I went to Florida. I saved up; I had to pay every single penny for my trip. I borrowed a hundred dollars from him and I've been paying him back as I get the money. He wrote in an extra twenty-two dollars that I needed and last night he brings up, "So, Gina, you owe me some cleaning." I said, "From what?" And he goes, "You said you'd do some cleaning to make up for that extra twenty-two dollars." When I was working to get enough money to go to Florida, I asked him if I could clean for him to get some money and he goes, "Well, don't you

271

still owe me some cleaning from two years ago?" He made me clean a whole day for nothing because he said I owed it to him from two years ago, which I did. I owed him a day of cleaning from two years ago to pay for going to camp.

If I want something and my mom doesn't have enough money for it, she'll say, "Why don't you try and get your father to do it for you?" You don't know how hard that is, getting something from my dad. It's like, "Well, are you going to work for me for it? Do you want a loan?" There's no way he will just buy it for me unless it's my birthday or Christmas. Even then, "That's your whole present, Gina." It makes me sick. He's got all this money and he won't spend it on anything.

So—no, he doesn't buy me anything. Even now he hasn't gotten me a birthday present. We're going to shop around for some sales. If he finds a good bargain, I guess he'll buy me something.

When I was little, I'd think my dad [was] the greatest guy in the world. I used to love him so much and I never thought there was anything wrong with him. Then when I saw him during the divorce, when I saw him lose his temper and throw things around, I used to hate him sometimes, for the things he'd do to my mom.

My mom used to have the biggest bruises all over the place and she'd always be a total wreck mentally. She started smoking cigarettes during the divorce and she still smokes them now. That really got me mad. You know, that was indirectly his fault.

I love him, but my opinion of him has changed.

He cares about me still. I like the time that I do spend with him, but I don't want to spend any more time with him because even when I see him for just a weekend, by the end of the weekend I'll think, I've got to get away from you. He'll start getting on my nerves.

Do you trust him?

Not as far as I can throw him. No, I don't trust him. Just from past experiences, like seeing the way he treated my mom. Lots of times he would say one thing and do another. He'd twist things around so it came out like he was doing the right thing and she was doing the wrong thing. Even things that he said to me. He'll say one thing and then—you know how you can say something and you can twist it around so that you were telling the truth then but you said it in a way that one person would infer it in a different way? He does things like that.

Did your father ever try to make you feel like you were leaving him and abandoning him and shit like that?

He did that all the time. When I'd come back to Derby to visit him, he'd go on and on about how nice Derby is and, "Gee, you've grown up here, you've lived here all your life and your family is here. I'm out here all alone in this big house and here I have all these bedrooms. You know, if you lived here, I would give you this and this and this."
It's such bullshit.
He always told my mom and me that he would take me to Europe before I was ten. I have never seen Europe. Even last night he was asking me about going on a trip and I said, "It would be nice to go to Europe." And he's sitting there. "Gee, really? Where would you like to go? Winter's really nice there." And he tells me where this really nice place is in Europe. He's been all over. and he said, "Yeah, let's go." He's said stuff like that so much. He said, "You know, Spain is kind of like Mexico." And I said, "Well, how about Acapulco?" And he said, "Oh, yeah, that's really nice."
We've had that same conversation so many times. We never go.

Does your mother ever guilt-trip you?

No, she never did. Well, she was lucky, too, because she always knew that she had us. Because we got to know how my father was by how he kept screwing around with the divorce. So we'd always back her [up] and support her. That got to be kind of hard, because I'd get to hate my dad.
I always wanted a different father. One [who] wouldn't [bullshit like] that.

Do you think you'll ever get married?

I doubt it, because of what happened to my parents. I figure, people change so much, just with their own lives. Two people just change. I wouldn't want to be stuck with one person all that time. I don't think that two people can really get along for that many years. Well, sometimes they can, but it would be hard.

Do you ever want to have a family, have kids?

That's a problem. See, I don't want to get married, but I would like to have some kids sometime and just settle down. But if I did get married, I'd definitely want to live with the person for a couple of years or so first because I figure that you don't really know the person until you live with them.

What's your overall feeling about divorce?

I think it's a good thing. I think it's good now that people are getting divorced when they don't get along because it saves a lot of people a lot of hurt and frustration. I think if it can be avoided, it should be, because so many people are getting divorced. I think the reason for that is they've been wanting to do it for a long time and it hasn't been out in the open. Ten years ago no one ever got divorced. I think it's a good thing if it's necessary, if it has to be done.

"Four times a year I'm part of his life for a week."

JANE (16)

They got divorced when I was five. I don't remember how I found out. All I remember is, my father moved out because he was going to school down in Virginia and then they decided they would get a divorce.

My mother tells me she got tired of not doing anything. She said my father never wanted to do anything and she was bored. There was never any hate or any anger during the divorce.

I was very upset. I was the classic divorced family child. I blamed it on myself. It took me a long time to get over it.

Did your parents help you with that? Did they tell you it wasn't your fault?

I can't remember that part. My mother helped me a lot just by being there. I can always remember that when I'd go down to visit my father, it was so traumatic to leave. I'd cry on the plane for an hour, all the way back to Buffalo. I'm not very close to him anymore.

My mother and I went through some hard times about two years ago. Really bad times.

I ran away once. One of those quick things. "You can't go out tonight."

"Why not?"

"Because you're going out alone."

"Yeah. Good-bye, Mom. I'm leaving."

Took off out the window and I stayed out until about one. When I got home, my stepfather—the only time he ever laid a hand on me was that night. I didn't think I deserved it, but now, thinking back, for what I did I deserved to get beaten.

Did he hit you hard?

Oh, yeah.

How old were you then?

Fourteen.

Did you have a choice who you would stay with?

No. I don't want one. Wherever I go, I'll always be with my mother.

Why?

Because my mother needs me more than my father would have. My father had his own life. I'm not part of my father's life, his everyday life. Four times a year I'm part of his life for a week.

What is your stepfather like?

Don't ask. He was really bad. He was on the verge of becoming an alcoholic and he's not a very nice person. He's very cold and distant, and he doesn't seem to give a damn about anybody except himself. He's very self-centered. My mother and my stepfather almost got a divorce about two months ago.

I wanted them to get a divorce. Jay's all right. He was nothing too spectacular in the past, but he's pouring on the sweetness now and we've been getting along really well.

Why are you so down on your father?

When I was in fourth grade, my parents had a fight over the house, about who was going to own the house. My mother had been making all the payments on it since they had gotten the divorce. My father said, "I want half the house. We're going to sell the house."

My mother said, "No way. I've paid for the house for the past four years."

My father said, "If that's the way you feel about it, until you decide to sell the house to me or sell it on the market and give me half of the profit, I won't talk to you or Jane again."

That destroyed me. I have never forgiven my father for that. He wouldn't speak to me for six months.

My father hasn't spent a dime on me since they got the divorce. He was supposed to. Not that much, because he's so far away, but he never paid a cent. My mother never took him to court for it. She said I was her responsibility. That's the way my mother is. She felt that responsibility.

My father has a daughter from his new marriage. She's six years old and she's a doll. And I have a three-year-old brother from my mother's new marriage.

My father's wife is very sweet, but she's also very stingy. I think she makes my father like that, too: his not paying for anything. Other than that, she's a really sweet person.

My stepfather was twenty-four when they got married and my mother was thirty. One of the reasons I don't get along with him now is because we are too close in age to have a father-child relationship. He wasn't ready for it. He was ready for a wife, but he was not ready to walk in on a situation where he had an almost-grown-up daughter.

What was the hardest part of the divorce for you to accept?

My mother getting remarried to somebody other than my father. It didn't bother me that much when my father got remarried because he was so far away. It didn't faze me that much.

Do you think your parents' divorce was a good or bad thing?

It was there. It wasn't good, it wasn't bad. It's just something that happened.

Did you wish they were back together?

When I was younger I did because I despised my stepfather.

My mother used to drive me down to somewhere in Pennsylvania and my father would meet me and pick me up and I always thought, maybe I can get them back together there.

The conflicts between me and my stepfather were always there. I always wanted my mother to leave him. I can always remember them fighting. For as long as I can remember, they were fighting. I remember sleeping in bed and him taking her out and them coming back drunk and him saying, "I'm leaving." My mother would be saying, "Go ahead." And then she'd break down and cry and say, "No, don't leave us" and all that kind of stuff. Until three months ago he was doing it. Now she doesn't let him drink anymore.

Did you ever use dope as an escape?

I used it to get away from my mother. I used to do Valiums.

I remember one summer when my mother and I had a really bad fight. My mother almost kicked me out. She [had already] kicked me out of the house twice and sent me down to my father's. She said she couldn't handle me. I wasn't half as bad as some of the people that you and I know.

I remember one time that I did the Valiums. So many that I was gone for a weekend. My mother found dope on me, just some weed, so she and her husband grounded me for a weekend. I was in my room without light, without TV, without a radio. The Valiums were my one thing, and I did six of those. That was the first time I did Valiums.

If a kid the age you were when your parents got divorced said to you, "My parents are getting divorced and I don't know how to cope with it," what would you say?

That you can't do anything about it; that you've got to face it; that you can't blame it on yourself.

Kids very rarely cause divorces. Very rarely. There will be fights over who gets the kids or who's going to pay child support, but all you can do is go with it. You can't fight it because it's like fighting the establishment. You can't do it.

How did the divorce affect your ability to handle problems?

I think I can handle things better than a lot of other people can. To a certain extent I can handle my parents' fighting. I get really pissed off when my mother and my stepfather fight. But I don't break down and say, "What are you doing to me and my brother?" I leave it up to my mother mostly and say, "It's your life." And I cope with other things more easily and readily than other people can, I think.

But I don't believe in marriage. My mother has blown away two marriages and so I think if people are going to get married and divorced, it's just not worth getting married.

"I was scared to be living without a dad."

ALICE (13)

They've been divorced for seven years—since I was six years old. My mom said that maybe he'd better try living by himself for a while, because he was getting frustrated and stuff, so she said, "Why don't you try living by yourself?"

He said, "Okay," and then he decided not to come back.

I wasn't mad at him, but I was scared to be living without a dad.

He used to come once a week and take us out to dinner. Then he stopped coming for three years. Now he takes us out to dinner every Thursday.

When he stopped coming, how did you feel?

I felt he hated me and I didn't mean anything to him. I felt pretty bad.

Did either of your parents say anything bad about the other one?

Yes, they did. Unmentionable things.

Can you think of what they said?

Yes, I can think of it.

Do you want to say it?

No. When they said those things, I felt awful. I didn't know why they were saying those things about each other. I remember when I was eight years old and my dad said something about my mom. Mom never said anything about my dad then, but sometimes my dad would say things about my mom that made me feel bad.

Did you ever say anything?

No. I didn't tell my mom and I didn't say something back to him. I don't know why.

My mom tried to make it easier for me. My mom kept saying that my dad just couldn't handle the situation, but he still loved me and it wasn't anything that I did that made them get a divorce.

Did they ever remarry?

No—I mean, not together. My mom got married again. Now she's separated. And my dad got married again and he's divorced again. I lived with my mom and I got along okay with my stepfather, but now I think he's a real asshole.

How about the person your father married?

I never met her. That was during the time my dad didn't come to see us.

How did you find out about it?

My mom told me.

How did you feel about him getting remarried?

I didn't think it was wrong or anything like that. I didn't feel good or bad about it. Mom getting remarried made me kind of glad, I guess.

Did you ever feel your father had abandoned you?

No, I didn't. I didn't think he just said, "Fuck it," and took off on us. That's what I thought about my stepfather. He just said, "I don't want to take this responsibility," and left. That was his attitude.

And how did you feel when your parents got divorced from the people they remarried?

I was kind of glad. I thought maybe my parents would get remarried again, but they didn't.

My mom and my stepfather would say bad things about each other. He'd always call her "bitch" and stuff like that. All these awful things. My mom said some things about him, too. They just didn't like each other after they separated.

I think Mom basically married him for his money. Because she couldn't go to school when we were in first and second grade and [make enough money to support us and have time for us, too.] It was just hard. She couldn't afford a baby-sitter because she didn't have a job and she was going to school. Where was she going to get the money to go to school? So then she did go to school and she got her bachelor's in social services. And now she has a job. So now we're doing okay, I guess.

If you had a friend whose parents were getting divorced, what advice would you give her?

I'd probably say what my mom said: "Don't think that your parents are getting divorced because it's your fault or something you did." I don't know what else. There's nothing really you can say.

I don't think my dad, my real dad, could hack kids. He wasn't the fatherly type, and I think that's one of the reasons he moved out. I remember one time we were playing and I spit in his teeth and he threw me across the backyard. Sometimes he just went into spastics and got really mad. My second dad liked kids, but he and my mom didn't get along too well.

The hardest part is just not having my dad around to talk to all the time, not being able to come home and see him every day.

I don't think divorce is fair to the kids 'cause it's sometimes hard for them to adjust. But if the parents are getting divorced for a good reason, it is probably better than if they stayed together, because then they'd just mess up the whole family.

"It's all your fault, it's all your fault."

JOSEPH (17)

How old were you when you found out your parents were about to be divorced?

I was about eight. They started having fights and then they got separated for about a six- or seven-year span before the actual divorce took place.

How did you find out?

My father left, and my mother told me they were breaking up because they couldn't get along and there were too many fights.

Some of them were really senseless. My father came in when my mother had one of her relatives over and he didn't like that relative, so he picked up the roast and threw it on the floor; then he poured chocolate milk all over the floor. And a couple of other incidents like that.

I was disturbed. I didn't like seeing it. But after a while you get used to it. It's the atmosphere you have to live with.

At first I was on my father's side. I'd say, "He is not really doing all that. He'll be all right." But then I realized that it wasn't going to work that way. And I just accepted what he was doing, and I was on my mother's side.

At first I used to go down to my father's office, like on weekends, just to visit him and to see him. But then after a while he ended that, and we ended contact, and that's been that way for five or six years.

My mother is set in her ways. She's old-fashioned. My father is—as well as I can remember him—he was nice, but he just got married to another woman. This woman that he's associated with was married five times before.

What my mother should never have done was talk to him about it. The only reason she did that is because the old husband of the woman that was running around with my father was giving my mother phone calls reporting on what they were doing.

Do you get along well with your mother now?

Now I do. Before, we were constantly fighting. I was opposing her views on everything: how late I was going to stay out, how I was going to run my life. Just little things; little things that set her off because she had a lot to handle: bringing my brother and me up and working.

We kids definitely got the worst of it, and it's still going on.

My father started sending alimony, and he was cutting us short each time. Sometimes he'd pay. He's really in debt with that. And sometimes he wouldn't pay for months. He's supposed to send a hundred twenty-five dollars a week. He sends a hundred.

I don't think it's right. It's been going on too long. I think the court should take over. It's been to the Supreme Court in New York, and it was the longest divorce case in the history of Buffalo. That's because there were so many controversies.

At first I hated my mother, just totally hated her. I didn't want to accept any opinion of hers; I just wanted to revolt against her and be me. Then, after a while, I'd help her. As I got older, I started to help, to grow up and do things that she wanted me to, not by force but just willingly.

Did your parents ever guilt-trip you?

Yes. They sort of made me feel, "It's all your fault, it's all your fault. You did it all to us. You broke us up." And they'd just go on and on. It made me feel pretty shitty most of the time. I really felt depressed for a number of years after the separation. My home life was my home life, outside was outside, and it was like two different worlds. I just cut life in half.

When you were outside the house, you just ignored your home life? It didn't bother you inside?

No. I couldn't let it, else how could I live?

Their separation went on for a long time. There were many indications of what was going to happen. One time my father physically attacked my mother. She was on the couch, and I heard some yelling and screaming, and I came down the stairs. My mother was knitting, and my father picked up the knitting needle and caught her right in the corner of the eye. It didn't blind her; it just caught in the corner there.

And verbally, it would be really bad for hours on end. I used to listen, and I understood it all. I knew what was going on and what the outcome would be, but I didn't want to accept it.

Did you try to forget it?

Yes, but I couldn't because I had to deal with it every day.

My mother made it hard, because she had all the stresses on her. She was raising us, going to work, doing everything. She got tired out; she got exhausted and she took out all her frustrations on us as we were growing up. After a while I understood why. Then I started using different things to my advantage—being very nice and accepting things, turning out the way she wanted me to.

I think if my father had never met the woman he was going with— he's married to her now—the marriage would have survived. It would have been with some faults, but I'm sure they could have been settled.

I've never met her. All I've heard is she's bad. She's been married five different times, all for money. That's what she married again for.

The divorce was a good thing because of everything that was happening with the other woman, and how he was treating us, and how the fights were going. It was a good thing, but it took too long. It took too long to resolve. It just drained my mother.

What's happening now is, my mother is going to take my father back to court for not paying. I don't know what's going to happen from there. He's a lawyer. The house he has now cost a hundred and ten thousand dollars, and it's in the name of his new wife. My mother is working as a clerk.

Since it was only my mother bringing me up, I could actually bring myself up to be what I wanted, to understand what I want to be and not be interfered with. I grew up by myself. It made me stronger, but it's not good to go through life with a broken family.

That's because the family structure is the first thing you learn as soon as you're born. It's the only thing. It is your world. And if you have a bad start, you're going to deal with problems [badly].

"She tried to kill herself with pills."

JUDY (15)

I was twelve when my mother told me they were getting divorced. She told me that they couldn't live together anymore because they fought too much. I was quite upset, to say the least. But it had been coming. It was better than them fighting. It had been coming on for a long time.

I lived with my mother, then I lived with my father. Then I lived with my mother and now I live with my father.

How come you had to switch back and forth so much?

Because my mother had a lot of drinking problems, and we couldn't live with her because she couldn't handle us.

Did she do a lot of irrational things?

No. She was just always vague about things. She was never really all there.

My mother is hyper; she's very tense. And my father is conservative and he works a lot [now]. He went through a time when he just played, and he got fired.

I'm closer to my father. I've built up a wall against my mother because I resent all the things she did.

She tried to kill herself with pills. And she would forget a lot. She would leave one of us somewhere and she'd forget to pick us up. She came close to smashing the car. She wrecked the car, but not by hitting anything. She just totally ruined it.

I was always closer to my father, and the divorce didn't make a difference. That wasn't the main problem. I was happy to have them divorced.

He did it all. That's what got her drinking, because he had an affair for six years. She always knew about it, but she never split up because of the kids. That's how her drinking problem started.

She drank to get away from the problems?

Yeah. She couldn't handle living with them and his fucking around on the side.

In a way it was hard to just get up and go from my mother because in a way I felt sorry for her, and I felt bad that I was doing it, that I was just leaving her. I felt bad about that, but it was better than living with her.

The divorce hasn't changed me, the divorce did not make a strong impact on me. It was basically the drinking that changed me.

How?

Just the way I am toward alcohol.

I have to be independent now: not having a structured life, never knowing where I'm going, how long I'm going to be living somewhere, who I'm going to be living with.

Do you ever play games between your parents? Do you use the split-up for your own benefit?

Yeah. I like it because I take advantage of my mother. I get away with a lot of shit when I'm with her because she doesn't want to lose me. She realizes the closeness between my father and me. She can't understand. She'll let me do what I want so she will not lose me. And I do take advantage of that.

What was the most painful or hardest thing to realize about it?

That he had been fooling around that long. The thing was, the woman was the best friend of the family. She was always over at all these dinner parties and other parties they had. I never knew about it until [my parents] got divorced.

They made it easy for me because I could always see him; it wasn't as if he had moved away. And they made it hard for me in the way that they still fought a lot. They'd try to take me, try to possess me from the other parent. It was like a game where they'd put me in the middle and sort of pull at me.

I just felt guilty about leaving her a lot of times.

In a year she will, if she keeps on drinking—she could die. And the reason for that is all the alcohol that is in her. She went to a place that dries you out. You're not allowed to drink and you learn about alcohol. That didn't work. The first time it didn't work, so they thought they'd send her back there, and that didn't work. She's been to AA and everything, but she still doesn't have the sense to stop drinking. She'll always be an alcoholic, all of her life. Even if she does stop drinking, she always will be. There's always that one drink that could start her drinking again.

If you were married and had a kid your age and you were getting divorced, what would you tell him?

I'll tell him that the reason I'm doing this is for myself, because it will make me happier. And that I should want them to be happy for me, that I can make a decision like that, a large decision like that. That it is better, it will work out better in the long run, because you won't be going through all the fighting and the changes.

Do you think your parents' divorce was a good or bad thing?

I think it was a good thing because it stopped a lot of tension. They

290

were just having a false relationship between them, and it stopped a lot of tension that was in the house. I think that they knew they were going to get divorced. It was just when they were going to do it; they didn't know. They waited until we were a little bit older.

"Your father's not coming home anymore."

BARBARA (17)

I was in eighth grade when they got divorced. They were separated for two years before that.

I came home and my mother said, "Your father's not coming home anymore. He's been under a lot of stress from work." And that was that.

That's all she said?

Yup.

How did you feel about it?

I laughed.

Why?

I got hysterical. I knew that if I didn't laugh, I'd start crying. I didn't cry about him leaving until about a year later. It was a delayed reaction.

How did it affect your relationships with your parents?

It worsened [my relationship] with my mother.
I never really knew my dad when he lived at home. He was just there. He went to work, he came home, he was there for dinner, and that was about the extent of it. He used to sing me songs and shit, but we never talked.
But now, ever since I moved in with him, I'd tell him anything. I adore the guy. I love the guy. It's like, I don't know . . . I can't explain it. It's just that I adore the guy. I worship him.
But [my relationship] with my mother went down the tubes.
I've been living with my father for about three months now.

Did you have to go through any trouble to move in with him?

Trouble—oh, yeah. I had to go to a lawyer. That didn't work. The lawyer told me there was no way I could get my custody changed until I was eighteen, that I had no say in the matter for another two years.
So then I had to go to a psychologist. The psychologist was the one that convinced my mother to let me stay with my father. I just put it to him bluntly, I just put the boots to the guy: "I don't like her. I don't feel comfortable there. I like my dad. I feel comfortable with him. I really want out." That's what I said.

And he got it for you?

Yup.

Do you feel that you got the worst of it?

No. I got the best of it.

How do you figure?

Because I'm with my dad now. And I think that's where I belong.

I meant, at the time, did you feel you got the worst of it?

No. It was like he wasn't there. It didn't faze me at all.

293

How has your opinion toward your mother changed?

I feel sorry for her. I pity the lady. She's worked up this big master plan for about [the past] twenty-five years and the way it turns out [now], she is going to be losing out.

When she married my father, she was engaged to this other guy. My dad was engaged to this girl. My father's father worked in Washington. They weren't rich, but they were upper-class compared to [my mother]. She set her eye on him because my mother was really smart. She was a baby genius. She skipped a year of college and all this bullshit. And she said to herself, I'm going to find somebody with as much potential as me. She wanted to be a high-class lady.

As soon as my father broke up with his old girl friend—they had a fight or something—[my mother] dumped her fiancé and took off after my dad. The whole thing is ridiculous because she didn't love the guy. She just wanted his money. She didn't have any at the time, but she knew that two chemists together would be well off. It was dumb. As it turns out, she's losing out, because all her children are going away from her.

My father will not say one bad word about her. Nothing. But every time she hears his name, she's crazy. She can't forgive him for leaving her. So every time she hears his name she throws these subtle digs. Really stupid things. And she makes up stories that he's a sick, deranged man; that he's having an affair with Greta; all this bullshit. It's ridiculous. But if he talks to her, she won't say a thing. She'll look at him and walk away. It's dumb.

If we ever got in trouble, our punishment was, "You can't go to your father's this weekend." That was the punishment.

Back up. Before my parents got married, they were engaged. And my dad wasn't going to marry her because of what happened with my grandmother. His mother said to my mother, "We have some furniture you can have."

My mother told her off. She said something like, "Go to hell. We don't want used shit. We want to get our own stuff." Which is really unlike my mother.

294

So my father's mother told my dad and he said, "Why did you do that?" and he got real mad.

She said, "Oh, no, Tom. I didn't do that. I didn't say a word to her."

And he said—of course you believe your mother, if you've been really close, and they were really close—"Well, forget it. I'm not going to marry you. We're not even married and you're lying to me already." The marriage was off.

But there was this bonfire that my mother had been absolutely begging my dad to take her to. And so he said, "All right, I'll take you," because she wouldn't leave him alone. That night he didn't go home. The next morning [when] he comes home: "Okay. We're getting married again."

My dad never said anything about this to me, but my grandmother told Greta, and Greta told me. [My mother] must have put it to him really good in bed to get him back.

So they got married. And six months after they got married, they got separated. The only reason my dad went back to her was because she was pregnant with Harvey. And they still never got along. So they had Tom. They had all these kids so they'd have something in common; they figured, we'll get along better. But it didn't work. So she said, "This isn't going to work. Let's adopt some." So they adopted two. And she was really angry all these years because they never got along.

All my dad would want to do is go to work, play handball or something, go out once in a while, and come home. And she'd say, "No. Come right home from work." She wouldn't let him do anything.

She took out all her frustrations on Greta. That girl was twelve years old when we got her. My mother treated her like shit. The things she did to her were really abnormal. She was going to have her put away in a mental [institution]. You know why? Because she didn't like her. I remember one time, I was about seven or eight, Greta came home and my mother said, "Some girl in your class says that you are really unhappy and that you'd like to go back to

Germany. Call up the next flight. I'll drive you to the airport."

You don't say something like that to somebody. You know how mean that is? You adopt the kid and then say, "Go home." You can't do that. She used to play these little games and do all this shit to Greta.

Greta said finally, "I can't take this anymore." And she got a place to live. My father used to go and see her, because you don't adopt a kid and then leave her, let her go out in the world at sixteen years to make it with nothing. She lived with her friend for a while and my dad used to go see her. Maybe she was fifteen. I'm not really sure.

My mother was nice to her the first year. She was on her own. Then, after that, everything went to shit. So my dad used to go out and see her. And my mother had somebody follow him. Bizarre, isn't it? And she said, "Oh, no. I don't want you seeing that kid anymore. Forget it. She's out of my life."

My dad said, "You forget it," and he went out there to see her as much as he could, which wasn't very often. Maybe once every three months or so.

That was the episode with Greta. She doesn't even consider my mother her mother anymore. She considers Jane her mother. That's how badly my mother treated her. Jane is my father's girl friend.

And then there was Frank. He's fucked up. The kid was a kleptomaniac when he was little. When we got him, he was one year old. After living in the orphanage, he never had gotten enough to eat, so he would eat as much dinner as he could possibly hold. Then he'd go out and, no matter how much he'd eaten, he'd take food from the garbage and eat it. At one o'clock in the morning he'd wake up and go in the garbage cans and eat the old chicken bones and stuff. I know: it's disgusting. And he used to be really clever about it. You don't expect this stuff from a four-year-old child. But he was sneaky when it came to taking food, just like an adult would be. Finally it got really bad and he started stealing money. One time he took fifty dollars from my mother's purse and fifty dollars from his teacher's purse and he took off. The police had to bring him back.

This was the year my father left, so he had to come home for that. [Frank] had to go through family court and all this other stuff, and my mother put him in this home, like a reform school. My father ended up paying twenty thousand dollars for it. And it wasn't doing anything for [Frank].

So my dad said, "Forget it. I'm not paying that." He took Frank to live with him. Frank's now getting Bs and As in all his classes. He got expelled from three schools before this. That was when he was living with my mother. Now he's getting Bs and As. He doesn't steal anymore. He's all better.

So Frank was gone, Greta was gone, and so it's my turn. Because I look like Daddy. I remind her of Daddy. She resented that. Said I had turned into the wild, young hippie daughter. Living in rags and smoking pot, quote-unquote.

She grounded me once. I could not leave her sight. At one time, me and [my friend] Debbie, were sitting there. It's seven o'clock at night. "Mom, can I go over to Debbie's until nine?"

"No."

"Why?"

"You're grounded."

"Why?"

"It's not even worth discussing."

"What do you mean, it's not worth discussing? I want to discuss it."

"No. You can't go."

We had to sit there and talk her into it for forty-five minutes to let me go over to Debbie's for another forty-five minutes and then come home. Is that ridiculous or is it my imagination?

Then she started to bullshit. My sister came home from school— Jodie—after my dad left. "Oh, by the way, your father is not coming home anymore."

Jodie cries. "Why?"

"Don't worry about it. He's a sick, deranged man."

The only way I could learn anything in that house was from eavesdropping. I used to hear her on the phone and she'd be saying stuff, like about Greta and my dad.

Greta was going to get married to this one guy and then she decided not to. She told me about it and said all he wanted to do was

297

get high and hop in bed. And she didn't like that shit because he was in the army and he never was around that much. So the announcement came out for her to get married and my mother says, "You watch. She won't get married. That announcement is just to show that there's nothing between her and your father."

[My mother] makes up lies like that.

And [my mother] used to throw Frank down the stairs. I've seen her pick the kid up, put him in a garbage can headfirst. When we were little, we all called him "pig." It was like, "Pig, go take out the garbage." We got it from my mother because my mother used to do that. She made him stand outside once holding a sign: "I am a pig." It was in front of the neighborhood.

She's weird. She's a strange lady.

One time she almost killed [Frank]. He was standing there and he did something bad. The kid could lie to your face. He lied through his teeth. So she grabbed him by the neck and she's going, "Don't you ever lie to me!"

My father goes, "Monique!" He had to pull her off. It was so weird.

And I'm just standing there. I didn't think anything of it because I was just a little kid. I figured, this is normal. But my sister was reminding me about it three months ago and then I realized how sick it was.

In my case the divorce was the best thing in the world, because now I can do what I want. And if I can't do something, there is a reason why not. My father is very reasonable with me. He said to me, "I just don't want you to lie to me." And I don't. Because he said, "If you do have to lie to me about going somewhere or where you're going to be, you'd better really think about why you're going there." And that makes sense.

I could say, "Dad, I'm going to a bar tonight," and he'd say, "Okay. Fine."

Are you ever going to get married?

I don't see the difference between living with someone and getting married. To me there's no difference. Wow: a piece of paper! It's written down! You don't need that.

Jodie and I were talking about that last night and she said, "The only difference is that if you get married and the guy wants to leave, it makes it harder."

That's ridiculous. If somebody wants to leave, you don't say, "Oh, no. I'm going to make it as hard as possible for you." You say, "Go." I wouldn't want someone living with me if they didn't want to do it. I'd just say, "You've got your freedom. Do what you want."

If you've gotten married, then you'd have to go through divorce instead of just packing everything up and leaving. It's ridiculous.

"Don't be manipulated like I was."

SHAUN (18)

My memory—that's one thing that got kind of hurt. It's really hard for me to remember anything before eight years old. I can't remember anything. I'm just starting to get my memory back. I think it's because, before all the divorce crap went on, those years were probably the best years in my life so far, and so now I'm starting to remember them.

I'm the oldest of the three [children]. I have two sisters. I was eight when it happened, and I think I'm the only one who knew anything about any of the divorce. I knew because I saw that my mother was crying a lot. My father wasn't there much. And everything started changing. One time I remember my mother was on the phone in her room and she was crying a lot. My sisters were saying, "What's going on?" and I kind of knew, so I just told them that she was sick or something like that.

Did {your parents} fight a lot?

Yeah. They yelled a lot at each other, especially over the phone. He has a real hot temper and she's a real withholder—she cries, won't say anything. They'd fight, but nothing happened. Most of the arguments were on the phone.

After a while they learned to talk on the phone. They've been kind of friendly. They still have arguments, but they understand each other and they're [getting along] for us.

When my father left, he told me, "Shaun, you're the man of the house. You've got to protect your mother, okay?" That's the only thing I remember about that time period that really [had] an effect on me. That's why I lived with my mother. I never could leave her. I felt obligated to stay with her. Finally, the only way I could get out of the house without going against what my father said was to start arguing with my mother.

When we started, it was unreal. We were almost bashing each other's ears out. We weren't hitting each other. I was pushing her around every so often, but I wasn't ever hitting her. It wasn't like that. It was just screaming, yelling, really bad. Finally she kicked me out of the house.

That made it easy for me: I didn't have to go against what my father said. She kicked me out so I didn't have any choice. I had to get out. She said, "Listen, Shaun, I want you out of here, but I'll give you enough time to go somewhere." She knew that I wanted to go live with my father.

This was last year, my junior year. I wanted to go spend my last year with my father just to see how it would be, just so I'd have time with him before I went to college. I did that and that turned out to be pretty bad.

I went down to Florida one time. I had a fight with my mother. Actually, it was more with my stepfather. I took off and thumbed all the way down to Florida. No friends. I knew someone down there, but I didn't go with anybody. That lasted for about a week and a half, and I came back. It was real hard coming back. I ran away a couple more times, but they were just to a friend's house and then back. And then I ran away to my father's house twice.

What did you fight about?

With my mother it was mostly that she wouldn't let me do something and I would argue about why not. She'd never give a good enough reason [to satisfy] me. And I was just probably so spoiled. My mother gave us everything, everything material. She used to give us all this good stuff, but she didn't give that much love or affection.

Did you ever use the divorce for your own benefit?

Yeah. I'd play martyr trips, if you know what that is: "You didn't do this for me. I'm such a poor soul. Look at me." Parents do that, too. "You've been so bad in my life. Look at me. Look at what's going on with me. It's all your fault."

I used to do that a lot. I think I picked that up from my mother. I was just a very manipulative person. I'd try to get anything that I wanted. I'd do other things for people, but I'd strongly try to get as much as possible. I still do, but not as much.

How do you feel about your parents' divorce now?

For them it was good, For us it was pretty bad. You knew someone was gone and we couldn't do anything; it was upsetting, but we had to face it.

For my father, it's been better lately. With my mother it was kind of good and bad. She was the one that took care of us. There wasn't any man around the house until three years later, and then she married again. And he wasn't a good substitute, if you want to call him that.

Did you get along with him?

At first I did, then about two years later we started having our differences. He's so different from me. We haven't been getting along that well. Same with my stepmother. My father remarried six months after he divorced my mother. I never got along with my stepmother. It was total argument, argument all the time. Especially when I moved up there; that was even worse.

Did you resent your parents' remarrying?

I did with my father, but I didn't with my mother. I felt like my father married so quickly. I didn't want [my stepmother]. It seemed like he didn't put much thought into it. But supposedly he did. I didn't like him getting married. With my mother, I felt that she needed and that I needed a man around the house, even though he wasn't the right person for me. He didn't do much with us.

My parents used us. We were in the middle. For a while there my father would tell me some things about my mother that he didn't like and he knew I would tell her. I'd go back and I'd tell her everything that he said and she'd say the same kind of thing about him. It went back and forth. After a while I figured out what was going on, so I just stopped it. I didn't want to do it anymore.

I was ashamed when my father left. He left my mother for another woman. He met her in New York City at a convention. I don't know what it was. He met this woman and he lived with her and he married her. I felt really crappy about how quickly they married each other. You know they didn't give it much thought, it seemed like. That pissed me off pretty much.

Did you feel abandoned?

I've been feeling abandoned all my life, it seems. One year after another. I've never really been close with any of my friends except for one. I feel abandoned by my friends in Virginia, where we used to live, and I'm sure they feel the same way about me. And with my mother, I feel like we keep in touch, but it's not the same way [as before]. With my grandfather. Everywhere I go, it seems like the places I left behind, and it's all over. There's no one there. So I've been feeling abandoned all my life. That's been a big effect from the divorce. My father abandoned me.

I left my father's house when I was seventeen and finished high school on my own. My father paid for my rent and my school, but I pay for my food. I've been living in this place for eight months now. I made it through school and I'm doing pretty well. I'm making it. Surprisingly. I didn't think I'd make it.

A big part of my life has been therapy. I don't think I would have made it without it. I made so many jumps. I changed my high school in my senior year three times—from Virginia to Pennsylvania to here. That's hard. And I was able to do it. Plus I was able to live on my own, not knowing that many people except for the group. I knew the people in my therapy group and they were able to give me a lot of support and help me out. And I made it. I don't think many people could do what I did.

My father and I—it's not like a father-and-son relationship. We are totally good friends. And with my mother it's okay. I still love her and everything, but I'm not as close to my mother as I am to my father. I'm really close to my father.

Does your father still pay your rent?

No. I'm completely on my own. I pay for everything.

I'm not going to school now. I'm skipping a year and then I'm going to college next year. I thought I needed a break. So I'm working as a physical therapist with kids. It's a good job. Full-time. That's where my income comes from.

What do you think is the biggest effect of the divorce on you?

My relationships with women. It's hard for me to hold down a relationship, especially with younger women. With older women it's not as hard. The longest relationship I ever had, solid relationship, was three months. That is not very long. That's been a big hang-up with me. I'm finally getting out of that, too.

And my relationships with people. It's hard for me, especially when I live with someone. I have a roommate now. I had a roommate before him, but he was in my group and we had that to turn to if we needed it and it still didn't work. We had a lot of problems. I'm not blaming myself for all of it, but half was my doing. I'm trying my hardest not to screw up this time the same way I did last time. I'm a hard person to live with. Ask my roommate.

If I knew a kid that was going through [his parents' divorce], I'd say, "Don't take a lot of guilt trips from them, 'cause they'll come." I'd tell him, "Don't let it get you too hard." It differs, it depends on the situation. With someone that was like me, that had the same background, I'd tell them to watch out. "Don't take these things too seriously, try to keep on good terms with both your parents. Don't play the middle guy. And don't be manipulated like I was."

"I'm a survivor."

MARY (16)

I was [a little over] two when they got divorced, so it wasn't like I knew what was going on.

When did you start understanding it?

When I was ten. I didn't really care, because I had a stepfather. Even though I never considered my stepfather a father, it was someone there. It wasn't complete, there was no father, but there was someone.

My father's Portuguese. He lives in Portugal now. He met my mother in Morocco. He managed a hotel and they met there. He came back to the States with my mother and they got married in New York. He worked in New York City for a while, then they split. My mother got married again about two years later. Two months after they first got divorced, I went to Portugal with my sister. We stayed there with him for a summer, and then we came back to the States, back to Buffalo.

That was the last I heard from him for twelve years. Nothing for twelve years.

Then this time last year, I didn't want to stay in Buffalo anymore. I was sick of everything—like living with my mother and my stepfather. I didn't want it. I guess my mother wrote a letter to his parents, and they told my father and he called my mother and said, "Sure, I want her to come." Two weeks after that I left for Portugal and I lived with him for five months. And then I traveled around for five months. And then I came back.

What was it like when you first saw him?

It was a trip.

What happened was, I was coming off the plane on one of these ramps. I had three or four big suitcases. I'm coming down the ramp and I see this guy standing there. He's real tall, thin, with a hat on and sunglasses. He's got a camera around his neck, he's wearing a T-shirt, a jacket, and a pair of bright yellow corduroys. He's smiling and I'm thinking, no, that can't be him, that's not my father, that can't be him. No. I saw him and he kept smiling and I just went, oh, wow. That's too much. So then we were both kissy, huggy, and that was it.

It was like nothing I expected. I expected him to look like what my mother looks like. Not because I thought they'd be the same, but I didn't know what he'd look like.

In all that time my mother never said one word about him. She never told me one thing about him—not where he lived, what he was doing, what he was like, what he looked like. Nothing.

He told me things that are important, that I should know about her, things I never knew about her 'cause she would never tell me. I mean things that she wouldn't like me to know: she had an abortion when they first met and things like that.

I asked my mother about it once. I said, "He told me you had an abortion," and she got so angry. She was really mad because he had told me. She said, "He's a wanderer, he's a dreamer, he doesn't like to make money, doesn't like to work."

Did you get along with your mother and stepfather after coming back from living with your father?

I had matured a lot. I used to be a real little stupid something-or-other. And the trip helped my head. My head is fine, it's in good shape. But to my parents, I came back like a hippie, just 'cause I wanted to go against a lot of things, like the system, the club, the bullshit. They like to put you right in a little box and completely close you in. Make you a basket case or something like that.

My stepfather's sixty-two and my mother's forty-four. He's very, very old-fashioned. He has a good business; he went to Nichols; he's like an Ivy League bullshit. He went to a fancy college; he wears pinstripe suits and still greases his hair. Not grease, but that stuff they put on to make it look wet. He's nice-looking, he doesn't look like he's sixty-two. He's very good-looking for his age.

When I came back, I understood that what I thought was right and what they thought was right were two different things. I'm for a lot of things they could never understand, just because they're parents. They don't really know that much about what's going on with kids now. They don't know how I feel because I can't talk to them. I can talk about surface things, but nothing important.

I have one sister who's my real sister. She's never seen my father. She didn't want to go with me. She could have gone, but she didn't want to go. She didn't want to leave her little social circle and bring herself down to another way of life. She's afraid.

I'm a survivor and I can do things. There are very few survivors around. I'm a survivor, you know? I just know I am. And I could take it.

[The trip] could have been unbelievably bad; [my father] could have been living in a slum. He wasn't, but it could have been like that.

[My sister] could have gone. She didn't want to because she can't leave her friends. I hadn't had friends for a year then.

My father—I didn't call him "Dad" or anything. He was like my best friend. The only real friend.

"You just can't know it all."

SUSAN (17)

Before they got the divorce, he'd stay out the whole night and he'd never tell us where he was. He'd come home drunk sometimes and he couldn't remember where he was. Thanksgiving, he stayed out all night and he knew we were having all the relatives for company the next day. He came in at twelve. He knew we were eating at one. He came in, took a shower, and was Mr. Host. All the relatives showed up, figured he had always been there, then he left right after dinner. He did things like that.

When we first got here, my mom got a job at a school. She's a teacher. My dad had already been here for a year. My mother paid quite a few of the bills—the food bills, the clothes, and others—with her paycheck. She couldn't figure out where the rest of my dad's paycheck was going. When he got the house sided, he took a loan for a lot more money than the siding cost. When the divorce came, he wanted my mother to pay him for the siding.

It was really strange things that I can't explain.

Money was disappearing and we didn't know where it was [going].

He had an account at OTB [Off-Track Betting]. And he used to drink. He would say, "This is just a social drink." But I used to find bottles: mayonnaise jars in his briefcase. About a year before the divorce, I started saving all these gin bottles. He used to drink martinis all the time. [The bottles] started piling up in the basement. Then he realized how much he did drink, but that didn't stop him. I found bottles behind the car seats for when he needed a drink at a certain time of day. I never saw him come home drunk. I was always in school and then I'd be in bed when he'd come home later on. He would never stumble. He never acted drunk.

Did your mother tell you he was drunk? How did you know?

I'd know. The only way you could really tell was when he had had a few drinks, he got surly. He was a bitch to everybody.

My mother said she had a class reunion one time and they went to it and she was just talking to one of her old friends and he got jealous. So he started talking to that guy's wife, then he was dancing on the tables and really making an asshole out of himself. It was just things like that.

I don't know everything. My mom hasn't told me and she doesn't want to.

Why doesn't she want to?

She doesn't. I know a lot more than my brother, but you just can't know it all. This has been going on ever since we were little, more than ten years.

They wanted the divorce before this, but because of his jobs, he would be in a different city, and he'd only come home for the weekend and he could make it. They could get along. It wasn't hard at all that way. But when we moved here and everybody was together, it was too much.

My brother is high quite a bit. It hurt him to lose a father. My mother wouldn't tell him what my dad did, and my dad would not talk to him like he talked to me, so [my brother] was out of it in a lot of ways.

My dad told me in my freshman year. He said, "Your mother and I

310

aren't getting along and we want a divorce, so we're going to get separated."

We knew it was going to happen, but it dragged on for two more years. He still lived in the house. I didn't see him too much because I would leave for school and then he would leave for work. I wouldn't even see him in the morning. At night, if I had something to do, I wouldn't see him. And he would sit home and watch TV or else come in real late.

Our neighbors went on vacation and he stayed at their house awhile. So he was living next door and that got him out of our house. When the divorce came, the agreement said he had to be out by a certain date. [My parents] knew an old lady that needed somebody to stay with her and keep the lawn up and stuff, so he's staying there right now.

We thought he had a girl friend. This didn't bug my mother at all; my mother was really glad. We used to get crank phone calls. The phone would ring once. And if he was home, fifteen minutes later he would get up and call her up. We would get on the phone and my mother would say, "Oh, excuse me. I'm sorry. I didn't mean to pick up the phone." He used to come in at two-thirty in the morning and the phone would ring once, and fifteen minutes later he'd be on the phone again.

She got pretty bold after a while. We used to talk to her on the phone. My mother would sit down and cheer whenever she got that one ring. I would tell my dad if the phone rang once and then he'd go up and call. He couldn't understand that we knew.

What did you think about him having a girl friend?

It didn't bother me at all. I could see how upset my mother was and they obviously weren't getting along. I thought it was good for him to have somebody else he could talk to.

My mom and dad didn't tell [my brother] that much. My dad did tell me quite a lot. And if I'd be talking to him, I'd say, "Yeah, Dad, I can understand that, why you'd be so upset about this." And then my mother would say the same thing, and I'd say, "Yeah, Mom, I understand."

I tried to be neutral. I would sort of bridge the gap between the two of them for a while. I would tell each of them things and I would try to explain to my dad maybe why this happened. He'd be upset about something my mother would do or say and I'd say, "Well, Dad, there's plenty of reasons for that."

But my brother never got [involved like that].

Did you favor one of your parents?

When I was little, I was Daddy's little girl. It was hard losing that image as Daddy's little girl. I'm not anymore.

I would come downstairs in the morning and he would yell at me. He would tell me I was an Amherst snob. He didn't like me.

My mother's reasoning on this is because I succeeded at things. I got the good grades at school and I did all these things. He loved my brother, but it was only because he didn't do well in school, because my brother didn't succeed at everything. That's her reasoning. It sounds logical to me, considering the way my dad is.

But then I think my mother and I, personality-wise, are pretty much alike. And so for the past few years I tended to be more on her side. I could understand her reasoning. I saw what he did to her. Equaling out what both people did, I think I was on her side.

He pays the mortgage and the taxes on the house. For support like clothing and food—nothing. The most he'll ever do for food is, he'll take us out every once in a while.

I think he should be contributing a lot more than he does. He's living with [that old] lady right now; her house is already paid for. I don't think he even pays rent to her. He just mows the lawn and does a few other things. And he does have a job. I don't know what the job pays, but he does have a job. I think we should be getting a little bit more.

The other day my mother was paying her bills. She went through her checkbook. She's a teacher and doesn't get paid from June until September. She said, "Well, I paid all my bills. We're all paid off. We have forty-three dollars from now until the middle of September when I next get paid." For food, clothing, gas.

I go, "Yeah, Mom. It's a good thing I'm working. At least I won't die."

Neither me nor my brother asks for money. Maybe once in a while my brother does for something. But I've never asked for money. If I need something, I go out and buy it with what I save from my job.

My grandfather died last winter and my grandmother got a little money. She's contributed a little bit because she stays with us quite a few days each week. Since she's here, she contributes. And we belong to a freezer plan. You buy three hundred dollars' worth of food all at once and it lasts you for three months. I've never been hungry.

Since about December, since the divorce, my mother and I have gotten along a lot better. A year ago she was horrid to me. She was a real bitch. I couldn't do anything right. I'd have to come in at eleven or twelve. But now we're getting along pretty well.

My dad says he misses us, which I believe. I think he really does miss us, and so I think I see my dad a lot more now than I did. He takes us out now, which he never did before. We go out to dinner or brunch.

As for talking to him, I don't think I talk to him that much more.

I stayed with my mother because she got the house. They were going to sell it and split the money between them, but that seemed to me impossible because then my mother would have had half that money and two kids, and my dad would just have half the money. And we really can't make it on my mother's salary.

I didn't want to stay with my dad. I still don't. My mother said to him the other day, "Why don't you take the kids for a week?" I wouldn't have gone. I would have lived out in the streets.

Why didn't you want to stay with your dad?

He gives me an uneasy feeling. Part of it is because I used to be "Daddy's girl," and I'm not anymore. And he's changed a lot. He's like a different person to me. Maybe it's because I'm growing up and I know him better. Or maybe he really has changed.

I think he's a lot happier now than he was before. I know my mother is.

What about you?

I am. I'm much happier.

And your brother?

I think so. He doesn't express his feelings to anybody. That is kind of hard on my mother because she doesn't know how he feels about anything. If he did feel anything about anything, she wouldn't know, and if he was having a hard time with it, we wouldn't know that either.

Between my brother and me, I had it a lot worse. A *lot* worse.

Tell me about it.

My dad would go through mood swings. One day he'd be a super-great guy and the next day you wouldn't even want to know him. They were that erratic. It got to be that he would be happy for one or two days, and then for the longest time he was really down. It was easy to tell when he was really depressed.

One day my brother, my dad, and I were just finishing dinner and he was quite upset. Not even about anything [special], just about things in general. My brother was done, so he got up and he went and lay down in the living room, and he fell asleep.

I guess it was just after the prom. The corsage was in the refrigerator and I was looking at it and talking about it. I was standing out by the kitchen and my dad got up. He didn't grab me around the neck, but he put his arms on the side of my neck and he just started crying and I could feel the tears running down my neck.

And he's going, "I don't know what I'm going to do without you kids. You're the only thing I have left in life."

It was sad, to have your own father cry, to just break down and cry. He was gone.

I just froze for a while. I didn't know what to do. Finally, I turned around and I gave him a hug and I said, "No, Dad. It's okay. You can cry, too. You're allowed."

He cried and he cried.

Having your own father break up on you like that—it crushed me for the rest of the day. I can remember I came out back here and I sat and I screamed. I said, "I just can't believe this is happening to me." I kept saying, "Why me? Why does it have to be me?"

Then I left the house. I can't remember where I went. I cried the rest of the night. I cried for eight hours straight, hard.

The next day I went to school and my eyes were so puffy and so red and I had the worst headache. Everybody was saying, "Susan, are you high?"

I said, "No, but I can't explain it so just leave me alone."

Did you ever tell your brother about that?

No, I don't think my brother knows. I did tell my mother. And I told a few of my friends.

That was one of the reasons I said I got the worst of the deal: because my dad would never have done anything like that to my brother.

Jessica Jackson: CONCLUSION

Divorce isn't just between two parents; it also affects the kids. Divorce is probably harder on kids than it is on parents. The kids have to adjust to a whole new way of life, and they have to get used to having one of their parents living somewhere else. Most kids are idealistic; they dream of the perfect family. Most parents don't realize that a divorce affects the kids for the rest of their lives.

When I did the interviews for this book, some of my friends were hesitant at first to say things, but I think it was much easier for them to talk openly to me than to an adult because they could identify with me. I could understand how they felt, because I had been through a divorce, too. Every divorce is different, but there is something in the experience we all share. The interviews helped some of my friends share feelings they'd never before expressed to anyone. And they helped me understand what had happened to me.

When divorce happens, some kids feel obligated to take over the role of the missing parent. I have one friend whose mother recently moved out and is filing for divorce. My friend's brothers and sisters are all away, so she is obligated to cook, clean, and keep the house together for her father. She submits to him for several reasons. One is that she feels he needs her. Another is that she's afraid that if she doesn't do what he says or if she moves out, he'll take her out of school, never give her money, and, worst of all, never talk to her. She feels trapped. She's usually awake until one A.M. doing the washing and cleaning. She doesn't get much sleep and has almost no time for schoolwork. She's not doing well in school anymore.

Sometimes the son feels obligated to take over the role of the father. Shaun's father said to him when he left, "Shaun, I want you to take care of your mother. You're the man of the house now." Shaun felt trapped. He was trying to get his own life together, to understand himself, and he was burdened with that responsibility, tied down by his promise.

I think most kids feel abandoned by the missing parent and sometimes resent him or her for leaving. When my parents separated, we were living in Berkeley. My father moved to San Francisco. My brother was furious at my father for leaving. He wouldn't speak to him. My father wrote all three of us a letter explaining the situation. I was six, and I didn't understand the letter very well.

I remember, before they were separated, hearing all their fights. They would usually go into their bedroom and close the door. It was pretty quiet then. But their bathroom connected to my room. I would sneak into the bathroom and open the door just a crack. I would sit on the floor and listen and cry. I wasn't sure what they were fighting about, but I got so scared.

After they separated, my father came over and brought us all lots of presents. He felt so bad for leaving. He realized how hard it was on us. It wasn't as if the presents made it all better, but they eased some of the pain at the time.

All three of us kids lived with my mother. I fought with her constantly. I love her, but we couldn't live in the same house.

If I'd want to go to a concert, her reason for saying no (she always said no) would be that she didn't want me to "follow in your brother's footsteps," "because people only go to concerts to do drugs," or "I don't have to give you reasons. I'm your mother."

My mother tried to say that Mike was incorrigible and bad. He was really just independent—he did whatever he wanted to do. She had no control over him, and she didn't want to be unable to control me, too.

I also had trouble with my stepfather. We didn't get along at all after the first year they were married.

Moving out was hard for me. Mike had already moved to my father's house. I couldn't convince my mother to let me move out. I could have just left, but I felt so guilty and I wanted her to say it was okay. She never said it was okay.

I couldn't handle it anymore. I couldn't handle my stepfather and the things he did, things I try to forget. I ran away and stayed at a friend's house for four days. I ran away with my bike, sixty-five cents, and a few clothes I grabbed as I left. I had been thinking about running away for a long time, and several people had offered me places to stay. When I did it, it was a spur-of-the-moment decision. After my final exam I just didn't come home. I called my father to tell him where I was staying so he wouldn't worry. I was so furious at my mother that I wanted her to worry.

One day while she was at work, I went to her house with my father to pick up all my stuff. Everything. I felt awful doing it that way, but I couldn't handle the guilt I would have felt if she had been there. She called me every night, crying, for about a week. Many times I almost went back because the crying made me feel so bad. But I realized I had to live my own life, not take care of my mother.

Once she told me that if I ever left her, she'd die. I know she loves me very much, but something like that is just too much for a kid to handle. I felt guilty for so long. I will always remember her saying that.

I don't think the divorce affected me too much until about four years after it happened. It helped me grow more independent and to learn to take care of myself. I was one of those idealists who imagine the perfect nuclear family, even with the arguments my parents used to have. The divorce ended that imagining.

For a while I took advantage of my father's living someplace else. I would bring friends to his house and they'd love him and we'd have a great time because we could do almost anything we wanted—within reason.

For the longest time I couldn't talk to my mother. The guilt and my fury at her prevented me from even being polite to her. It's taken me the last year to have a good conversation with her. I used to have to force myself to be nice, and it was just awful.

I think the divorce affected my relationships with people enormously. I used to want to trust people so much, but I was so scared of letting myself get too close to anyone for fear of being hurt.

The divorce also affected my relationships with boyfriends. For a long time I used to look for someone who was considerably older than me, someone who would take care of me, as if I was looking for a father figure. I only wanted to feel cared for. I'm sure that both my parents love me, but I wasn't sure I trusted their love. It took me a long time to get my life together and to figure out who I am, most of all, to let me be me.

The divorce, for a while, brought my brother and me together. He would tell me everything. When he moved out of my mother's house, we grew apart. I rarely saw him because when I'd go to visit my father, Mike would be in Amherst going out with his friends. For a while I felt that I hated him. I felt he betrayed me. He didn't seem interested anymore.

I became much closer to my father. At the beginning I would get furious at him because he said bad things about my mother. (My mother would always say, "I never say anything bad about your father, but . . ." and then she'd go on and say it), and I was in the middle—defending them both. Now they've pretty much stopped saying things, but they still can't be pleasant to each other. The only time they talk to each other is when they're fighting about visitation rights for my sister Rachel. My mother doesn't let Rachel visit us much.

I had always liked my stepmother, Diane. I remember liking her when my father moved in with her. I resented her for just a short time then (if I did at all) because I thought she was taking my father away.

It's so common today to have divorced parents that people marvel over a "happily" married couple. I saw a movie recently that is a parody of marriage. It mocks an elderly couple that are still very much in love. Everyone says, "What? You're happily married? In love? You never cheated on your wife? Crazy! What a square!"

By reading this book, I hope that kids going through these things now can identify with some of the people Mike and I talked with and come to understand that these things happen to other people, too, and to understand that they're normal. I hope that parents can realize that they should talk to their kids, tell them what's going on, and they shouldn't use them. The kids are affected forever by a divorce, and if parents could realize that it's just as hard or harder on the kids, maybe they could make it easier for them.

You are about to read stories of violence and incest, drug and alcohol abuse, betrayal and abandonment, love, faith and hope; stories of survival through that all-too-common experience—divorce.

Jessica and Michael Jackson, themselves children of divorce, selected thirty-eight interviews with teenagers between the ages of thirteen and twenty-one from the multitude they conducted for this book. The Jacksons bring not only their own knowledge and empathy to their subjects—average American kids from average middle-class American homes who have gone through average American divorces —but also a fresh, unrelentingly realistic approach.

As no two divorces are the same, so is each child's story different. For many of them, it was the first time they had spoken of the shattering of their families and the aftermath. Many are forced to mature way before their time; others seem locked in preadolescence. Too many